"We have seen a spate of bool the arts or a 'sacramental' aes something we have been waitir a pneumatology. Unafraid to engage popula... art, Guthrie challenges the latent gnosticism in so much talk of 'spirituality,' returning Christian spirituality to the rehumanizing work of the Holy Spirit. The result is a kind of chemical reaction of mutual illumination: I have a new appreciation for the Spirit's work and a new excitement about the arts. I hope this book finds many, many readers."

—**James K. A. Smith**, Calvin College and Calvin Institute of Christian Worship

"Talk of the relationship between spirituality and aesthetics has become so commonplace in our culture that it has become both cacophonous and banal at the same time. In the midst of this situation Guthrie has produced a theology of the Spirit and the arts that brings welcome clarity to the conversation while retaining an appropriate sense of mystery and openness. *Creator Spirit* is a compelling example of the sort of generous orthodoxy that is in keeping with the best intuitions of the Christian tradition."

—**John R. Franke**, First Presbyterian Church, Allentown, PA

"A brilliant book! Guthrie makes nuances exceedingly accurately, so that his readers are able to distinguish various ideas in Christianity from their mistaken use in historical and postmodern philosophies about the arts. Guthrie consequently frees us to recognize more clearly and biblically the labors of diverse artists and the liberating presence of the Holy Spirit. You will devour this volume, and it will increase your faith!"

—**Marva J. Dawn**, Regent College, Vancouver; theologian; speaker

"Guthrie has offered to a varied audience a study that is both challenging and captivating as it traces how and in what way the Holy Spirit is active in sanctified human artistry. Indeed, *Creator Spirit* itself reflects the beauty that its author seeks to describe. First, the book displays admirable proportion, balancing an analysis of the arts (music, visual art, dance) with theological, philosophical, and cultural concerns. Next, it provides keen pleasure for the reader in terms of its lively and compelling style and its rich content. Finally, it moves admirably toward a satisfying telos, even if, with all other human projects, it is not perfect. That perfection is instead attributed to the Author and Creator of all, whom this book glorifies, as Guthrie rejoices in the gifts and in the Gift, the Spirit who humanizes those who receive."

—**Edith M. Humphrey**, Pittsburgh Theological Seminary

"This book participates in a growing movement interested in the intersection of art, faith, and spirituality. But this book also stands out as a leading voice in this field because of its breadth of vision for the sources and functions of the arts in human life and because of the specificity and clarity of its theological convictions about the work of the Holy Spirit and the expansive nature of salvation offered in and through Jesus Christ. The book's particular interest in Athanasius is especially welcome, inviting all of us to sharpen and deepen our theological vision and to wrestle with the astonishing implications of the incarnation for human flourishing."

—**John D. Witvliet**, Calvin Institute of Christian Worship, Calvin College and Calvin Theological Seminary

Creator *Spirit*

THE HOLY SPIRIT AND THE ART OF BECOMING HUMAN

Steven R. Guthrie

Foreword by Jeremy S. Begbie

BakerAcademic
a division of Baker Publishing Group
Grand Rapids, Michigan

For Dick and Sally Guthrie
and Ron and Mary Waterloo.
My parents and parents-in-law,
and people of the Spirit.

Published by Baker Academic
a division of Baker Publishing Group
P.O. Box 6287, Grand Rapids, MI 49516-6287
www.bakeracademic.com

Printed in the United States of America

Library of Congress Cataloging-in-Publication Data

Guthrie, Steven R., 1967–
Creator Spirit : the Holy Spirit and the art of becoming human / Steven R. Guthrie.
p. cm.
Includes bibliographical references and indexes.
ISBN 978-0-8010-2921-9 (pbk.)
1. Holy Spirit. 2. Christianity and the arts. 3. Theological anthropology—Christianity.
I. Title.
BT121.3.G88 2011
261.5'7—dc22 2010053036

In keeping with biblical principles of creation stewardship, Baker Publishing Group advocates the responsible use of our natural resources. As a member of the Green Press Initiative, our company uses recycled paper when possible. The text paper of this book is composed in part of post-consumer waste.

11 12 13 14 15 16 17 7 6 5 4 3 2 1

Contents

Foreword *Jeremy S. Begbie* vii

Acknowledgments ix

Introduction xi

1. Is There Anything to Talk About Here? Spirit and Mystery 1

Part 1 The Making of a Human

2. Remaking Humanity: John Coltrane and a Love Supreme 25
3. Remaking Human Bodies: Kingdom Come and the Kingdom of the Abstract 47
4. Remaking Community: Singing to One Another in Songs, Hymns, and Spiritual Songs 71

Part 2 The Spirit's Making and Ours

5. Ionized Inspiration: Can a Human Voice Be Heard? 95
6. The Gift-Giving Spirit: De-Ionized Inspiration 115
7. Finding Our Voices: The Spirit of Freedom 131

Part 3 A World Remade

8. Seeing the Spirit in All Things, Seeing All Things in the Spirit: Discernment and the Restoration of Vocation 153
9. Beautiful, Beautiful Zion: The Spirit and Completion 177
10. Perfection, Proportion, and Pleasure: The Spirit and Beauty 197

Epilogue: The Museum of Spirituality 211

Subject Index 216

Scripture Index 220

Foreword

Jeremy S. Begbie

This book has been provoked by something widespread in our culture: talk about the arts has a habit of veering into talk about "spirit," "the spiritual," and "spirituality"; and likewise, "spiritual" talk often slides into talk about the arts. In our culture, there seems to be an intuitive sense that "the spiritual" and the world of the arts are somehow intimately related.

And yet when we dig a little deeper we find that language about "the spiritual" covers, if not a multitude of sins, at least a multitude of meanings. We find ourselves in something of a semantic chaos. This might not matter much, if it weren't for the fact that Christians, eager to find connections with the religious impulses of our culture at large, are prone to use the language of "spirit" in ways quite alien to the biblical texts. Most worrying, talk of "spirit" is used to justify a neglect, even a denigration of our humanness, especially our embodied, physical nature: to be "spiritual" is somehow to rise above our earthy, common humanity. And when the arts are drawn into this kind of confusion, the problems multiply.

Guthrie brings a welcome dose of fresh air into this foggy territory. He is immersed in the biblical texts, with an acute grasp of the multidimensional moves of the Spirit portrayed in the New Testament. He shows us that at the heart of the Spirit's work is the renewal of our humanity—through the Spirit, as we are changed into the likeness of Christ. We are re-humanized by the Spirit, not de-humanized. With this perspective in mind, he invites us to enter the world of human artistry and reenvision the arts in ways that are illuminating, compelling, and always down to earth. Throughout, Guthrie is careful not to denigrate or downplay the stirrings of the Spirit beyond the church: this is a charitable, hospitable theology, eager to listen as well as speak. (Indeed, the book breathes the generous spirit of its author, with whom I was once fortunate enough to coteach a course on the Holy Spirit at the University of St. Andrews.) But Guthrie's is a discerning generosity—as he shows, the eagerness to baptize everything in the arts that attracts the language of "spiritual" is naïve and in the end helps nobody.

In these pages, you will encounter John Coltrane, Annie Dillard, and Wassily Kandinsky. You will rub shoulders with Augustine, Miroslav Volf, Gordon Fee, and—Guthrie's main theological companion—Athanasius. You will encounter a first-rate teacher who seems to be able to draw on a vast range of images and metaphors to press each point home. You will encounter a theologian who can bring clarity out of confusion without ever stifling a sense of openness and wonder. And most important, you will, by God's grace, encounter the work of the Spirit, sharpening your thinking and enlarging your vision, the Spirit who alone can, and will, remake all things.

Acknowledgments

I am grateful to Brian Bolger of Baker Academic for inviting me to write this book and for continuing to pursue the idea despite my initial uncertainty. I am also very grateful to Baker Academic for not giving up on this project when significant health and family concerns forced long delays.

I thank my students from St. Mary's College, University of St. Andrews. In particular, I am grateful for the thoughtful and enthusiastic reception of this material given by the students who took my class "The Holy Spirit: An Exploration through the Arts" the first time it was offered in Autumn 2001: Henriette Guthauser, Jen Kilps, Catriona Lang, Jeff McSwain, Andrew Rawnsley, and Dave and Chelle Stearns.

My students at Belmont continue to shape this material semester on semester, and I thank them for the creativity and energy they bring to our studies together. I owe a special debt to the students who took "Faith and Beauty" in the Fall of 2007: Luke Barnhart, Luke Baugher, Johnny Beach, Sarah Bennett, Mikey Brackett, Jess Brandhorst, Rachel Cope, Lucas Cummins, Sharon Dale, Ashley Eayre, Meghan Gwaltney, Meredith Harlin, Kailey Hussey, Giorgio Kemp, Anthony Mangin, Steffie Misner, Rachel Mueller, Allie Peden, Greg Privett, Matthew Ross, Taylor Shade, Kelsey Siebold, Anna Skates, Nate Sutliff, Jessica Waltrip, Melissa Wheatley, and Rachel Williamson. I gave these students the assignment of reading and critiquing an early draft of chapters 1–5. Their assessments were invaluable and strengthened the book immensely.

I am grateful to Jim and Kim Thomas, the pastor and curate of my church, The Village Chapel. In addition to their friendship and spiritual leadership, they generously provided me with a writing space away from the distractions of my university office.

A number of friends read portions of this manuscript at various points in its development: Oliver Crisp, Tim Gombis, Bruce Hansen, Trevor Hart, Matt

Jenson and Pat Manfredi. I couldn't have completed the book without their encouragement and their insights.

I owe several debts to Jeremy Begbie—first of all for inviting me to co-teach the course that gave rise to this book; additionally, for agreeing to write a foreword for the book; and finally, for urging me to continue work when I hit some difficult points in the writing process.

My dad and the Friday morning men's group at Upper St. Clair Christian and Missionary Alliance Church prayed for me and for the completion of this book over (too) many years. I couldn't possibly compose a book equal to the prayers offered on its behalf. I thank these older brothers with great respect and affection.

Every day I am grateful for my children, Joel, Noah, Sophie, and Lucy, and for the memory of my son Samuel. Their lives fill and animate these pages in more ways than they could know.

My deepest thanks are due to my wife Julie: for reading drafts, for listening to me think through chapters aloud, and for offering both criticism and encouragement. Comforter, counselor, and giver of gifts are all names of the Spirit, but they characterize Julie's part in my life remarkably well.

Introduction

> The LORD God formed man from the dust of the ground, and breathed into his nostrils the breath of life; and the man became a living being.
>
> Genesis 2:7

> And all of us, with unveiled faces, seeing the glory of the Lord as though reflected in a mirror, are being transformed into the same image from one degree of glory to another; for this comes from the Lord, the Spirit.
>
> 2 Corinthians 3:18

> For we are God's masterpiece. He has created us anew in Christ Jesus.
>
> Ephesians 2:10 (NLT)

Theology involves careful thought and speech about God. The theologian employs words and concepts in reflecting on God and God's ways with the created world. But while words are the tools of the theologian's trade, they are not, on the whole, dedicated tools. Words and concepts are not kept encased in glass, awaiting the moment they are required by theologians. They are tools already in daily use, and they are formed, shaped, and bent by their employment.

Here is one such word: *spirit*.

Plainly, it is an important word for the theologian. It is also—plainly—a word that does a good deal of work outside of Christian academic theology, particularly as the root of the word "spirituality." Everything from home decorating to corporate management techniques are addressed in that nebulous region of the local bookstore labeled "Mind, Body, and Spirit." Cooking, exercise, sex, and travel are likewise just a few of the activities that popular publications characterize as spiritual. So a Christian might well wonder: what does "spiritual" mean, what do the people who use this word mean by it when they employ it in these settings? And do these uses bear any resemblance to the word as it is used in a specifically Christian sense, such as when it is used to speak of the Holy Spirit of Christian belief?

The Spiritual and the Aesthetic

Years ago, as an undergraduate student in music, I was struck by the number of times I heard the language of spirituality used to characterize art and beauty. (In particular, I can remember a long conversation in the student lounge with a *very* intense vocal performance major who explained to me that one *could not* be a real musician without also being a deeply spiritual person!) A whole raft of popular publications bears witness to the fact that this association between the aesthetic and the spiritual is not idiosyncratic, nor is it unique to the music school I attended. Consider just a few titles from the past decade:

- *Creativity: Where the Divine and the Human Meet*[1]
- *The New Creative Artist: A Guide to Developing Your Creative Spirit*[2]
- *The Spirit of Silence: Making Space for Creativity*[3]
- *Releasing the Creative Spirit: Unleashing the Creativity in Your Life*[4]
- *The Spirit of Creativity*[5]
- *The Soul's Palette: Drawing on Art's Transformative Powers*[6]
- *Art Heals: How Creativity Cures the Soul*[7]
- *The Zen of Creativity: Cultivating Your Artistic Life*[8]
- *Spirit Taking Form: Making a Spiritual Practice of Making Art*[9]
- *Drawing as a Sacred Activity: Simple Steps to Explore Your Feelings and Heal Your Consciousness*[10]

1. Matthew Fox, *Creativity: Where the Divine and the Human Meet* (New York: Tarcher/Putnam, 2002).
2. Nita Leland, *The New Creative Artist: A Guide to Developing Your Creative Spirit* (Cincinnati: North Light Books, 2006).
3. John Lane, *The Spirit of Silence: Making Space for Creativity* (Foxhole, Dartington, UK: Green Books, 2006).
4. Dan Wakefield, *Releasing the Creative Spirit: Unleashing the Creativity in Your Life* (Woodstock, VT: SkyLight Paths, 2001).
5. Joseph Curiale, *The Spirit of Creativity* (Philadephia: Xlibris, 2006).
6. Cathy A. Malchiodi, *The Soul's Palette: Drawing on Art's Transformative Powers* (Boston: Shambhala, 2002).
7. Shaun McNiff, *Art Heals: How Creativity Cures the Soul* (Boston: Shambhala, 2004).
8. John Daido Loori, *The Zen of Creativity: Cultivating Your Artistic Life* (New York: Ballantine, 2005).
9. Nancy J. Azara, *Spirit Taking Form: Making a Spiritual Practice of Making Art* (York Beach, ME: Red Wheel, 2002).
10. Heather C. Williams, *Drawing as a Sacred Activity: Simple Steps to Explore Your Feelings and Heal Your Consciousness* (Novato, CA: New World Library, 2002).

- *The Soul of Creativity: Insights into the Creative Process*[11]
- *Seeing in the Dark: A Vision of Creativity & Spirituality*[12]
- *The Artist Inside: A Spiritual Guide to Cultivating Your Creative Self*[13]
- *The Soul Tells a Story: Engaging Creativity with Spirituality in the Writing Life*[14]

The best known book in this vein is probably Julia Cameron's *The Artist's Way: A Spiritual Path to Higher Creativity.*[15] This book has sold more than a million copies since its publication in 1992, and Cameron has followed it with a host of companion volumes, seminars, conferences and workshops.[16]

Why should so many identify art (or beauty or music) as spiritual? What could it mean to characterize a painting, or a Brahms string quartet, or the act of drawing in this way? Is the description even meaningful? Or is "spiritual" in this context simply shorthand for "things-I-really-like" or "that-which-gives-me-goosebumps"?

The association hasn't only been made frequently, however. It has also been made thoughtfully, in careful and considered ways. When we move beyond the realm of popular and self-help books and back behind the last couple of decades, we continue to find the aesthetic and the spiritual set alongside one another. Tolstoy, Plato, Schleiermacher, Augustine, Tillich, Schopenhauer, Santayana, and Schiller are just a few of the notable thinkers who have believed that spirit and art (or beauty) are—in one way or another—closely related to each other.

It is this "in one way or another," in fact, that I want to consider in the pages that follow. We will survey some of the various ways and some of the various reasons the aesthetic and the spiritual have been paired. In light of the preceding lists of thinkers and publications, it should go without saying that my survey will not be exhaustive. I do hope, however, that it is representative. I also have made an attempt to listen to the voices of artists as well as those of theologians and philosophers; similarly, I've tried to attend not only to scholarly works but also to popular ones.

11. Tona Pearce Myers, *The Soul of Creativity: Insights into the Creative Process* (Novato, CA: New World Library, 1999).

12. Beverly J. Shamana, *Seeing in the Dark: A Vision of Creativity & Spirituality* (Nashville: Abingdon, 2001).

13. Tom Crockett, *The Artist Inside: A Spiritual Guide to Cultivating Your Creative Self* (New York: Broadway Books, 2000).

14. Vinita Hampton Wright, *The Soul Tells a Story: Engaging Creativity with Spirituality in the Writing Life* (Downers Grove, IL: InterVarsity, 2005).

15. Julia Cameron, *The Artist's Way: A Spiritual Path to Higher Creativity* (New York: Tarcher/Putnam, 1992).

16. Details about Cameron and some of the publications and activities connected with *The Artist's Way* can be found at http://www.theartistsway.com.

In chapter 1 the proposed connection we will explore is *mystery and ineffability*. Some have suggested that art and spirituality are closely related because in each we move into a realm beyond words and concepts.

In chapter 2 the proposed resemblance has to do with *expression and emotion*. A number of artists and philosophers have suggested that art is spiritual because it arises from and gives voice to the deepest places in us (our "spirit"). Art on this account is spiritual because through it we are enabled to give voice to who we are most truly—or enter most deeply into the humanity of another.

The third chapter considers the idea that *spiritual* means something like "non-material" or "non-physical." Taking this as a starting point, many artists and philosophers have argued that art and spirituality each take us beyond the world of matter and appearance, into a world of spiritual realities.

Chapter 4 observes that art and religion have been regularly paired not just within various philosophical systems but also in the actual worship and religious rituals of nearly all human cultures. Art—particularly music—is the persistent counterpart to human religious practice. In light of this, some have suggested that art is connected to spirituality because of its *power to enact and embody the shared life of a community*.

Chapters 5, 6, and 7 consider an idea from ancient philosophy that continues to find currency on the lips of artists and lovers of art: *the artist is literally in-spired*—enspirited—and creates by virtue of allowing the unimpeded flow of the Spirit (or the Muse, or some other sort of "Higher Power"). Here, then, the connection between spirit and art is that of direct cause and effect.

Chapter 8 explores a related idea, that art is a matter of *discernment*. On this account, art arises from unusually sensitive individuals who are able to recognize the "spiritual meaning" latent in all things. The world is full of spirit. The artist is the one able to see this and is also the one through whom others' eyes are opened.

Finally, in chapters 9 and 10 we will consider the idea that the connection between the spiritual and the aesthetic is *eschatological*. The artist has caught a glimpse of heaven and provides an "advance screening" for those of us on earth. Beauty is spiritual, according to this account, because it offers us a foretaste of the better and brighter world to come.

Right away this outline of the chapters alerts us to the fact that spirituality and the aesthetic enjoy not just one but several areas of verbal and conceptual overlap. Mystery, ecstasy, inspiration, creation and creativity, "giftedness," the relation of the seen to the unseen, "taste" and discernment, completion and perfection: each of these is an important issue in theology as well as in the realm of art and beauty.

Theologies of the Spirit

The preceding outline of chapters also draws our attention to an even more important point: every association, every proposed connection between art and spirituality is also a *theology of the Spirit*. The person who says "thus and such is spiritual," also advances—often by implication—a particular understanding of "spirit." They offer, in other words, a pneumatology. One of the central tasks of the chapters that follow will be to evaluate these pneumatologies (some secular, some religious; some popular, some scholarly), comparing and contrasting them with an explicitly biblical and Christian theology of the Holy Spirit.

This is different, then, from a "natural theology" of the Spirit, in which one might attempt to extrapolate from an experience of beauty to a theology of the Spirit, or work one's way up from some instance of art to a full-blown pneumatology. We won't undertake to prove—or disprove—that any particular experience of art or beauty is an experience of the Holy Spirit (who, after all, "blows where it chooses" [John 3:8]). Instead we will be comparing and evaluating various ways of talking and thinking about the Spirit.

This sort of comparing and contrasting is helpful and instructive, not because at every point the theologies in question turn out to be entirely different, nor because at every point they end up being entirely the same. But rather, setting various conceptions of spirit alongside one other provides an occasion for sharpening and refining our words and thoughts. It is an opportunity to say both "Yes, that's *exactly* what I mean as well" and "No, I don't mean *that*, I mean *this*."

Spirit-uality

Finally, in the chapters that follow I will outline a Christian theology of the Spirit. Based upon this pneumatology, I also will propose one reason why so many have sensed an affinity between the aesthetic and the spiritual.

As I do this I will be thinking about the aesthetic in relation to one very particular Christian understanding of "spirituality"—one that I believe is foundational to all other Christian uses. Namely, I will be thinking about Christian spirituality as, in the first instance, *Spirit*-uality. For Christian theology, the "spiritual" is manifestly the realm of the Holy Spirit. This conviction is firmly rooted in the biblical use of the adjective *pneumatikos* ("spiritual"). The word occurs twenty-six times in the New Testament, with twenty-four of these occurrences arising within the Pauline epistles. Plainly, then, the word has a "strong Pauline stamp."[17] It does not occur in the Septuagint, and it is not often found in Hellenistic texts. So what does Paul mean when he uses the word "spiritual"? In its Pauline usage, Gordon Fee writes, "the word functions primarily as an adjective for the Spirit, referring to *that which belongs to, or pertains to, the Spirit*."[18] In the New Testament, "spiritual" is not simply a way

17. Gordon D. Fee, *God's Empowering Presence: The Holy Spirit in the Letters of Paul* (Peabody, MA: Hendrickson, 1994), 28.

18. Ibid., 29, emphasis original.

of denoting one's own beliefs, tendencies, practices, or experiences (except insofar as those relate to the Holy Spirit of God). For Paul, a "spiritual person" is "a person of the Holy Spirit."

On this account, understanding spirituality will mean first of all arriving at an understanding of the person and work of the Holy Spirit. Throughout this book I will argue that one of the principal works of the Holy Spirit is to make and remake our humanity. In creation, incarnation, and redemption, the Holy Spirit is *the humanizing Spirit.*[19]

In creation, the Spirit is the Breath of God that animates the dust of the ground and creates a living human being. Similarly, in the coming of Jesus Christ, the Holy Spirit is *the incarnating Spirit*. It is by the Spirit that the eternal Word of God becomes truly and fully human. The Spirit likewise rests upon and empowers the humanity of Jesus, and so we call him the Christ, the Messiah—that is, the one anointed with the Spirit. Finally, in the work of redemption and consummation, the Holy Spirit is *the re-humanizing Spirit*. The Spirit is poured out on God's people, so that by the Spirit they may become truly and fully human, recreated in the Image of the perfect humanity of Jesus Christ.

This theme is likewise reflected in the structure of the book.

After the first chapter, chapter 2 makes the basic argument that the work of the Spirit is *to restore, rather than extinguish, our humanity*. Chapter 3 focuses on the role of the Spirit in the creation and re-creation of *our physical bodies*. Chapter 4 explores the work of the Spirit in re-making *human community* (as well as the role of Spirit-filled community in remaking us individually).

Chapters 5, 6, and 7 look at the Spirit as the bringer of *human freedom*, re-creating persons who are, in turn, able to create. The Spirit's work includes the restoration of *our voices*. And not only does the Spirit recreate, but God's Spirit also invites and enables us to share in his work of re-creation. In light of this, chapter 8 considers one way in which the Spirit restores not only human volition and the human voice but also *human vocation*. Finally, the work of the Spirit has an eschatological orientation. The Spirit's work is to perfect and complete our humanity—and not our humanity only, but all things. Chapters 9 and 10 are devoted to this *eschatological and perfecting work* of the Spirit.

If the work of the Spirit is to make and re-make our humanity, then this suggests a couple of interesting possibilities with respect to the "spirituality" of the arts. First, it may be that human beings have associated the arts with spirituality precisely because art-making is a *paradigmatically human activity*. The work of the Spirit is to restore our humanity, to restore our bodies, to restore community, to restore our voices, to restore our freedom and our

19. I have borrowed the term "humanization" from Dumitru Staniloae, *The Experience of God: Orthodox Dogmatic Theology*, vol. 2, *The World: Creation and Deification*, trans. Ioan Ionita and Robert Barringer (Brookline, MA: Holy Cross Orthodox Press, 2005).

vocation. Artistic activity, likewise, is a powerful means of connecting us to our physical selves. It is one of the fundamental ways human beings have of establishing a community's identity. And for cultures around the world and across time, artistic activity has been a powerful way of "finding one's voice" and shaping one's environment. Perhaps it is not surprising, then, that many have had the intuition that there is something spiritual about art. The work of the Spirit is to restore our humanity. To the extent that artistic activity helps us realize and connects us more deeply to our humanity, art may indeed be said to be not only "spiritual," but *Spirit*-ual.

Second, the pneumatology I have described gives a distinctly artistic character to the Spirit's work. Making and remaking; perfecting and forming—this is what the Spirit does. The Spirit is involved with bringing human beings into right proportion, rightly arranging them both within themselves and in relation to the world around them. Moreover, the Spirit's re-creative work takes the form of following a pattern—that of Jesus Christ—and then of creatively re-imagining that pattern in new and varied settings. We become, Paul says, God's *poiema*—"his masterpiece" (as the *New Living Translation* vividly renders Eph. 2:10). Not only does our theology of the Spirit enable a better understanding of art and why it moves us, in addition to this, the world of art provides us with helpful and appropriate imagery for thinking about the work of the Spirit.

Athanasius and the Re-creation of Humanity

In developing this material we also will have a theological traveling companion—through the first half of the book in particular. In these chapters I will often turn for help to one of the greatest theological minds of the early church, St. Athanasius (c. 296–373). Some might find this surprising; Athanasius's theology has at times been criticized (his early theology in particular) for neglecting the Holy Spirit.[20] His mature work, however, more than makes up for any early deficiency. In fact, his *Letters to Serapion* is the first Christian theological treatise devoted entirely to the doctrine of the Holy Spirit.[21]

But the main reason for turning to Athanasius is that at every point in his long career he powerfully articulated the theme at the center of this book: humanity made and remade. Athanasius recognized, as clearly as any theologian has, that the story of *redemption* is the story of *re-creation*. This re-creation includes especially the remaking of our humanity, in and through the humanity of Jesus Christ. Athanasius also draws attention to a critical role that the Holy Spirit has in this work of re-creation. It is by the Holy Spirit that we are joined to the perfect humanity of Christ and remade in his image.

20. See for instance Thomas Weinandy, *Athanasius: A Theological Introduction* (Burlington, VT: Ashgate, 2007), 26, 48.

21. Khaled Anatolios, *Athanasius* (New York: Routledge, 2004), 82.

Who This Book Is For

This book arose from lectures I gave at the University of St. Andrews in the Autumn of 2001. Jeremy Begbie, then my colleague at St. Andrews, invited me to co-teach a course with him entitled "The Holy Spirit: An Exploration through the Arts." The idea was to teach an upper-level undergraduate course on the doctrine of the Holy Spirit in which the arts would act as a primary conversation partner, opening up and focusing important issues in pneumatology. We ended up teaching the course three times together over the next few years—Jeremy lecturing one week and I the next. (Anyone who has ever heard Professor Begbie speak will know what a fool's mission I had accepted!)

In 2005 I came to Belmont University in Nashville, Tennessee, to help launch a new program in religion and the arts. In my teaching at Belmont, I continue to use some of the same material I developed in St. Andrews, but now primarily in an upper-level undergraduate course called "Faith and Beauty: An Introduction to Theological Aesthetics."

So, in St. Andrews, this material was presented to students with some background in theology, but who in many cases had not spent much time thinking about the arts. At Belmont, I teach this material to students who have some training and a great deal of interest in the arts—but who for the most part have relatively little background in theology. My hope is that this book will prove useful to readers who fall into each of these categories. For this reason, I often will provide background information or definitions for names and terms that will seem awfully basic to an art or music student ("John Coltrane," for instance, or "mimesis") but which may be new to a student of theology. Similarly, terms and names already very familiar to students of theology ("Athanasius" or "perichoresis") will be briefly explained for the benefit of those whose primary experience is in the arts. I hope that all of those reading will be patient at these points where I pause and offer a bit of explanation for the benefit of readers entering the conversation from a different direction.

Finally, I should say that although this book originated in (on the one hand) a course on the doctrine of the Holy Spirit and (on the other hand) a course on theological aesthetics, it does not itself aspire to function as a comprehensive introduction to either area. A discussion of the *filioque* controversy, for instance, could hardly be omitted from a general introduction to pneumatology. Here it is barely mentioned, however, and this is because this book is not a general introduction to pneumatology. Instead, it is an evaluation—from the perspective of Christian theology—of the ways and reasons art and beauty have been linked with spirit.

1

Is There Anything to Talk About Here?

Spirit and Mystery

"Holiness"—"the holy"—is a category . . . peculiar to the sphere of religion. . . . It contains a quite specific element or "moment," which sets it apart from "the rational" . . . and which remains inexpressible . . . in the sense that it completely eludes apprehension in terms of concepts. The same thing is true (to take a quite different region of experience) of the category of the beautiful.

Rudolf Otto[1]

There is probably no conviction more deeply rooted in modern aesthetics than this, that works of art express what cannot be expressed in ordinary discourse.

W. E. Kennick[2]

Why a Theology of the Spirit?

What exactly is so "spiritual" about the arts? Among the many answers to this question that have been suggested, there is one we should consider right at the beginning. If it is correct we can stop—in fact, we will have to stop—before going much further.

1. Rudolf Otto, *The Idea of the Holy*, trans. John W. Harvey (Oxford: Oxford University Press, 1958), 5.

2. W. E. Kennick, "Art and the Ineffable," *The Journal of Philosophy* 58, no. 12 (June 8, 1961): 309–20.

There is an anonymous but often repeated quip that goes: "Talking about music is like dancing about architecture."[3] The conviction behind this one-liner is that words and music, concepts and song, are not only different but incommensurable media. Words and music each have a kind of meaning, certainly. But what is "said" in one domain really cannot be said in the other. "Is there a meaning to music?" asks composer Aaron Copland. "My answer would be 'Yes.' . . . 'Can you state in so many words what the meaning is?' My answer to that would be, 'No.' "[4]

Here, some have said, we've found the important resemblance between the spiritual and—not just music, but art generally. Each, it seems, moves us out beyond words and definitions, beyond concepts and logical distinctions. Each opens us up to realities and experiences of great profundity, but realities that wither on the examination table of the philosopher or the theologian. And—if this is the case—then ineffability, the "unsayable-ness" of art and spirituality, isn't a limitation to be overcome. It is instead precisely the virtue we value. In these areas we are given the privilege of speaking languages beyond language and knowing truths beyond knowing.

So, theologians, go home! If art and the spirit reside entirely within the domain of ineffability, then our study has both begun and ended. The last thing we should want in this case is a *theology* of the spirit, or a *theological* reflection on the arts. If the spiritual always runs out beyond our words and categories, then a conceptual, theological analysis of spirit seems misguided, or maybe even distasteful. Like producing a study titled *The Exhaustive Mechanical Physics of Lovemaking*, it misses the point entirely. The first proposal we must consider is this: the most important resemblance between art and Spirit is that we really can't talk about either one.

Art and Mystery

This is an idea that appears throughout a study by Princeton sociologist Robert Wuthnow, titled *Creative Spirituality: The Way of the Artist*.[5] The book's dust jacket claims that "artists have become the spiritual vanguard of our time." Increasingly, Wuthnow says, when Americans look for spiritual guidance and insight, they are turning not to priests or theologians, but to poets, musicians, sculptors, and dancers.

Why should artists—artists particularly—be singled out as the spiritual vanguard of our time? Why would people be inclined to seek spiritual insight

3. The quotation has been variously attributed to Elvis Costello, Martin Mull, David Byrne, and even Clara Schumann.

4. Aaron Copland, *What to Listen For in Music* (New York: Mentor, 1988), 12.

5. Robert Wuthnow, *Creative Spirituality: The Way of the Artist* (Berkeley: University of California Press, 2001).

from a poet or a painter, rather than (say) a dentist or an electrician? A number of the artists Wuthnow interviews answer along the lines we have just suggested. The arts usher us into the "spiritual" realm of ineffability. They invite us to stand open-mouthed before the mystery of things, and this, Wuthnow suggests, is the "spirituality" of art.

This is not a new idea. Particularly during the Romantic era the idea that the arts "say the unsayable" becomes something of a philosophical cliché.[6] In a famous study of Beethoven's music, the nineteenth century critic E. T. A. Hoffmann insists that "music *reveals* to man *an unknown realm* . . . a world in which he leaves behind all precise feelings in order to embrace an *inexpressible* longing."[7] It "comes to us from an unknown domain and kindles in the breast an inner bliss, *a higher significance than feeble words*, confined to the expression of banal earthly pleasures, can communicate."[8] In Hoffmann's breathless tribute music "reveals," though what it reveals remains somehow "unknown" and "inexpressible." Music has "significance," but what it signifies escapes—and in fact, exceeds—words.

These same ideas appear in Wuthnow's book, in an interview with wood sculptor David Ellsworth. Ellsworth creates free-form wooden objects that are difficult to define, and in fact, Wuthnow writes, "This is the essence that he is most intent on expressing. 'Without a definition,' he explains, 'we're left with wonderment.' "[9] "Being without definition is the key to Ellsworth's understanding of spirituality," Wuthnow continues, observing that an "emphasis on mystery occurs repeatedly in artists' accounts of their work."[10] Wuthnow believes that artists are sensitive and responsive to mystery because they recognize the futility of attempting to explain, define, or categorize their own creative work. He notes that the artists he interviews likewise place mystery and ineffability at the center of their spiritual lives and "emphasize the impossibility of fully understanding God."[11] Ellsworth for instance explains: "I believe in God, in a higher order that is above the human species. . . . There's something bigger than us. But it cannot be defined. If we could quantify it, identify it, catalog it, it would lose its value."[12]

For Ellsworth, then (as for many of the other artists Wuthnow interviews), mystery (what cannot be fully known or seen), and ineffability (what cannot be defined or spoken of) are the hallmarks of "the spiritual." And an interesting

6. David E. Cooper, "Ineffability," in *A Companion to Aesthetics*, ed. David E. Cooper (Oxford: Blackwell, 1995), 221–25.

7. E. T. A. Hoffmann, "Beethoven's Instrumental Music," in E. T. A. Hoffman, *Musical Writings: Kreisleriana, The Poet and the Composer, Music Criticism*, ed. David Charlton (Cambridge: Cambridge University Press, 1989), 96, emphasis added.

8. Ibid., 102, emphasis added.

9. Wuthnow, *Creative Spirituality*, 3.

10. Ibid., 2.

11. Ibid., 3.

12. Ibid.

conviction follows from this belief, namely, that those who are at the *furthest* possible remove from spirituality are theologians and clerics—those who deal in reason, words, and explanations.

According to Wuthnow, artists insist "on the limits of rationality in spirituality."[13] They recognize "that spirituality is more than a system of knowledge," and so, for them, the value of Scripture "lies less in its theological propositions than in its accurate description of human experience."[14] "They agree that God is ultimately too great to be fully comprehended by fallible human intellect."[15] Moreover they emphasize a lifestyle of faith "as opposed to simply ascribing intellectually to a set of abstract doctrines."[16] This, Wuthnow observes, "is a corrective to those philosophers and theologians who seem to think that the key to faith is having logical answers to every conceivable question."[17]

Artists, Wuthnow says, are unwilling to "settle easily for a faith that emphasizes intellectual arguments. They are drawn to artistic expressions of spirituality because they have experienced life in a way that cannot be reduced to words."[18] They are "uneasy with theological systems that claim to understand God through reason alone. Indeed, reason compels them to believe in a God who ultimately defies rational understanding."[19] Author Madeleine L'Engle echoes these sentiments in her interview, quoting one of her poems:

> This is the irrational season
> When love blooms bright and wild.
> Had Mary been filled with reason,
> There'd have been no room for the child.

"She elaborates: 'We try to be too reasonable about what we believe. What I believe is not reasonable at all.' "[20] L'Engle tells Wuthnow that theology "in today's complex world" must be "more about questions than answers." She recalls that when her children were young, she removed them from Sunday school when she discovered that "they were being taught questions that had answers."[21]

According to this perspective, knowledge, answers, and reason are toxic to mystery. Wuthnow reports that artists believe the "mysteries of life are too great

13. Ibid., 159.
14. Ibid., 162.
15. Ibid., 267.
16. Ibid., 273.
17. Ibid. (Who *are* these logic-obsessed theologians, by the way? I haven't yet met any of this crowd of theologians who believe that logic can answer "every conceivable question.")
18. Ibid., 59.
19. Ibid., 159.
20. Ibid., 143.
21. Ibid., 141.

to be captured fully in any religious community."[22] They insist that "spirituality should not be reduced too readily to doctrines or creeds."[23] The verbs—*capture*, *reduce*—insist upon a hostile relationship between what is fixed and known (religious communities, creeds, doctrines) and mystery. These are alternatives between which one must choose: "faith is more important to spiritual life than abstract knowledge."[24] Doctrinal formulations and theological systems obstruct rather than illuminate spiritual realities. Wuthnow believes that this may be why "many Americans," when faced with difficulty "turn more often to the music of Aretha Franklin or Jessye Norman than they do to theologians. Their spirits are uplifted as much by the concert on Saturday night as by the sermon on Sunday morning."[25]

The Spirituality of Non-Knowing

Perhaps the artists interviewed by Wuthnow would be surprised to learn that this same antipathy toward creeds and precise theological description is also common *among* theologians. At about the same time that "ineffability" assumed a prominent place in philosophical aesthetics, the idea of the "unknowable" and "unnameable" became important in theological discussions. The great theologian Friedrich Schleiermacher (1768–1834) would be especially influential in moving the verbal and the conceptual away from the center of the Christian faith. While we must speak and reason, Schleiermacher argued that whatever can be contained in words and concepts is not "the essence of religion."[26]

This idea and its connection to the arts is at the heart of Schleiermacher's beautiful little dialogue, *Christmas Eve*.[27] The dialogue describes a pleasant gathering of friends in a middle-class German home on the eve of Christmas. Much of the dialogue revolves around the contrasting characters of Sophie, a deeply pious and musical little girl, and Leonhardt, a skeptical, analytical lawyer. While Sophie displays "that childlike attitude . . . without which one cannot enter the kingdom of God,"[28] Leonhardt is (only somewhat teasingly)

22. Ibid., 9.
23. Ibid., 10.
24. Ibid., 22.
25. Ibid., 10.
26. Schleiermacher's best known exposition of this theme is found in the second speech in *On Religion: Speeches to Its Cultured Despisers*, trans. Richard Crouter (Cambridge: Cambridge University Press, 1988), 96–104.
27. Friedrich Schleiermacher, *Christmas Eve: Dialogue on the Incarnation*, trans. Terrence N. Tice (San Francisco: Edwin Mellen Press, 1990). The following discussion is drawn from Steven R. Guthrie, "Carmen Universitatis: A Theological Study of Music and Measure" (PhD diss., University of St. Andrews, 2000), 26–66.
28. Schleiermacher, *Christmas Eve*, 53.

described as "the evil principle . . . among you."[29] While Leonhardt represents learning, Sophie's piety is marked by a "deep underlying intelligence of feeling."[30] While Leonhardt analyzes things rigorously, Sophie feels things deeply and musically. "She knew how to treat each note aright; her touch and phrasing made each chord sound forth with an attachment which can scarcely tear itself from the rest but which then stands forth in its own measured strength until it too, like a holy kiss gives way to the next."[31] In Schleiermacher's dialogue it is the child—who sings, who feels, and who does *not* think and analyze—who shows us what true piety is.

In the same way, Agnes, one of the women participating in the conversation, admits that Leonhardt can reason and speak "better and finer than I,"[32] but this does not cause her any distress. Words are not at the heart of faith.

> For I do not know how to describe with words how deeply and ardently I [have] felt that all radiant, serene joy is religion; that love, pleasure, and devotion are tones making up a perfect harmony, tones which fit in with each other in any phrasing and in full chord.[33]

Agnes's relative awkwardness with words is no great deficit in the religious sphere, nor are Leondardt's rhetorical and conceptual powers any great advantage. Leonhardt summarizes Agnes's perspective: "You have yourself stated how you would have [the truth] expressed," he says, "namely, not by words, but in music."[34]

Music and religion, the dialogue suggests, reside primarily in the domain of experience and feeling, not that of ideas and knowledge. That is why, as one of the characters observes,

> we can well dispense with particular words in church music but not with the singing itself. A Miserere, a Gloria, or a Requiem: what special words are required of these? Their very character conveys plenty of meaning and suffers no essential change even though accompanying words may be replaced with others, so long as they fit the timing of the music; and this is true no matter what the language. Indeed, no one would say that anything of gross importance was lost even if one didn't get the words at all.[35]

Karl Barth sums up the message of Schleiermacher's dialogue: "*Exactly because of its lack of concepts*, music is the true and legitimate bearer of the message

29. Ibid., 85.
30. Ibid., 36.
31. Ibid., 31.
32. Ibid., 63.
33. Ibid.
34. Ibid.
35. Ibid., 47.

of Christmas, the adequate expression for the highest and final dialectical level, a level attainable by singing, by playing on flute and piano."[36]

More recently, the philosopher John Caputo stakes out similar territory in his essay *On Religion*,[37] claiming a central place for the unsayable in religion. The spiritual life, according to Caputo, has to do not with answers but with mystery, not with knowing but with uncertainty, not with theological definitions but with that which is unspeakable. In fact, he goes so far as to say that non-knowing is "*the condition of* [religious] *passion*."[38] From Caputo's perspective, the danger against which the spiritual person must guard is precisely the tendency to try to nail things down, tie things up, draw things to a close—choose your metaphor—through answers and definitions, creeds and doctrines. In so doing we deaden ourselves to the limitless possibilities and unfathomable mysteries of God and "close down" faith.[39] "The name of God," he insists, "is the name of the ever open question . . . the name of infinite questionability."[40] Caputo, then, advances the same opposition between faith and knowledge we find in Wuthnow: "The very highest passion is driven by non-knowing."[41]

Caputo is frustrated with those who think that the spiritual life is about having all their theological *i*'s dotted and all their doctrinal *t*'s crossed. Schleiermacher likewise feels that the one who stands closest to the kingdom is not the lawyer, the philosopher, the dialectician—but the musician. This is the case, not *despite* the absence of words and concepts in instrumental music, but *because* of it. It is the musician who says what cannot be said in words. On these points the theologian Schleiermacher and the philosopher Caputo stand cheek to cheek with artists like L'Engle and Ellsworth. All locate both art and spirituality in the domain of mystery—that which cannot be fully explored, understood, or known—and ineffability—that which exceeds verbal, rational, or conceptual articulation.

Ruach and Untameable Mystery

As I explained in the introduction, for Christians spirituality is most properly *Spirit*-uality—life in and by the Spirit. And certainly if we are thinking in terms of *Spirit*-uality there is some validity to the connection between spirituality, mystery, and ineffability that Schleiermacher, Caputo, and Wuthnow have

36. Karl Barth, *Theology and Church, Shorter Writings 1920–1928*, trans. Louise Pettibone Smith (London: SCM, 1962), 157, emphasis added.

37. John D. Caputo, *On Religion* (New York: Routledge, 2001).

38. Ibid., 19, emphasis added. It's not clear whether by this Caputo means that religious passion always and only exists in the state ("the condition") of non-knowing, or that non-knowing is the prerequisite ("the condition") of religious passion.

39. Ibid., 130.

40. Ibid., 134.

41. Ibid., 129.

highlighted. It is difficult to say much about the work of the Holy Spirit in Scripture without employing adjectives like *mysterious*, *untamed*, *unseen*, and *surprising*.

The very name "Spirit" (*ruach* in Hebrew; *pneuma* in Greek) has an element of uncharted wildness about it. The words *ruach* and *pneuma* mean not only "spirit," but also "breath" or "wind." *Spirit*, then, is a word that suggests movement, and movement of an organic (rather than a mechanically regular) sort. Neither breath nor wind can easily be seen or kept contained. The wind comes unexpectedly and cannot be directed or turned aside.[42] Both breath and wind are connected with natural processes, processes that are difficult to control or map with precision.[43] Who knows when the wind will turn or in which direction? Though we may try—for a little while—to hold our breath, or do our best to catch our breath, ultimately it is our breath that holds and catches us. It is most intimately connected to us; we could not survive apart from it, yet we cannot dictate its arrival or cessation.

It is this unpredictable and mysteriously sovereign character of the Spirit's work that Jesus seems to have in mind as he speaks with Nicodemus: "Jesus answered, 'Very truly, I tell you, no one can enter the kingdom of God without being born of water and Spirit. What is born of the flesh is flesh, and what is born of the Spirit is spirit. Do not be astonished that I said to you, "You must be born from above." The wind [*pneuma*] blows where it chooses, and you *hear the sound of it, but you do not know where it comes from or where it goes*. So it is with everyone who is born of the Spirit'" (John 3:5–8, emphasis added).

Interestingly, these words are also a good description of the Spirit's descent upon the church at Pentecost: "They were all together in one place. And suddenly from heaven there came a sound like the rush of a violent wind, and it filled the entire house where they were sitting. . . . All of them were filled with the Holy Spirit" (Acts 2:1–2, 4). Just like the wind in Jesus's dialogue with Nicodemus, a rushing sound is heard, but they "do not know where it comes from" (we read that it descended upon the believers "suddenly"). Certainly they could not have known where the wind was going. By the end of

42. "*Ruach* as 'wind' commonly refers to the strong wind of the storm, the raging blast from the desert, like the one that divided the Red Sea at the Exodus (Exod. 14.21). This driving wind is not identical with the *ruach* of God himself, but its elemental power made it a powerful image of divine strength" (Alasdair Heron, *The Holy Spirit* [London: Marshall, Morgan, and Scott, 1983], 4). See also Hendrikus Berkhof, *The Doctrine of the Holy Spirit* (Atlanta: John Knox, 1964), 13–14.

43. "Perhaps the first thing that strikes us as we come to the Old Testament is the tremendous emphasis on the Spirit of God as a violent, invading force. It is like the wind that hurtled across the desert or whistled through the cedars or rushed down the wadis. . . . In speaking of the 'Spirit of the Lord' the Old Testament writers significantly retain this emphasis on God's violent invasion from outside our experience, disturbing and mysterious like the wind. It is their way of stressing that the Beyond has come into our midst, and we can neither organize nor domesticate him" (Michael Green, *I Believe in the Holy Spirit* [London: Hodder and Stoughton, 1975], 19–20).

the book of Acts it would sweep them all the way to Rome! The Spirit comes roaring in—unexpected, irresistible, and with extraordinary effect. These pneumatic traits of movement, power, and spontaneity mark the work of the Spirit throughout the New Testament.

Holy Spirit as Boundary-Breaker

Throughout the New Testament the Spirit drives the church along like a skiff out ahead of a gale, scuttering across geographical, social, and racial boundaries, out into uncharted waters. At Pentecost Peter declares that when God pours out his Spirit upon all flesh "your sons and your daughters shall prophesy, and your young men shall see visions, and your old men shall dream dreams. Even upon my slaves, both men and women, in those days I will pour out my Spirit; and they shall prophesy" (Acts 2:17–18).

In Acts, the Spirit is "poured out" with such force as to burst the channels and banks of social division. Not only sons but daughters, not only youths but the aged, not only masters but slaves now have a share in the Spirit. The implications of this become increasingly clear to the church. As Peter will recognize to his astonishment a little later in the book of Acts, if both Jews and Gentiles have the same Spirit, then these two "unlike" parties are now, in a very significant sense, alike. Those with the same Spirit can eat at the same table and stay under the same roof: "While Peter was still speaking, the Holy Spirit fell upon all who heard the word. The circumcised believers who had come with Peter were astounded that the gift of the Holy Spirit had been poured out even on the Gentiles. . . . Then Peter said, 'Can anyone withhold the water for baptizing these people who have received the Holy Spirit just as we have?' So he ordered them to be baptized in the name of Jesus Christ. Then they invited him to stay for several days" (Acts 10:44–48).

In fact, the apostle Paul will observe, those who share the same *pneuma*—the same Spirit, the same breath—may well be said to be "one body." "For in the one Spirit we were all baptized into one body—Jews or Greeks, slaves or free—and we were all made to drink of one Spirit" (1 Cor. 12:13).

In this way the powerful and unpredictable Spirit breaks through impassable barriers, opening up new paths and allowing free converse between those who were once separated.

Holy Spirit as Plan-Disrupter

Not only does the Spirit-wind blow down social fences and cultural boundary markers. In the New Testament the Spirit also disrupts plans and itineraries, like electrical lines tangled in the gusts of a thunderstorm.

Philip, after baptizing the Ethiopian eunuch, is "snatched away" by the Spirit of the Lord (Acts 8:39) and finds himself at Azotus—traveling north to Caesarea, though previously he had been journeying "towards the south . . .

down from Jerusalem to Gaza" (Acts 8:26). In a similar way, Paul and Timothy believe they are headed to Asia, but when they attempt to enter Bythynia, "the Spirit of Jesus did not allow them" (Acts 16:7). And so a new, unexpected itinerary takes shape, carrying them through the regions of Phrygia and Galatia, and eventually bringing the gospel to the city of Philippi in Macedonia. Later in his career, Paul would be led back to Jerusalem, "as a captive to the Spirit . . . not knowing what will happen to me there" (Acts 20:22).

Even Jesus, who calms the winds of the storm, is "driven" by the wind of the Spirit. The Spirit, in the form of a dove, descends upon Jesus at his baptism. After this, "immediately" the Spirit "*drove him* out into the wilderness" (Mark 1:12, emphasis added). The powerful and unpredictable Spirit literally "casts Jesus out" (*ekballei*) into the desert—the word is the same forceful term used to describe the "casting out" of demons (cf. Mark 3:22).

Holy Spirit as Surprise-Bringer

So the Spirit often disrupts settled plans already in place. What is more, the Spirit also brings about *new* and altogether *unexpected* states of affairs. We've already mentioned some of these surprising incidents: a sudden relocation to a different region; a church composed of Jew and Gentile—none of these would have seemed very likely developments. Other Old and New Testament events connected with the Spirit seem almost worthy of tabloid headlines: "Virgin expecting baby!" (see Luke 1:34–35); "Dead raised to life!" (see Rom. 8:11); "Man kills lion with bare hands!" (see Judg. 14:6); "Fire falls from heaven!" (see Acts 2:3).

The *ruach* of God "blows where it listeth," unable to be contained by social boundaries, human plans, or expectations of what is and is not possible. We cannot say with certainty, "the Spirit will lead this way or that," or "the Spirit is at work over here but not over there."

It seems fair, then—entirely appropriate—to associate *Spirit* with mystery and the ineffable, as Wuthnow's artists have done. The Spirit moves in ways we do not expect and acts with a power we cannot easily describe. This is a point at which artistic intuitions can serve as a powerful reminder and opportunity for Christian theology.

When we recognize the Spirit as the *ruach*—the breath, the wind—of God, it is right that we should be put in mind of the wild, uncharted regions of which we can say little. When we remember that the Spirit is the *ruach*, we remember to be humble before a sovereign God, whose thoughts are higher than our thoughts and whose ways are higher than our ways. We remember that while we may hold doctrines, our doctrines don't hold God—neither controlling him nor containing all there is of him.

If we were to describe all of this in terms other than *mystery* and *ineffability*, we might say that the work of the Spirit is characterized by *dynamism*. The

Spirit is active and agile; the Spirit moves. Moreover, the movement of the Spirit cannot be contained or constrained. The Spirit moves in ways we may not have expected, to places we may not have chosen to go, bringing about effects we may not be able to put into words. The energy and motion of the Spirit is not like that of a billiard ball, which shoots off in this way or that because it has been struck or aimed. The activity of the Spirit is more like that of the wind: who can see its source or how it has been set in motion? It is a *sovereign dynamism*.

The Communicative Spirit

But this is not all that we can say of the Holy Spirit. At the very same time, Scripture connects the work of the Spirit with understanding, knowledge, guidance, and speech.

Jesus speaks of the Spirit as the one who "will guide you into all the truth" and who will "declare to you the things that are to come" (John 16:13). The apostle Paul also identifies the Spirit as a teacher—the one from whom Paul and his associates have received their message and training: "We speak of these things in words not taught by human wisdom but taught by the Spirit" (1 Cor. 2:13). Later in the same letter, wisdom and knowledge are the first two examples that come to mind when Paul speaks of the gifts given by the Spirit: "To one is given through the Spirit the utterance of wisdom, and to another the utterance of knowledge according to the same Spirit" (1 Cor. 12:8).

Actually, it would be more accurate to say that in this passage Paul associates the Spirit with wise and knowledgeable speech (rather than simply with wisdom and knowledge). And this raises an interesting point of contrast with the suggestion advanced by Wuthnow and Caputo. Our artists have suggested that whatever else we may say about spiritual reality, we must say that it is unsayable. The spiritual (it is claimed) has to do with mystery and ineffability, and the ineffable is that which cannot be spoken or fully articulated. We've seen that within the Christian Scriptures there are grounds for this association of the Spirit with the ineffable. The Spirit brings surprises and makes possible what would have seemed impossible. The Spirit (Paul says in a well-known passage) prays for us "with sighs too deep for words" (Rom. 8:26).

And yet, the wisdom and knowledge that the Christian Scriptures associate with the Spirit's work is not simply an inward and inarticulate wisdom—a "secret knowledge" as it were. Rather, over and over again, the Spirit is specifically connected with communicative action. The Spirit, Jesus says, "will take what is mine and *declare* it to you" (John 16:14). The Spirit gives not only inward illumination but—specifically, particularly—words, speech, language, communication. Jesus comforts his followers by assuring them that when persecution comes, and when they are made to answer for their beliefs, "the Holy Spirit will teach you at that very hour what you ought to say" (Luke 12:12; cf. Mark 13:11).

Indeed, when Peter and others begin to speak up in challenging situations, they speak "by the Holy Spirit": "Then Peter, filled with the Holy Spirit, *said to them*, 'Rulers of the people and elders . . .' " (Acts 4:8, emphasis added). We read that the rulers in turn recognized that this was no ordinary display of rhetoric. "Now when they saw the boldness of Peter and John and realized that they were uneducated and ordinary men, they were amazed and recognized them as companions of Jesus" (Acts 4:13).

Where the Spirit is given, there is speech: "All of them were filled with the Holy Spirit and *began to speak*" (Acts 2:4, emphasis added). Or, perhaps we should say, where the Spirit is given there is communication. At Pentecost the followers of Jesus speak, but what is more remarkable is that those to whom they speak—those who are in Jerusalem "from every nation under heaven"—are able to declare: "*In our own languages we hear them* speaking about God's deeds of power" (Acts 2:11, emphasis added). And of course the supreme instance of the Spirit bringing the Word and knowledge is the incarnation. By the Spirit (Luke 1:35; Matt. 1:20) the Word became flesh and dwelt among us (John 1:14), revealing, declaring, and giving knowledge of the unseen God (John 1:18).

Ruach and *pneuma*, as we've said, mean not only wind, but breath. Spirit is not only the mysterious wind that blows "wherever it listeth," but is also the breath that carries speech from speaker to listener. We've said that the activity of the Spirit can be characterized as a *sovereign dynamism*. In addition to this we can say that the movement of the Spirit is *fertile*. The *ruach* not only moves, but *carries*—gifts, power, words, insight, and so on. It is *movement-between*. (John V. Taylor's apt description of the Holy Spirit is *The Go-Between God*.) What belongs to Jesus is *carried to* his followers (John 16:14); the words of the Pentecost believers are *carried to* their hearers (Acts 2:11); the gospel is *carried to* Gentile believers, out beyond the ordinary boundaries of the Jewish believers (Acts 10:47–48).

Knowledge *Toward*

We've arrived at an interesting paradox. The Christian Scriptures associate the Spirit with both mystery and knowledge. Despite the criticisms of theologians we surveyed earlier, *both* poles of this paradox are embraced in the earliest Christian theological writings on the Spirit.

In fact, Athanasius's *Letters to Serapion* is written to counter precisely the sort of small-minded rationalism about which Wuthnow and Caputo are concerned. The letters were prompted by the teaching of a Christian group who were unwilling to acknowledge the full divinity of the Spirit. If both the Spirit and the Son share in the being of the Father, they reasoned, then doesn't this amount to saying that God has two Sons? Or, if we say that the Spirit comes to us from the Son, then it seems we are saying the Spirit is the Son of the Son, which would make him the Father's Grandson! In countering these complaints Athanasius reminds his opponents of the ineffability of God. "It is only in the Godhead," Athanasius declares, "that the Father is *properly* Father and the Son *properly* Son."[44] In other words, we learn what fatherhood is and what sonship is by looking to God; we do not deduce what God can or cannot be by logical analysis of human categories. God cannot be forced into the constraints of our words and concepts. "For what discourse can suitably interpret the things that are above originated nature?" he asks. "Or what hearing can understand what it is not possible for human beings to either hear or speak?"[45]

In his *Fifth Theological Oration: On the Holy Spirit*, Gregory of Nazianzus (c. 330–90) speaks to the same sort of complaints Athanasius countered. Like Athanasius, Gregory argues against the petty rationalism of those who denied the Spirit's divinity. And like Athanasius, Gregory insists that while we must use words to speak of God, our words cannot contain all the reality of God. Just because we speak of God as "Father" and Christ as "Son," he points out, "it does not follow that we ought to think it essential to transfer wholesale to the divine sphere the earthly names of human family ties."[46]

Basil the Great (c. 330–79) in his treatise on the Holy Spirit also addresses a group who seem unable to accept mystery and ineffability. These teachers complain of the mathematical irrationality of Trinitarian teaching. How can God be three *and* one? they ask. Isn't this just numerical nonsense?

Basil replies, "The Unapproachable One is beyond numbers, wisest sirs; imitate the reverence shown by the Hebrews of old to the unutterable name of God. Count if you must, but do not malign the truth. Either honor Him Who cannot be described with your silence, or number holy things in accord with true religion."[47]

Each of these theologians insists that our speech and our categories must conform to who God is, and not the other way around. We must begin with

44. Athanasius, *Letters to Serapion on the Holy Spirit*, in Khaled Anatolios, *Athanasius* (New York: Routledge, 2004), 215, emphasis added.

45. Ibid., 216.

46. St. Gregory of Nazianzus, *On God and Christ: The Five Theological Orations and Two Letters to Cledoniius*, trans. Lionel Wickham (Crestwood, NY: St. Vladimir's Seminary Press, 2002), 121. T. F. Torrance summarizes this insight of the Greek Fathers: "We cannot but use language taken from our common experience in this world when we make theological statements, but even so it is the subject that must be allowed to determine the meaning. It would be inherently wrong to use expressions like 'right hand' or 'bosom' or even 'father' and 'son' as if they meant when applied to God the same thing they mean when used of creatures" (T. F. Torrance, *Theology in Reconstruction* [London: SCM Press, 1965], 30).

47. St. Basil the Great, *On the Holy Spirit*, 18.44, trans. David Anderson (Crestwood, NY: St. Vladimir's Seminary Press, 1980), 71.

the mystery of God rather than trying to squeeze God into our philosophical systems—and here Athanasius is in hearty agreement with the criticisms of Wuthnow, L'Engle, and Caputo. "It is not fitting to enquire in this way about divinity," writes Athanasius. "God is not as a human being, so that anyone should dare to ask human questions about him."[48]

At the same time, however, this does not mean that Athanasius thinks of the Spirit-life as permanently inhabiting Caputo's "condition of non-knowing." It is precisely because "it is impossible for . . . us human beings to speak appropriately of the things that are ineffable,"[49] that Athanasius emphasizes the indispensable role of the Holy Spirit. As T. F. Torrance observes, "It is only the Spirit of God who knows the things of God, [so] it is only in the Spirit and by his power that we may really know God and apprehend his Truth. *The revelation of the unknowable is the peculiar function of the Spirit.*"[50]

In the *Letters to Serapion* Athanasius identifies the Spirit with this work of opening ears and eyes, of making us *participants* in the revelation of God in Jesus Christ. While Jesus is "the exact imprint of God's very being" (Heb. 1:3), this image must be *seen*, must be *recognized* as the image of God for it to be of value to us. For revelation to become knowledge there must be eyes that see and ears that hear. Athanasius appeals to the biblical image of light. The Father is light, he writes, and the Son is the radiance of the Father's glory; but it is the Spirit "in whom we are enlightened."[51] Changing metaphors, he writes, "The Father is fountain, and the Son is called river, [yet] we are said to *drink* of one Spirit."[52] The Spirit's distinctive work is to make God's revelatory work in Christ actual and effective.[53] The metaphors of fountain, river, and drink make clear that Athanasius is not talking about the kind of static rationalism caricatured by Caputo and Wuthnow. It is an image of intimacy, nourishment, and life; it is knowledge *set in motion* toward the one known. By the Spirit, we are given the knowledge that enables us to *respond*, to drink, to actively participate in the life of God. Athanasius's theology of the Spirit can comfortably accommodate both knowledge and mystery because it is built on a broader foundation of participation, worship, and love.

48. Athanasius, *Letters to Serapion*, 215.

49. Ibid., 217.

50. Torrance, *Theology in Reconstruction*, 30, emphasis added.

51. Athanasius, *Letters to Serapion*, 218, emphasis added.

52. Ibid., emphasis added.

53. In his discussion of Athanasius's *Letters to Serapion*, Alan Torrance offers a powerful exposition of this theme. "The transforming presence of the Holy Spirit who is 'of one Being with the Father' is the necessary subjective condition for the recognition of Jesus as the incarnate Word. . . . If God is not present as the Holy Spirit in and with the 'mind' of the church, then there is no possibility of that 'mind' recognizing or being informed by the presence with humanity of God the Son—'flesh and blood' does not, cannot, and will not reveal this in and of itself!" ("Being of One Substance with the Father," in *Nicene Christianity: The Future for a New Ecumenism*, ed. Christopher R. Seitz [Grand Rapids: Brazos, 2001], 55).

Love as Source and Goal

The life of the Spirit arises in love and culminates in participation, and the route along which we travel the spiritual life is neither that of blind mystery nor dogmatic knowledge, but of worship. We know the Spirit in and through response and adoration. At this point we find ourselves in agreement with Caputo, who expresses this idea eloquently. "The love of God is my north star," he writes; "Love is the measure."[54] As we've seen, however, Caputo believes that knowledge must be set aside in order to make room for the highest passion, the greatest love.[55] We find better guides in Basil, Gregory of Nazianzus, and Athanasius. They are convinced that the pursuit of knowledge springs from the experience of worship. In particular, they believe that worship nourishes a passion for the kind of doctrinal, theological knowledge disparaged by Wuthnow's artists. Moreover, they are convinced that this pursuit of knowledge finds its consummation in worship, in a richer and fuller adoration of the beloved.

Basil's treatise on the Holy Spirit is a good example of this. It was not written for an academic conference or in the hopes of achieving tenure. Basil is defending his congregation's practice of prayer, which had recently been criticized by the *Pneumatomachoi* (literally, "the fighters against the Spirit," a group who denied the Spirit's divinity). Basil explains, "While I pray with the people, we sometimes finish the doxology to God the Father with the form 'Glory to the Father with the Son, together with the Holy Spirit,' and at other times we use 'Glory to the Father through the Son in the Holy Spirit.' "[56] The arguments that follow are offered in support of what the worshiping congregation *does*. Likewise, for both Basil and Athanasius, one of the strongest arguments in favor of the Spirit's divinity is the church's *practice* of baptism—in the name of the Father and of the Son and of the Holy Spirit. In each of these cases, then, doctrine arises in large part as men and women reflect on the practices of the worshiping church. For his part, before he begins arguing with his opponents concerning the interpretation of various biblical passages, Gregory declares, "For the present it will be sufficient for us to say just this: it is the Spirit in whom we worship and through whom we pray."[57]

And as we've said, for Basil, Gregory, and Athanasius, a right theology of the Spirit is not only grounded in, but oriented toward, adoration. Athanasius urges his readers "to confess and cling to the Truth," not because he has a compulsive addiction to logic, but "according to the model of true worshippers."[58]

54. Caputo, *On Religion*, 3.
55. See, for example, ibid., 115, 129.
56. Basil, *On the Holy Spirit*, 17.
57. Gregory, *Orations* 31.12, 125.
58. Athanasius, *Letters to Serapion*, 233.

Art and Ineffability

It is here, in fact—in worship, in adoration—that we find a far richer resemblance between art and spirituality; not in ineffability understood simplistically as "not-knowing," but in a movement that arises from love, is carried along in worship, and finds fulfillment in participation.

In terms of Christian spirituality we have seen that "ineffability" captures only part of what the Scriptures want to say about the activity of the Spirit. The same is true of the arts. Certainly, ineffability captures something of the artistic experience. A verbal or conceptual description of a painting will fall far short of the experience we have when standing before it; a written review or a thematic analysis of a play by Shakespeare is not even a pale substitute for attending in person. When it comes to beauty, "our findings are, as one might say, all first-personal, and discussions of a piece of music that is described but never heard are necessarily vacuous."[59]

But, of course, the same frailty of explanation applies to all first-person experience. A wasp sting, David Cooper points out, "also causes a feeling that a description of the sting fortunately does not."[60] Artistic ineffability "is simply a special case of the ineffability of first-person awareness—the impossibility of translating 'what it is like' into a description."[61] What we value in art is not merely unsayable-ness.

Rather, the *distinctive* feature of artistic ineffability lies close to what Calvin Seerveld calls "allusivity."[62] Works of art both beckon and point beyond by "hinting or referring indirectly, referring to without explicit mention, referring to in a covert, or passing way."[63] Why should this indirectness be an artistic value? Because in this way the artist invites us not merely to exist in the vicinity of the work, but to *participate* in it. We are drawn in, drawn out of ourselves. To be experienced as art it must be received, reconstructed, as it were, in the perception of the listener or viewer. By enlisting our active perception, the work of art "depicts the subject-matter *as experienced*."[64] There is a paradox here: the expressive character of art is directly related to what it does not say (explicitly). In support of this point Roger Scruton sets out the rich allusions in several lines of poetry by Rimbaud. He observes that none of these resonances and connections are explicitly stated by the poet, "but precisely because it is not stated, the lines can be understood only by a leap into subjectivity—by attaining the first-person perspective that binds these images together."[65]

59. Mary Mothersill, "Beauty," in *Companion to Aesthetics*, ed. Cooper, 46.

60. Cooper, "Ineffability," 223.

61. Roger Scruton, *The Aesthetics of Music* (Oxford: Clarendon, 1997), 364.

62. Quoted in Hilary Brand and Adrienne Chaplin, *Art and Soul: Signposts for Christians in the Arts*, 2nd ed. (Carlisle, UK/Downers Grove, IL: Piquant/InterVarsity, 2001), 123.

63. Ibid.

64. Ibid.

65. Scruton, *Aesthetics of Music*, 364.

Scruton concludes that "the expressive and the ineffable go together." In gesturing and beckoning rather than exhaustively defining, the work of art invites us "to 'enter into' its expressive content."[66] In the artwork there is veiling as well as disclosure, and as in some exotic dance, it is the veil as well as the disclosure that we find alluring. Not all the work is done for us, precisely in order to enlist us in the work of making meaning and experiencing delight. Micheal O'Siadhail gives an eloquent poetic testimony to the power of allusivity.

Revelation

Our train gains ground into the evening light.
Among the trees the sun catches in its fall
Glints and anglings of a stone in a distant gable,
A broadcast of facets, one and infinite.
I glance at you. There's so much unexplained.
Plays of your light keep provoking my infinity;
Already something in your presence overflows me,
A gleam of a face refusing to be contained.
How little I know of you. Again and again
I've resolved to be the giver and not the taker,
Somehow to surpass myself. Am I the mapmaker
So soon astray in this unknowable terrain?
Twenty-one years. And I'm journeying to discover
Only what your face reveals. Stranger and lover.[67]

We could offer (forgive me!) a prosaic exposition of at least some of the elements of the narrator's experience:

> Once my wife and I were riding on a train—and actually, it occurs to me that there's a sense in which in our married life, she and I are on a "journey" together as well. Anyway, we were on this journey and I looked out the window and saw a stone in the archway of a building. It kind of shimmered and glittered in the sun, and that got me thinking about how you can look at something simple and familiar but continue to see it from different angles and discover new things in it. I guess it's kind of that way with the face of someone you love or know very well. Really, it's that way with my wife's face, the one I know best. It continues to surprise and reveal more; it's both familiar and mysterious.

Clearly this description is a desecration of the original. While the prose paraphrase articulates at least some of the conceptual material from O'Siadhail's sonnet, the artistic beauty, the allusiveness, and the poetic ineffability are lost. In a word what is lost is *love*: the allure of beauty and the experience of participation. In

66. Ibid.

67. Micheal O'Siadhail, "Revelation," in *Poems: 1975–1995: Hail! Madam Jazz/A Fragile City* (Tarset, UK: Bloodaxe Books, 1999), 173. Used by permission.

the original the narrator is on a journey, sees a gable, sees a face, and various connections among these experiences begin to play in his mind. Through what is said and, equally, what is not said, the poem invites us to participate in these experiences—rather than simply offering us a prepared explanation of them. The poem draws us into a similar first-person experience of discovery. If we set out to understand the poem then we, like the narrator, will have the experience of actively making connections between one image and another and exploring the richness of these juxtapositions. In this way the poem reproduces in us the narrator's experience of discovery and "revelation." In the same way, Anne Sheppard observes that often we do not respond as deeply to a *trompe-l'oeil* painting (that is, a painting designed to "deceive the eye" into believing that it is reality) as we do to less literal, less illusionistic representational works. Rather "we value representational art which gives scope to [the] capacity of the imagination." In the *trompe-l'oeil* work "there is little room . . . to exercise the imagination and no opportunity for the mental balancing act involved in seeing a picture both as a representation of something else and as a configuration of shapes and colors."[68] The illusionistic painting, like the prose description, "does the work for us." While in the case of the *trompe-l'oeil* painting there may be other elements we enjoy, there is less of a fascination, less a sense of the ineffable. "That which cannot be uttered" (Latin, *ineffabilis*) *has* been uttered. So we admire the skill of the artist, but are not ourselves drawn into the work.

And this "drawing in" is what artistic ineffability reaches toward. We value artistic ineffability, not because it leaves us in a state of perpetual unknowing, but because of the way description is set aside in favor of invitation: *come and see*. The poet limits what her words reveal, not to bar the way but to draw us forward. O'Siadhail's poem not only embodies but illuminates this dialectic of mystery and participation. The face of his beloved is mysterious, and this mystery draws him forward toward continuing and deepening consummation. The mystery keeps him "journeying to discover only what your face reveals." And not only mystery, but also beauty. "Beauty brings copies of itself into being," Elaine Scarry observes. "It makes us draw it, take photographs of it, or describe it to other people."[69] The work of art calls forth a response. It is desirable and calls for our gaze; it is allusive and asks us to enter into first-personal experience. The narrator continues to gaze at the face of his wife because she is beautiful, because she is his beloved. Through desire and beauty he is drawn out beyond himself: "Plays of your light keep provoking my infinity." Mary Mothersill argues that this is one of the "fundamental truths"[70] of beauty: that it is "linked with pleasure and inspires love."[71] In fact, she believes, "falling

68. Anne Sheppard, *Aesthetics: An Introduction to the Philosophy of Art* (Oxford: Oxford University Press, 1987), 14.

69. Elaine Scarry, *On Beauty and Being Just* (Princeton: Princeton University Press, 1999), 3.

70. Mary Mothersill, *Beauty Restored* (Oxford: Oxford University Press, 1984), 262.

71. Ibid., 274.

in love" is a singularly appropriate description of the aesthetic experience.[72] A similar idea has a prominent role in R. G. Collingwood's influential aesthetic theory. Collingwood argues that an artifact only functions as a work of art as it is "reimagined" in the mind and "reexperienced" in the perception of a viewer or listener. "The kind of contact that is required," he writes, "is a collaborative contact in which the audience genuinely shares in the creative activity."[73] Significantly, Collingwood likens aesthetic activity to speech, and he points out that "speech is speech only so far as it is both spoken and *heard*. . . . *Mutual love is a collaborative activity*."[74]

A communicative act that aims at the collaborative activity of mutual love—here we have a much richer, much more satisfying way of thinking about artistic ineffability. And it is fair to say that in this richer conception there is indeed a structural similarity between the aesthetic and the spiritual experience. In each case the experience (1) communicates and reveals and yet (2) cannot be reduced to words; each (3) originates in love and (4) culminates in participation. Madeleine L'Engle, Caputo, and the others we've heard are right to sense that the experience of art—and the experience of spirituality—cannot be reduced to receiving information or dogmatic answers. The role of mystery, however—again in both art and the life of the Spirit—is not that we would remain in a constant state of "not knowing." Rather, we are given a taste—but only a taste—that we might accept the invitation to come to the fountain.

> "Come and see!" (John 1:46)
>
> "Taste and see that the LORD is good." (Ps. 34:8)

This is perhaps the best answer to the question with which we opened this chapter: if God is mysterious, then isn't any sort of "theology of the Holy Spirit" profoundly misguided? The Spirit's work is to call forth response, to give us speech, and to make us participants in truth. There are many ways of responding to such an invitation, but the proper response of friend to friend, or lover to beloved, is not enduring silence. The Spirit, like beauty, draws us toward participation: "The Father is fountain, and the Son is called river, [yet] we are said to *drink* of one Spirit."[75] "All God's deeds are inexpressible," acknowledges Hendrikus Berkhof. "We can dishonor them all by speaking about them in an irreverent way. But all God's deeds want to be confessed, in spite of—no, on account of—their inexpressibility. God wants us to love him with all our mind and with all our strength. True theology is an act of love. In this act we cannot be silent about a single one of God's mighty inexpressible deeds."[76]

72. Ibid.

73. R. G. Collingwood, *The Principles of Art* (London: Oxford University Press, 1975), 331.

74. Ibid., 317, emphasis added.

75. Athanasius, *Letters to Serapion*, 218.

76. Berkhof, *Doctrine of the Holy Spirit*, 9.

The goal toward which the Spirit carries us is not numinous silence but the ecstatic speech of Pentecost, not simply standing in wordless awe over the unknowable depths but kneeling down at the spring *to drink*. We account for the ineffability of biblical *Spirit*-uality not by denying but by insisting that the Spirit also invites us to *speak*. *Spirit*-uality may be described as ineffable not only because of the Spirit-Wind who rushes in unexpectedly, but also and precisely *because* of the Spirit-Breath who brings word and speech. The Spirit's ineffability is not the refusal of words. Quite the opposite. It is an invitation and an enabling by which we speak and respond.

The Personal Spirit

There is one other observation worth making here. We have been speaking about communication and desire, love and participation, invitation and response, all of which place us squarely in the realm of the personal. Acts like love and invitation are—or find their archetypes in—the acts of a person. It is interesting, then, that the artists in Wuthnow's book generally describe a spiritual reality that is nonpersonal—as a force, an energy, or a "Reality." Artist Jon Davis speaks of "some form of Truth or Reality"[77]; dancer Jamal Gaines "regards spirituality as a kind of energy that flows through and empowers people."[78]

The biblical portrayal of the Spirit, however, is able to hold together ineffability and knowledge precisely because it understands the Holy Spirit as person. It is persons with whom we speak and who speak to us, and it is persons who remain always beyond what we can say about them. It is persons whom we most genuinely speak of "knowing," and it is persons who are most truly always beyond our knowing, who always remain, to some degree, mysterious. Indeed, the mysterious is preeminently the domain of the personal. Things (how a television works; how many galaxies there are in the universe) may be *unknown*—but they are not mysterious per se. They are things that could be known, given additional research and exploration. But no amount of data or scientific analysis could ever eliminate the ineffable wonder I felt when I first held my children; no philosophical speculation could ever resolve the mystery of my wife's face. With artistic ineffability as well, I have argued that what we value is allusivity. An artist calls us out of ourselves; a person beckons us to experience something from a first-person perspective. It is not the stone as a brute material fact that is ineffable, but, rather, considering it from the perspective another has inhabited.

Some of the artists and authors we have surveyed have insisted that God and spirituality cannot be defined nor contained and analyzed by rational formulations. But we should notice at once that it is precisely impersonal

77. Wuthnow, *Creative Spirituality*, 26.
78. Ibid., 33.

things, things like forces, energies, and so on, that can be quantified, defined, and plotted out mathematically. We can articulate rules and generalizations and principles when we speak of a force; we can apply the physical principles of gravity, electromagnetism, weak and strong nuclear force. It is when we enter the realm of personhood that we move outside of definitions and enter into mystery. It is precisely because the Holy Spirit is a person, and not a force, that we cannot box him into doctrinal formulations. It is *because* he is a person that he is mysterious.

At the same time, it is his personhood that provides boundaries and precision and definition. When we speak of the Spirit, we are not speaking about an amorphous field of force, but about a person. To be a person is to have a name; it is to be a particular, to occupy a particular "space," to have a particular history. What is more, we more naturally speak of knowledge or wisdom coming from persons rather than things. We may study a force or a natural phenomenon, but it is only in a metaphorical sense that these can "speak to" us or "teach" us. In fact, they do not teach—we observe, study, and learn, and draw our conclusions. Neither can a "power" or "energy" reveal something to us. To "reveal" requires both self-awareness ("here is something I know") and intention ("this thing I know, I will make known"); and self-awareness and intention are things, once again, that we associate with persons.

As stunningly complex as some of the universe's systems and forces may be, it is still surprising that so many would believe that a force, or a cosmic energy of some sort, or a divine Ground of Being, might be more mysterious or possess greater "depths" than a person. Colin Gunton urges us that when speaking of God we "should not be afraid of . . . personal language, as if it were somehow inappropriate to the divine mystery. There is . . . nothing higher than the personal."[79]

Because the Holy Spirit of God is personal, it is right that we react against sterile definitions—in the same way we would if someone were to describe a friend or a family member entirely in terms of her chemical composition. But precisely because the Spirit is personal, neither should we abandon all attempts to develop a theology of the Spirit. The response of friend to friend, or lover to beloved, is not silence. Because the Spirit is a person who encounters us, the proper thing—really the only polite thing—is to respond, to say something, whether in paint or tones or words on paper, however inadequate, about the One who meets and remakes us.

79. Colin Gunton, *The Christian Faith: An Introduction to Christian Doctrine* (Oxford: Blackwell, 2002), 6.

PART 1

The Making of a Human

2

Remaking Humanity

John Coltrane and a Love Supreme

In the last chapter we considered the suggestion that art and spirituality are alike because they both have to do with ineffability—with what cannot be spoken. There is another idea about the connection between spirituality and the arts that seems to stand this proposal on its head. Some believe that art is a spiritual activity because it communicates, because of its *expressiveness*.

For some Christians, for instance, words like *worship* and *spirituality* function as near synonyms for *emotion*, *deep feeling*, or *passion*. To have a "spiritual" experience means to experience certain deep or powerful feelings. And the arts are thought to have a connection to spirituality at this point, since they too (so this way of thinking goes) are more or less in the business of expressing or arousing emotions. This association between spirituality and art is further strengthened by the fact that in many churches *worship* has come to mean "that part of the service when we sing." Art and music speak to the heart of the worshiper—her passions and emotions, her deepest and truest self—while likewise allowing her to express her heart to God.

This line of thinking might be described as a layperson's variation on a philosophical theory of the arts known as *expressionism*. The great Russian author Leo Tolstoy provides us with one of the earliest and best known versions of this theory. In *What is Art?* Tolstoy defines art as "a human activity, consisting in this, that one man consciously, by means of certain external signs, hands on to others feelings he has lived through, and that other people are infected by these feelings, and also experience them."[1]

Here, as at several key points in his treatise, Tolstoy explains art through the metaphor of infection—something like a flu virus. An infection of this sort spreads when there is an infectious person (someone who has contracted the contagion), a medium through which the infection is carried (a hand for instance, a doorknob, or the air), and a person who is infected (someone who, through contact with the carrier medium, comes to carry the virus). This is the picture Tolstoy provides of the artistic experience. First there is someone who "has the infection"—someone who feels something deeply. If this person is an artist, she may pour that feeling into the medium of word or dance, paint or song. This work of art carries the artist's emotion out into the world. When another person encounters this work, he meets much more than just a great piece of art. Much more importantly, he "receive[s] another man's expression of feeling, and experience[s] those feelings himself."[2] When listening to Beethoven, I do not just become aware of *his* sadness; it is not even just that I hear the piece and feel sad. Tolstoy believes that as I listen I actually experience the *same sadness* that Beethoven felt. Beethoven's sadness becomes mine; carried from his heart to mine through the music.

This communication of feeling does not in and of itself make art worthwhile, however. There are some feelings and emotions worthy of being communicated and others that are not. The highest and best art, Tolstoy believes, corresponds to the highest and best passions, and most cultures have felt that these noblest passions are those connected with religion. So, Tolstoy writes, "special importance has always been given by all men to that part of this activity [of art] which transmits feelings flowing from their religious perception, and this small part of art they have specifically called art, attaching to it the full meaning of the word."[3] Here is where Tolstoy locates a connection between (what we might call) spirituality and the arts. Art is the communication of emotion. The greater and more significant the emotion, the greater and more significant the art. ("Art is a human activity having for its purpose the transmission to others of the highest and best feelings to which men have risen."[4]) And, generally speaking, these highest and best emotions arise from "religious perception."

Philosophers and art critics have recognized many problems with expressionism.[5] To begin with, it doesn't do a good job of accounting for

1. Leo Tolstoy, *What is Art?* trans. Aylmer Maude (New York: Crowell, 1899), 43.

2. Ibid., 41.

3. Ibid., 44.

4. Ibid., 57.

5. There are particular problems with Tolstoy's rather extreme version of expressionism. A much more carefully articulated and philosophically rigorous version of expressionism is found in R. G. Collingwood's *The Principles of Art* (London: Oxford University Press, 1975).

certain works that are commonly recognized as instances of art. The Parthenon, for instance, is one of humanity's great architectural achievements. It feels like quite a stretch, however, to describe this monument as "an expression of emotion." Likewise, it is unlikely that one's principal impression when looking at the Parthenon is that the structure is somehow communicating the architect's or designer's emotions to us. This is not the most natural way of describing our experience of this masterpiece.

Not only does the theory of expressionism *exclude* some works that we would want to call art (like the Parthenon), it also *includes* much that we would *not* want to call art. We might imagine a painter arguing with her boyfriend, and becoming so angry that she hurls a can of paint at his head. The can of paint (fortunately) misses the young man, but splatters spectacularly against a canvas on the far wall of the studio. Here then is an artist experiencing deep emotion (anger), using an artistic medium (paint) to express this emotion, and as a result, producing an artifact that could conceivably be displayed in a museum. Nevertheless, our artist's "Angry Splat" is not an obvious candidate for inclusion in the pantheon of great works. Expressionism, in other words, provides neither a necessary nor sufficient condition for art.

If we are students of history, we might also notice that the rise of expressionism corresponds to the rise of *romanticism* in the late seventeenth century and the emergence of the modern stereotype of the artistic genius. If we think of the artist as an Artist—a genius, a noble spirit, a high priest of the emotions—then we might well long for his insights into the subtleties of the soul. But this is a relatively recent way of thinking. For much of Western history the artist was more like a skilled tradesperson, someone with undeniably valuable and maybe even remarkable abilities, but someone who rendered a service according to the specifications of a patron or employer (rather than according to the deepest movements of his own soul). During his tenure in Leipzig, Bach produced something like 295 cantatas, motets for important funerals, music for civic functions, and larger pieces for special holy days.[6] He composed these works, not out of a compulsion to express his inner angst, but because this was his responsibility as town cantor. Likewise, it seems improbable that the princes of renaissance Europe would have been terribly interested in the emotional lives of the composers on their payroll. These musicians were not hired to plumb the depths of the human condition but to write something the members of court could dance to after dessert. This doesn't mean these musicians weren't great composers, however, or that the music they wrote was not art.

In addition to this, there is a special problem with how expressionism has made its way into popular thinking. In the popular imagination art is often understood to be entirely a matter of the emotions—and entirely *other than*

6. Tim Dowley, *Bach* (London: Omnibus, 1981), 75.

rational. This way of thinking is especially problematic in a church setting, where music comes to be understood as the nonrational, emotional supplement to the rational content of preaching.[7]

Having said all of this, for "the person on the street," the most obvious virtue of art is still likely to be its power over our emotions, and such a person is not entirely wrong to think in this way. While expressionism fails to give us a complete account of art, it nevertheless identifies something vitally important in the artistic experience. Writers across many centuries and throughout many cultures have spoken of the power of music, story, poetry, and image to arouse the passions and stir the soul. This is indeed one of the things we value in great art.

In the same way, I believe that it is not entirely unreasonable for people to associate the expression of emotion or deep passions with spirituality—even if we take spirituality in its strong and explicitly Christian sense (*Spirituality*). Though we will need to qualify this association in important ways, this intuition does have some theological merit. To explore this idea more fully we will consider a great work of twentieth-century art—one that sets out to be an expression of both deep feeling and spiritual devotion.

John Coltrane at Prayer

> During the year 1957, I experienced, by the grace of God, a spiritual awakening which was to lead me to a richer, fuller, more productive life. At that time, in gratitude, I humbly asked to be given the means and privilege to make others happy through music. I feel this has been granted through His grace. ALL PRAISE TO GOD. . . . This album is a humble offering to Him. An attempt to say "THANK YOU GOD" through our work even as we do in our hearts and with our tongues.[8]

This is part of jazz great John Coltrane's address to the listener, found on the inner sleeve of his 1964 recording, *A Love Supreme*.

John Coltrane is one of a handful of musicians—along with monumental figures like Louis Armstrong, Charlie Parker, and Miles Davis—who have defined the genre of jazz. And in many ways, *A Love Supreme* is Coltrane's definitive statement.[9] Like the man itself, the work is profound, brooding,

7. See Steven R. Guthrie, "Music and Lyrics," in *Worship Leader Magazine* (January/February 2009): 24–30.

8. John Coltrane, *A Love Supreme*, deluxe ed. sound recording, 2002, The Verve Music Group, LC 00383. This quotation appears on p. 26 of the original liner notes in the booklet accompanying the recording.

9. "To jazz cognoscenti, it is the pinnacle of Coltrane's Classic Quartet, the collective high-water mark of the saxophonist in the company of pianist McCoy Tyner, bassist Jimmy Garrison, and drummer Elvin Jones. To generations of music lovers whose general embrace elbows aside considerations of category, the album resonates with a universal pull. To Coltrane devotees, it proves as self-revealing a statement as any he recorded. 'If you want to know who John Coltrane

intense, and musically demanding. It is an intensely personal statement, a prayer, John Coltrane's offering to God. Coltrane tells us that he had asked God that he might "be given the means and privilege to make others happy through music," and in that sense, one might say that *A Love Supreme* is not only an offered prayer, but an answered prayer. It has become one of the most influential and best-selling recordings in jazz history.

In addition to the intimate expression of gratitude in the address, the album sleeve includes a lengthy devotional poem written by Coltrane ("A Love Supreme"). The titles of the four movements of the piece likewise suggest moments in a spiritual pilgrimage: I. Acknowledgement; II. Resolution; III. Pursuance; IV. Psalm. Listeners have been drawn to the album, not only because of its musical interest, but because many have heard in its melodies and harmonies the kind of intensity of devotion and spiritual yearning that Coltrane intended.[10] Perhaps few works of art have been characterized as "spiritual" as regularly as Coltrane's suite.

Tenor sax player Frank Foster assesses Coltrane's playing as having "a more intelligent, complicated, and then, spiritual, style. . . . I was very much in agreement, spiritually in line, with what Coltrane was doing."[11] Archie Shepp (saxophone) believes that Coltrane took the ideas of the jazz avant-garde of the time and added "a spirituality" to it.[12] He remembers that listening to Coltrane "was like being in church."[13] The suite has similar associations for pianist Tommy Flanagan: "His solos on *A Love Supreme*, they're like small sermons to me."[14] Coltrane's bass player, Jimmy Garrison, says that what was so unique about Coltrane's group was not so much its musical material, but rather, he says, "it had to do more with the sheer energy of the band—I could say the spirituality of the band."[15]

Others, outside the world of jazz, responded in similar ways to the recording. Singer Patti Smith recalls, "R&B music I loved because it spoke to my awkward teenage self, and I like to move and dance to it. But Coltrane spoke to my soul."[16] Roger McGuinn of The Byrds remembers the rapturous reception *A Love Supreme* had among the Flower Children of the mid-1960s. "It gave people an opportunity to experience spirituality on a general level," he says.[17] David Murray (saxophonist) makes a similar assessment: "Coltrane had pierced into

---

was,' maintains Elvin Jones, 'you have to know *A Love Supreme*'" (Ravi Coltrane, "A Note on the Contents," p. 8, in *A Love Supreme*).

10. The following comments and interview excerpts are drawn from Ashley Kahn, *A Love Supreme: The Creation of John Coltrane's Classic Album* (London: Granta Books, 2002).

11. Ibid., 66–67.

12. Ibid., 67.

13. Ibid., 68.

14. Ibid., 97.

15. Ibid., 63.

16. Ibid., 73.

17. Ibid., 161.

the whole 'flower-child,' hippie base. They might not even know about any other jazz album, but they knew about *A Love Supreme*. . . . They connected to spirituality in music."[18]

The listeners I've quoted—and many others beside—feel they hear something spiritual in *A Love Supreme*. Their statements also imply that this is something extraordinary, or at least notable. We don't hear each and every piece of music ("The Pennsylvania Polka" for instance, or "Pop! Goes the Weasel") as a great spiritual work; not even every jazz performance, or all recordings by Coltrane, strike listeners in this way. Likewise, anyone who has sat through a certain number of church services can testify that it is possible for a piece of music to flop as an act of devotion. So what allows *A Love Supreme* to succeed as an expression of deep passion and spirituality? What musical or aesthetic conditions must be met for us to hear it as a credible act of devotion?

The Musical Character of *A Love Supreme*

We can identify a number of distinctive musical features of Coltrane's suite, qualities that contribute to the piece's credibility as a prayer and expression of emotion—and which also, by the way, make it challenging listening.[19]

Structural Openness

Many early reviews of the suite expressed surprise at its very limited musical material. Its architecture and harmonic palette is extremely simple. Branford Marsalis observes that the bass line repeated throughout the first movement of *A Love Supreme* is more or less the same blues riff that opens Led Zeppelin's "Whole Lotta Love." The insistent repetition of this four note riff led one critic to complain that the piece was "wearing" and lacking "any real development."[20] Sy Johnson likewise remembers that his first impression of the work was that "it was simplistic musically." He continues, "I had no connection at that point with the spiritual aspect of it. . . . I wasn't ready for that when it first came out."[21] One person who did resonate with the music was minimalist composer Terry Riley. Riley, Kahn observes, was already writing music "based on repetitive cycling of basic patterns."[22] Riley found the repetitive rhythm of the piece "riveting . . . like a mantra."[23]

18. Ibid.

19. "The unusual structure of the piece is dictated, in part, by the extramusical meanings Coltrane wishes to convey." Lewis Porter, "John Coltrane's 'A Love Supreme': Jazz Improvisation as Composition," *Journal of the American Musicological Society* 38:3 (Autumn 1985): 612.

20. Kahn, *A Love Supreme*, 158.

21. Ibid., 157.

22. Ibid., 163.

23. Ibid., 163–64.

After an opening fanfare, the first movement of Coltrane's suite, "Acknowledgement," settles into a four note riff that is, indeed, mantralike (fig. 2.1). For more than seven minutes, the rhythm section hovers around the F minor sonority traced out by the riff. Finally, in the last forty-five seconds of the movement, the bass moves from F to E flat, and continues to repeat the riff in E flat until the end of the piece.

Fig. 2.1. The bass figure from "Acknowledgement" by John Coltrane. (Lewis Porter, "John Coltrane's 'A Love Supreme,'" *Journal of the American Musicological Society* 38, no. 3 [Autumn 1985]: 606)

In this respect, "Acknowledgement" is similar to the "modal jazz" compositions that Coltrane had helped Miles Davis pioneer a few years earlier. These works tend to be relatively static harmonically. Earlier jazz compositions are often structured by a melody that stretches out over twenty-four, thirty-two, or more measures, driven along by the harmonic motion of a series of chord changes. In fact, most popular music derives its sense of direction from its structural organization. We listen and at some level recognize: "here's the verse, here's the chorus, now we're going to that third part. . . . Oh—here comes the theme again," and so on. We typically discern this structural organization in one of a few ways: we follow the progress of a melody (recognizing, for instance: "when that catchy bit comes around—with the big skip up and then the fast notes moving down—then we're back at the chorus"). Or similarly, we recognize some harmonic variation: we notice that the song shifts from an A section in a major key to a B section in the relative minor. We may also orient ourselves within a song by noting some sort of rhythmic development, as in the jazz standard "On Green Dolphin Street," which shifts from a Latin beat in the A section to a swing feel in the B and C sections. Through the 1930s, '40s, and '50s, an improviser's competence—and a jazz performance's appeal—were often established by the soloist's ability to skillfully "make the changes," that is, to invent patterns and new melodies that seamlessly moved through the different chords and harmonic areas being sounded out by the rhythm section.

In the first movement of Coltrane's suite, by contrast, we have simply a repeated four note riff and seven minutes of hovering around a single sonority. As Coltrane improvises, one gets the feeling that he is meditating on a tiny kernel of musical material, turning it over and over, rather than being driven along by the logic of a song structure. Throughout all of this, what holds our attention as listeners? Not an inventive melody or interesting chord progression; not some interesting compositional architecture as the piece moves from section A to section B, or from a major key to the relative minor. Whatever structure and direction the piece has must be provided entirely by the invention and interaction of soloist and band.

This, as I've said, makes the piece more demanding listening. But it also means that the piece has an extraordinarily intimate, personal, and even autobiographical quality. We are not listening to a particular tune, or chord progression, we are not listening to "Bye Bye Blackbird" or "Heart and Soul"; we are only listening to John Coltrane, and his quartet—their own statement, their own prayer.

Harmonic and Rhythmic Openness

Other musical features contribute to this sense of intimacy and personal authenticity. The chords pianist McCoy Tyner uses to support Coltrane's solos, for instance, tend to feature quartal voicings (chords built up out of musical intervals of fourths) rather than tertiary harmonies (built up out of musical thirds). A chord that is built up of thirds has an easily identifiable "major" or "minor" quality. Sonorities built up out of fourths are more ambiguous—both harmonically and in terms of "mood." In this sense, quartal harmonies leave more space, literally and figuratively, for the improviser (fig. 2.2). Moreover, the typical associations of mood and character that accompany major and minor keys are not as pronounced. This means, once again, that the feel, mood, and even the harmonies of *A Love Supreme* are more deeply shaped by the decisions Coltrane is making as a soloist.

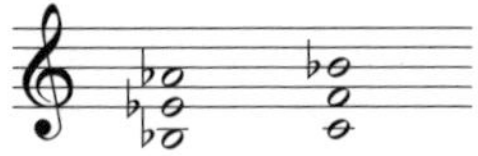

Fig. 2.2. Quartral chord voicings in piano part of "Acknowledgement" by John Coltrane. (Porter, "John Coltrane's 'A Love Supreme,'" 607)

The work is marked by a similar rhythmic openness. On earlier recordings such as "Giant Steps," "Mr. P.C.," or "Syeeda's Song Flute," Coltrane is locked in tight with his rhythm section, sitting back "in the pocket" of the band's groove. By contrast, *A Love Supreme*—particularly Coltrane's solo in the first movement—finds Coltrane pushing and pulling the tempo, ranging further and further outside of the pulse of the rhythm section. Here, as well, rhythmic openness contributes to the sense of spontaneity, immediacy, and urgency. The pacing and phrasing are being determined by Coltrane and the other soloists, rather than being dictated by the click of a metronome. Coltrane lingers over this note and rushes through that passage, like an orator straining to communicate his vision to an audience.

A "Vulnerable" Tone

One of the striking features of Coltrane's playing on this recording is its vulnerable and unaffected quality. As with some of the other musical elements we've mentioned, this makes the work more challenging to listen to, but adds considerably to the impression of expressiveness and spiritual depth. Coltrane's tone on *A Love Supreme* is not pretty or polished; his phrases do not sound well rounded, balanced, or carefully constructed. His tone is often tense, strained, hoarse; he uses overblowing to make his sax growl and shriek, he rasps the reed to get a throaty quality. His phrasing is sharp and jagged, and he leaps across registers. Joshua Redman—a contemporary jazz great—says that Coltrane "sounds like he's screaming and praying at the same time. . . . It's like he's trying to blow the horn apart and just play his emotions through the instrument."[24] (Redman says this, by the way, of a Coltrane piece titled "Transition," recorded with the same quartet but shortly after the *A Love Supreme* sessions. Redman had been asked by the *New York Times* to offer an analysis of some important jazz performances. He knew he wanted to talk about Coltrane, but felt that *A Love Supreme* "was too sacred to pick apart."[25])

Coltrane's sound suggests that we are listening to someone desperate to say something—however he can say it. Indeed, the passions he needs to express exceed his instrument's capabilities, even his own abilities. He is not concerned with "making a good impression" or using correct grammar. It is raw, unadorned, immediate, and heartfelt.

The Sound of a Voice

All of this means that as we listen to *A Love Supreme*, we feel we are hearing Coltrane's voice. This is literally the case at the end of the first movement, "Acknowledgement." There, following his sax solo, he chants the words "a love supreme" in time with the bass riff, repeating the phrase nineteen times.

There is another striking instance of a kind of speech in the fourth movement of the piece. The title of this movement is "Psalm," which is also the name of a poem composed by Coltrane that is included in the liner notes to *A Love Supreme*. Careful listeners soon realize that in the musical piece "Psalm," Coltrane is "reciting" the text of his poem on the saxophone.[26] The rhythm and phrasing of the poem provide the rhythm and phrasing of his musical improvisation. One can follow the poem while listening to the recording of "Psalm." Coltrane works his way through the text, word for word and line by line, in his own improvised musical phrases. Listeners may or may not be aware of the fact that Coltrane is playing along to the text of a written prayer. What is undeniable, however, is that Coltrane was aware of it. As a result his solo has a speechlike, preacherly quality, and this, again, adds to the sense that we are listening to the performer's prayer, his personal confession of faith.

24. Ben Ratliff, "Playing the Diplomatic Changes," *The New York Times*, May 27, 2005. Available at http://www.nytimes.com/2005/05/27/arts/music/27redm.html.

25. Ibid.

26. See the discussion in chapter 17 of Lewis Porter, *John Coltrane: His Life and Music* (Ann Arbor: University of Michigan Press, 1998).

A Human Being, Being Human

In considering the elements that contribute to the "spiritual" character of *A Love Supreme*, we have mentioned spontaneity, immediacy, vulnerability, expressiveness, and a speechlike, even autobiographical, quality. Taking these together, we arrive at an interesting conclusion: the traits that make the work seem most "spiritual" are also what make it seem most human. In order to convey "spirituality" Coltrane has employed musical devices that intensify our sense of his humanity, devices that encourage the impression of intimacy, of encountering the performer's voice.

Though it is emphasized in Coltrane's suite, this element of intimacy and encounter is one of the things we value in art generally. The very persistence of performance testifies to this. Why should we continue to value live musical performances, when works can be flawlessly generated and reproduced digitally? And why should we value improvisation at all? Wouldn't it be better if each soloist took the time to sit down and plan out precisely the notes to be played? Why not write out everything ahead of time and ensure that each musical event will be exactly right? Improvisation begins to seem of pretty limited musical value if it is just a way of showing off what one can play off the cuff.

But of course performance is more than an opportunity for ticket sales, and improvisation is more than a party trick. One reason we continue to value these dimensions of music-making is that they add to our sense of encounter, of meeting a person. In performance we hear an inward impulse externalized, a personal creative vision given public expression. Because of this we feel that there has been some sort of communication or shared experience between ourselves and the performer. In public improvisation we are even more aware of the creative process unfolding in our presence. This (at least in theory) is not the carefully edited and prepared statement but the immediate response. We hear musicians interacting with one another, reacting to the musical material presented to them, thinking, sensing, feeling, and creating. What we hear and enjoy is a human being, being human.

This aspect of art is at least something like what Tolstoy had in view. The great value and virtue of art, he argued, is its ability to powerfully communicate to others the deepest concerns and experiences of the artist. Tolstoy believed in the spiritual importance of art, not because it transports us to another plane or some heavenly realm, but because through it we encounter the depths of another's humanity. However inadequate this may be as a complete theory of art, it identifies an important dimension of artistic experience. And there is a kind of Christian theological insight here as well; namely, the spiritual is not opposed to the human. Quite the opposite. There is in fact a deep and intimate connection between *Spirit*-uality (the work of God's Holy Spirit) and our own deepest and truest humanity. We might even say that the Holy Spirit is the *humanizing* Spirit, the breath of God that transforms dust into a living soul. The work of the Holy Spirit is to fulfill, complete, create, and re-create our humanity, remaking us after the perfect humanity of Jesus Christ.

The Breath of Life

This human-making activity of the Spirit is evident from the first chapters of the biblical narrative. In Genesis 2, lifeless dust is transformed into a living human being by the breath that proceeds from the mouth of God: "Then the LORD God formed man from the dust of the ground, and breathed into his nostrils the breath of life; and the man became a living being" (Gen. 2:7). It is an account that underlines the *glory* and the *frailty* of humankind. On the one hand humanity is the glory of creation. We are fashioned "by hand," and in an act of extraordinary intimacy, brought to life by the breath of God's own mouth. "You have made them [humanity] a little lower than God," the psalmist writes, "and crowned them with glory [*kabod*] and honor" (Ps. 8:5).

Genesis 2 also tells us that God's intention is for humanity to be the kind of creature in which his breath can dwell. The Lord God breathes "the breath of life" into Adam's nostrils. God draws very near—much nearer, and in a much more intimate posture, than the moment of life-giving famously portrayed by Michelangelo on the ceiling of the Sistine Chapel. God does not simply reach out to the human, with one majestic, omnipotent finger. God's intention is for this creature to be filled by God's own breath, to have and enjoy life in a relationship of intimacy and dependence.

On the other hand this account tells us we are dust. The *adam* is taken from the *adamah*—the Hebrew word for "earth" or "ground." This speaks of a deep connection between humanity and the rest of the created world, but it also reminds us of the extraordinary contingency of the *adam*. He is human (rather than dust) only by the breath of God. Adam is not "a living being" until or apart from God's *ruach*. It is a complex and nuanced picture of the human condition. We are creatures of glory, creatures of dust.

Throughout the Old Testament *dust* continues to suggest the frailty and contingency that epitomize the human condition. "All are from the dust," the Preacher declares, "and all turn to dust again" (Eccles. 3:20). God may in a moment declare to mortals: "turn back to dust" (see Ps. 90:3). Indeed, if God "should take back his spirit (*ruach*) to himself, and gather to himself his breath, all flesh would perish together, and all mortals return to dust" (Job 34:14–15; cf. Ps. 104:27–30).

When Adam and Eve choose independence, then, they choose dissolution over glory, dwelling in the dust rather than rising to the humanity God intends for them:

> By the sweat of your face
>   you shall eat bread

until you return to the ground,
  for out of it you were taken;
you are dust,
  and to dust you shall return.

Genesis 3:19

The Disappearing Man

Athanasius, with whom we spent some time in the last chapter, spelled out this dilemma with great clarity. Apart from God's Spirit, we are not simply less good or less pleasant human beings. Apart from God's Spirit, we sink further and further away from our humanity. More than that, separated from the source of life, we sink further from *being* into nonexistence. "Instead of remaining in the state in which God had created them," Athanasius writes, human beings "were in the process of becoming corrupted entirely, and death had them completely under its dominion. . . . And as they had at the beginning come into being out of non-existence, so were they now on the way to returning, through corruption, to non-existence again."[27]

On this account, the great crisis of human history is that God's intention—to create human beings in his image, filled with his Spirit—is in danger of being undone. The urgent and necessary thing is that our true humanity be restored; that we be rehumanized. Friedrich Nietzsche complained that we are "human, all too human," but from a biblical perspective, our problem is that we are not nearly human enough. We have turned away from the humanizing Spirit and are sinking slowly back into dust.

Faced with this crisis, Athanasius continues, "the incorporeal and incorruptible and immaterial Word of God entered our world."[28] He took our very humanity to himself "that He might turn again to incorruption men who had turned back to corruption."[29] This is the work of God, Athanasius says: to restore us to humanity.

The Incarnating Spirit

The biblical narrative declares that in the same way that humanity was first animated by the breath of God, so the re-creation of humanity takes place by the agency of the Spirit. When Gabriel announces to Mary that she is to give birth to a child, she asks, how can this be, since I am a virgin? The angel

27. Athanasius, *On the Incarnation*, 1.4, trans. and ed. by A Religious of C. S. M. V. (Crestwood, NY: St. Vladimir's Seminary Press, 2003), 29–30.

28. Ibid., 1.8., 33.

29. Ibid., 1.8., 34.

replies: "The Holy Spirit will come upon you, and the power of the Most High will overshadow you; therefore the child to be born will be holy; he will be called Son of God" (Luke 1:35). An angel also reassures Joseph: "Joseph, son of David, do not be afraid to take Mary as your wife, for the child conceived in her is from the Holy Spirit" (Matt. 1:20).

The work of the Spirit at Jesus's birth is that of incarnation—*enfleshment*. By the power of the Spirit, the Word of God takes humanity to himself so that broken humanity might be restored.

We Have Seen His Glory

In remaking humanity the Word also displays the *glory* of God. John writes that "the Word became flesh and lived among us, and we have seen his glory, the glory as of a father's only son, full of grace and truth" (John 1:14). In Jesus, God's intention is fulfilled—that humanity should declare the glory of God (Ps. 8:5).

There is another biblical resonance to the word *glory*, and one specifically connected with the work of the Spirit. In the Old Testament, *glory* (Hebrew, *kabod*) is often associated with the overwhelming radiance of God on those occasions when God reveals his presence. So, when God makes a covenant with Israel at Mount Sinai, we read that "the glory of the Lord settled on Mount Sinai, and the cloud covered it for six days. . . . The appearance of the glory of the Lord was like a devouring fire on the top of the mountain" (Exod. 24:16–17). When the tabernacle is constructed, and then later, the temple in Jerusalem is dedicated, these places of meeting are filled—dramatically!—with the glory of the Lord: "Then the cloud covered the tent of meeting, and the glory of the Lord filled the tabernacle" (Exod. 40:34; cf. 1 Kings 8:10–11).

Glory, then, is a way that God's powerful, active presence is made visible among his people. This glory of God can also be imparted or can attach to God's servants. This glory may be a visible brightness, as in the case of Moses after his time on Sinai (Exod. 34:29). Or the glory of God may be the power and presence of the Lord, given to an individual specially appointed to lead or minister to God's people—a prophet or a king for instance. Such a person is said to be empowered by the spirit, an "anointed one" or "messiah." A standard reference work draws attention to the connection between "anointing" and "glory": "The act of anointing confers [*kabod*]; it is thus to be regarded as an act of enablement. . . . Anointing by Yahweh Himself is a conferring of [*kabod*], and is thus authorization by Him."[30]

A number of Old Testament passages further connect this anointing with the power and presence of the Spirit. So for instance, in 2 Samuel 23, King

30. Franz Hesse, "מׁשח and מָשִׁיחַ in the Old Testament," in *Theological Dictionary of the New Testament*, vol. 9, Φ–Ω, ed. Gerhard Friedrich, trans. Geoffrey W. Bromiley (Grand Rapids: Eerdmans, 1974), 498–99.

David is described as "the anointed [Hebrew, *Mashiach*, "the messiah"] of the God of Jacob," and in this capacity he declares: "The spirit of the LORD speaks through me, his word is upon my tongue" (2 Sam. 23:1–2). In Isaiah 61 the prophet declares, "The spirit of the Lord GOD is upon me, because the LORD has anointed me" (Isa. 61:1).

Drawing some of these threads together, we can say that God's glory is associated with his powerful, radiant presence as in the tabernacle. It is also associated with the powerful, enabling presence of his Spirit as it is made manifest among his anointed ones. Humanity was created to reflect, indeed to be inhabited by, the glory of God—which is also to say that humanity was created to be filled by the Spirit of God.

Returning to John's gospel, we are now better situated to understand the declaration, "the Word became flesh and lived among us, and we have seen his glory" (John 1:14). As we have seen, in the Old Testament the tabernacle (and then the temple) was the place on earth where God's glory—his powerful radiant presence—was made fully manifest. Now, John's gospel says, that glorious presence of God is made manifest in Jesus, who "became flesh and dwelt [Greek, *skene*—literally, "tabernacled"] among us" (John 1:14 NASB). Jesus, John is asserting, is the one anointed with God's Spirit, and the bearer of God's glory. The early church agreed with this assessment, insisting that Jesus is truly the Messiah (or in Greek, "the Christ"). He is the anointed one and the radiant presence of God among us.

Anointed by the Spirit

Luke's gospel is particularly interested to portray Jesus as the one anointed and empowered by the Spirit in this way. Near the beginning of Luke's gospel we read that "when all the people were baptized, and when Jesus also had been baptized and was praying, the heaven was opened, and the Holy Spirit descended upon him in bodily form like a dove. And a voice came from heaven, 'You are my Son, the Beloved; with you I am well pleased'" (Luke 3:21–22).

This anointing is also an act of re-creation which gestures back to another act of re-creation: God's renewal of the world after the great flood. In the beginning, God created the heavens and the earth, and also humankind in God's own image, and "God's Spirit [*ruach*] brooded like a bird above the watery abyss" (Gen. 1:2 Message). After the great de-creation of the flood (Gen. 6–8), God once again creates a place where human life can flourish: "and God caused a wind [*ruach*] to pass over the earth, and the water subsided" (Gen. 8:1 NASB). Once again, the life-giving *ruach* of God broods over the deep. A dove is sent out over the waters, and returns with an olive branch—a sign of new beginnings. In the same way, Jesus comes into a world "corrupt" and "filled with violence" (Gen. 6:11). There at the River Jordan the Spirit hovers over the waters. Once again a dove descends, signaling new life, an end to chaos and darkness, and a new beginning for humanity. The new humanity stands in the River Jordan, born again, of "water and Spirit" (John 3:5).

In the chapters that follow this Spirit anointing, Luke draws special attention to the activity of the Spirit in and through Jesus. First, we read that "Jesus, *full of the Holy Spirit*, returned from the Jordan and *was led by the Spirit* in the wilderness" (Luke 4:1, emphasis added). After this time of testing, "Jesus, *filled with the power of the Spirit*, returned to Galilee, and a report about him spread through all the surrounding country" (Luke 4:14, emphasis added). This leads on to the remarkable scene in the synagogue at Nazareth:

> When he came to Nazareth, where he had been brought up, he went to the synagogue on the sabbath day, as was his custom. He stood up to read, and the scroll of the prophet Isaiah was given to him. He unrolled the scroll and found the place where it was written: "The Spirit of the Lord is upon me, because he has anointed me to bring good news to the poor. He has sent me to proclaim release to the captives and recovery of sight to the blind, to let the oppressed go free, to proclaim the year of the Lord's favor." And he rolled up the scroll, gave it back to the attendant, and sat down. The eyes of all in the synagogue were fixed on him. Then he began to say to them, "Today this scripture has been fulfilled in your hearing."
>
> Luke 4:16–21

Luke has Jesus appropriate the words of Isaiah 61:1 for his own ministry, publicly identifying himself as the one powerfully anointed by God's Spirit, for the purpose of ushering in God's kingdom.[31]

A few chapters later, this powerful anointing of the Spirit overflows in radiant glory—just as the cloud once filled the tabernacle with the dazzling presence of God.

> Now about eight days after these sayings Jesus took with him Peter and John and James, and went up on the mountain to pray. And while he was praying, the appearance of his face changed, and his clothes *became dazzling white*. Suddenly they saw two men, Moses and Elijah, talking to him. *They appeared in glory* and were speaking of his departure, which he was about to accomplish

31. James Dunn summarizes his discussion of this passage, concluding, "*Jesus believed himself to be the one in whom Isa. 61.1 found fulfillment; his sense of being inspired was such that he could believe himself to be the end-time prophet of Isa. 61.1*: he had been anointed with the Spirit of the Lord. Luke is quite justified therefore when he depicts Jesus as opening his public ministry in the full conviction and inspiration of the Spirit upon him" (James D. G. Dunn, *Jesus and the Spirit: A Study of the Religious and Charismatic Experience of Jesus and the First Christians as Reflected in the New Testament* [Grand Rapids: Eerdmans, 1975], 61, emphasis original). Dunn does not believe that the synagogue episode recorded by Luke is historical; nevertheless, he believes that the story accurately reflects Jesus's self-awareness as bearer of the Spirit.

> at Jerusalem. Now Peter and his companions were weighed down with sleep; but since they had stayed awake, *they saw his glory* and the two men who stood with him. . . . *A cloud came and overshadowed them*; and they were terrified as they entered the cloud. Then from the cloud came a voice that said, "This is my Son, my Chosen; listen to him!" When the voice had spoken, Jesus was found alone. And they kept silent and in those days told no one any of the things they had seen.
>
> Luke 9:28–32, 34–36, emphasis added

This, like Jesus's baptism, is a kind of anointing—a filling with the radiant glory of God. And, as at Jesus's baptism, a voice speaks from heaven, affirming the Sonship of Jesus.

Why Would God Need to Be Anointed?

Athanasius's opponents in the early church were followers of Arius, who rejected the idea that Jesus was "of one substance" with God the Father. They seized upon these references to Jesus's anointing. Here, they argued, is biblical evidence that Jesus is not of the same substance as the Father! Why would one who is fully God need to be anointed by the Holy Spirit? If Jesus is fully God would he not shine forth with his own glory? They pointed to Jesus's declaration that he drove out demons "by the Spirit of God" (Matt. 12:28). If Jesus were God, they argued, why would he require the Spirit's power?

In response, Athanasius reminds his opponents of the fundamental Christian affirmation that Jesus is not only fully and perfectly God, but also fully and perfectly human. It is as a man that Jesus receives the anointing and enabling of the Spirit.[32] His anointing, then, does not represent any sort of deficiency in his deity; far from it, it points to the perfection, the glorification (*glory*-fication) of his humanity. Athanasius writes that "the Savior . . . being God, and forever ruling the kingdom of the Father, and being himself the supplier of the Spirit, is nevertheless now said to be anointed by the Spirit, so that, being said to be anointed as a human being by the Spirit, he may provide us human beings with the indwelling and intimacy of the Holy Spirit, just as he provides us with exaltation and resurrection."[33]

Humankind was originally created by God to be filled with the breath of God. The dust is made to be the dwelling of God's radiant glory. Now this

32. "It is not so often recalled that when [Athanasius] came to speak clearly and fully of *deification* in the *Contra Arianos* . . . he insisted that this takes place through our participation in the human nature of Christ by the power of the Spirit" (T. F. Torrance, *Theology in Reconstruction* [London: SCM, 1965], 217, emphasis original).

33. Athanasius, *Orations against the Arians*, 1.46, in Khaled Anatolios, *Athanasius* (New York: Routledge, 2004), 103.

broken race is being re-created in Jesus—the prototype and pioneer of a brand new humanity. Again, Athanasius explains,

> The descent of the Spirit upon him in the Jordan was a descent upon us, because of our body which he carried. This did not take place for the advancement of the Word but for our sanctification, so that we may share in his anointing and so that it may be said of us, "Do you not know that you are the temple of God, and the Spirit of God dwells in you?" (1 Cor. 3:16). For when the Lord was washed in the Jordan, it was we who were washed in him and by him. And when he received the Spirit, it was we who were made recipients of the Spirit by him.[34]

As the one who is both fully God and fully man, Jesus shines with a two-fold glory. As the divine Word made flesh, he is the "radiance of God's glory" (Heb. 1:3 NIV). As the New Human he is the one anointed with the power and glory of the Spirit. His glorification by the Spirit, far from being a point of embarrassment for orthodox belief, is essential to an orthodox understanding of salvation. "It is not the Word, as Word and Wisdom, who is anointed by the Spirit which is given by him," writes Athanasius. "But it is the flesh assumed by him that is anointed in him and by him, in order that the sanctification which came to be in the Lord as a human being may come to be in all human beings from him."[35] As the prototype of the new humanity, Jesus remains dependent upon God's Spirit for life. Jesus does not re-create our race as some sort of superhumanity that stands independent of God. We remain dust—mortal and contingent—but dust once again filled with the breath (and glory) of God. In Jesus, humanity is again a place in which God dwells. In Jesus, humanity is no longer dust only, but "crowned with glory" (see Ps. 8:5), filled with the glorious presence of God's Holy Spirit.[36]

The Transforming Spirit

> We must understand that as long as Christ remains outside of us, and we are separated from him, all that he has suffered and done for the salvation of the human race remains useless and of no value for us.[37]

John Calvin offers this often-repeated observation at the beginning of a section titled "The Holy Spirit as the Bond That Unites Us to Christ." Calvin's

34. Ibid., 1.47, 104.

35. Ibid., 1.47, 105.

36. "In this one Man the divine life and love overflowed into creaturely and human being, so that Jesus, Man on earth, received the Spirit of God without measure, for the fullness of the Godhead dwelt in him bodily. Jesus became the Bearer of the Holy Spirit among men" (Torrance, *Theology in Reconstruction*, 241).

37. John Calvin, *Institutes of the Christian Religion*, 3.1.1, trans. Ford Lewis Battles (Philadelphia: Westminster, 1960), 537.

point is simply this: it is one thing for Christ to obtain some benefit for us; it is another thing for that benefit to be actually applied and enjoyed. So, we might say, it is one thing for Jesus's humanity to be filled, transfigured, and glorified by the Spirit. But I need this transformation to be made actual in my life. This, Calvin says, is accomplished by the Spirit. The work of the Spirit, then, is not only re-creating broken humanity in the person of Jesus, but also re-creating us in the image of Jesus's perfect humanity.

Athanasius points to this work of the Spirit—remaking us in the image of Jesus Christ—as evidence that the Spirit is fully God, of one substance with God the Father. "It is in the Spirit that the Word glorifies creation and presents it to the Father by divinizing it and granting it adoption. But the one who binds creation to the Word cannot be among the creatures. . . . Therefore, the Spirit is not among the things that have come into being but belongs to the divinity of the Father."[38]

It is not enough, Athanasius says, for God to descend to us in our lowly condition (as he does in the incarnation). We must also be raised from our lowly condition to God, a raising-up that Athanasius calls "divinization" (Greek, *theosis*). Athanasius does not mean by this that we are to become, like Jesus, "of the same substance" as God the Father—as if we were being remade into additional members of the eternal Godhead. But in our humanity, we are made to be dwelling places of God's own Spirit, filled with the radiant glory of God.[39] This is what Athanasius has in mind: a re-union, an "at-one-ment" of humanity and the God who made us for relationship with himself. "The Word, in the Spirit, fashioned and joined a body to himself, wishing to unite creation to the Father and offer it to the Father through himself and to reconcile all things in his body, 'making peace among the things of heaven and the things of earth.'"[40]

The work of the Spirit is to bring dust to life and fill it with glory, in other words, to make us truly human, the image bearers of God. In Jesus, the eternal Word of God is made flesh by the power of the Spirit. In his humanity, he is the Messiah—the one anointed with the Holy Spirit and filled with the presence and glory of God. In him, the image of God is restored in humanity. By the power of the Spirit, Jesus is the True Human. By the power of the Spirit, we are likewise united to the humanity of Christ. Dust that we are, we are transformed and remade in the image of the perfect, glorified humanity of Jesus Christ.

38. Athanasius, *Letters to Serapion on the Holy Spirit*, in Anatolios, *Athanasius*, 225.

39. What the Greek fathers called *theosis* "is usually unfortunately translated *deification*, but it has nothing to do with the *divinization* of man any more than the Incarnation has to do with the humanization of God. . . . *Theosis* describes man's involvement in such a mighty act of God upon him that he is raised up to find the true centre of his existence not in himself but in Holy God, where he lives and moves and has his being in the uncreated but creative energy of the Holy Spirit" (Torrance, *Theology in Reconstruction*, 243, emphasis original).

40. Athanasius, *Letters to Serapion*, 232.

In thinking about the glory of Jesus Christ, and our glorious re-creation in him through the Spirit, the apostle Paul remembered the old story of Moses, his face shining with the *kabod* of the Lord. This radiant glory in his face was so unsettling to his fellow Israelites that he took to covering his face with a veil. But "when one turns to the Lord, the veil is removed. Now the Lord is the Spirit, and where the Spirit of the Lord is, there is freedom. And all of us, with unveiled faces, seeing the glory of the Lord as though reflected in a mirror, are being transformed into the same image from one degree of glory to another; for this comes from the Lord, the Spirit" (2 Cor. 3:16–18).

By the Spirit, we are united to the glorified humanity of Christ. Because of Jesus, we may also be filled with the Spirit, made into glorious, radiant dwelling places of God. In fact, Paul observes that it is not too much to say that we are also "anointed ones"—little "christs" (or "Christians"!): God "establishes us with you" in the Anointed One [*christon*]—and has anointed us!—"by putting his seal on us and giving us his Spirit in our hearts as a first installment" (2 Cor. 1:21–22).

Raised from the Dust

If anointing with the Spirit is the "first installment" of our glorification, then the consummation of this "being raised up to God" is our bodily resurrection. Here too the Spirit is at work. The Spirit of Jesus Christ is in you, Paul says, and "if the Spirit of him who raised Jesus from the dead is living in you, he who raised Christ from the dead will also give life to your mortal bodies through his Spirit, who lives in you" (Rom. 8:11 NIV).

The first human was formed from the dust. Filled with the breath of God, he nevertheless ultimately turned away from the source of life and so, tragically, returned to the dust. The True Human, however, is Jesus Christ, the man filled with the Spirit—the one upon whom the breath of God has descended and remained. All who are in turn anointed with this same life-giving Spirit are reborn into the new, and true, humanity of Jesus Christ. "Just as we have borne the image of the man of dust, we will also bear the image of the man of heaven" (1 Cor. 15:49).

Breath and Dust

To sum up, from the beginning of the biblical story to its consummation, the Spirit is at work fashioning and refashioning our humanity. The Holy Spirit is the humanizing Spirit. In the first chapters of Genesis, lifeless dust is transformed into a living human being by *the breath that proceeds from the mouth of God*. When humanity falls into ruin once again, it is the Spirit—the breath of God—who *re-creates* humanity as Jesus is "conceived by the Holy

Spirit" (Apostles' Creed). The Spirit then rests and remains upon Jesus, so that he is truly called "Messiah" ("anointed one," bearer of the Spirit). As the human being filled with God's Spirit, Jesus is the second Adam—the True Human. At the end of his earthly ministry, Jesus pours out the Spirit on his disciples that they may be remade after the likeness of Jesus's own perfect humanity. The Spirit's presence in Jesus's followers is also the guarantee of their bodily resurrection, the pledge that God will bring their humanity to completion—completely healed, completely restored, completely whole: no longer dust only, but dust raised up and filled by the glory of God.

Tolstoy argued that we value art for the way it expresses and communicates our deepest humanity. In *A Love Supreme* we discovered that the "spiritual" qualities of the work are also those that give us a sense of a deeply *human* encounter with the musicians. Strikingly, we find the spirituality of the work *is* its humanity. We could give other examples of this same phenomenon. The sorts of experiences that people in a post-Christian culture characterize as "spiritual" might include the birth of a child, a quiet moment with an old friend, a wedding ceremony, holding someone's hand while they pass from this life, a "coming of age" moment, making love. In such moments we do not transcend our humanity, but rather, inhabit it most deeply. We see the frailty of our humanity while catching a flickering glimpse of its glory.

Jean Bethke Elshtain quotes a beautiful passage from Czeslaw Milosz's *The Captive Mind*. Milosz is walking through a train station in Ukraine in the chaotic days at the beginning of the Second World War:

> A peasant family—husband and wife and two children—had settled down by the wall. They were sitting on baskets and bundles. The wife was feeding the younger child; the husband who had a dark wrinkled face and a black, drooping mustache was pouring tea out of a kettle into a cup for the older boy. They were whispering to each other in Polish. I gazed at them until I felt moved to the point of tears. What had stopped my steps so suddenly and touched me so profoundly was their difference. This was a human group, an island in a crowd that lacked something proper to humble, ordinary human life. The gesture of a hand pouring tea, the careful, delicate handing of the cup to the child, the worried words I guessed from the movements of their lips, their isolation, the privacy in the midst of the crowd—that is what moved me. For a moment, then, I understood something that quickly slipped from my grasp.[41]

These are profoundly, even paradigmatically *human* experiences. We sense that somehow these moments participate in what belongs to human beings universally. These are the things that human beings *do*, and are proper to their humanity. Elshtain reflects on the "something" that Milosz understood

41. Quoted in Jean Bethke Elshtain, *Who Are We? Critical Reflections and Hopeful Possibilities* (Grand Rapids: Eerdmans, 2000), 151–52.

for a moment upon seeing that peasant family. "Perhaps," she says, "one might suggest, that the 'something' concerns the fragility and miracle of the quotidian."[42] In these profoundly spiritual human moments we recognize the frailty and glory of our humanity. We are dust, created to be filled with the breath of God.

Perhaps this is what some have heard in *A Love Supreme*: a musician of extraordinary power whose voice cracks as it tries to sing of God's love. We hear the fragile and the miraculous side by side, and this gives the performance a power and poignancy that it would lack if it were *only* "miraculous." One can think of flawlessly virtuosic performances that are soulless. But here are a group of improvisers—creatures living and working through time, pushing and pulling at the corners of musical meter to say something about the One who is eternal. And for a moment we hear—whether in fact or only as a kind of parable in sound—dust inhabited by glory.

If we are moved, then, it may be because of an intuition that there is something properly spiritual—spiritual in the biblical sense, having to do with the work of the Holy Spirit—about the moment when dust is filled with glory. We may sense that there is something properly spiritual about becoming truly human. And that intuition is correct.

42. Ibid., 152.

3

Remaking Human Bodies

Kingdom Come and the Kingdom of the Abstract

Veni Creator Spiritus[1]

CREATOR SPIRIT, by whose aid
The world's foundations first were laid,
Come, visit every pious mind;
Come, pour thy joys on human kind;
From sin and sorrow set us free,
And make thy temples worthy thee. . . .

Refine and purge our earthy parts,
But O, inflame and fire our hearts,
Our frailties help, our vice control;
Submit the senses to the soul,
And, when rebellious they are grown,
Then lay thy hand, and hold them down.

Some of this material has appeared in Steven R. Guthrie, "Singing: In the Body and in the Spirit," *Journal of the Evangelical Theological Society* 46:4 (December 2003): 633–46; and Steven R. Guthrie, "Temples of the Spirit: Worship as Embodied Performance," in *Faithful Performances*, ed. Trevor A. Hart and Steven R. Guthrie (Burlington, VT: Ashgate, 2007).

1. *Hymns of the Christian Church*, vol. 45, part 2, of The Harvard Classics (New York: P. F. Collier & Son, 1909–14). Available online at www.bartleby.com/45/2/. Attributed to Charlemagne, trans. John Dryden.

Spirit versus the Body?

The work of the Spirit is to remake our humanity. But, of course, there is more than one way of remaking or restoring. In some instances, a doctor might need to remove a diseased organ or kill off cells that are malignant. In these sorts of treatment, not every part of the patient is restored and strengthened. Rather, in order to save the whole person, some parts are put to death.

In the history of Western spirituality, something like this strategy of treatment has occupied a prominent place. One part of the person—namely the body and its senses—must be put to death, so that the spirit might live. We find elements of this idea in the poem I have quoted above. The supplicant asks that the Holy Spirit might "refine and purge our earthy parts," and "submit the senses to the soul"—rather forcefully, in fact ("then lay thy hand and hold them down")!

The poet sets out a series of oppositions—good things and bad things. On the "good side" of the divide is the heart, the soul, and the work of "thy hand" (that is, the work of the Spirit). The "bad side" of this opposition is populated by our "earthy" parts, frailties, vices, and the senses—which, the poet points out, tend to grow rebellious. A clear and starkly drawn picture of the spiritual life emerges:

GOOD	BAD
HEART	"EARTHY" PARTS
SOUL	WEAKNESSES
THE WORK OF THE SPIRIT	VICES
	SENSES
	REBELLION

According to "Veni Creator Spiritus," when it comes to the body and the senses, the role of the Spirit is largely negative. These "earthy parts" are to be *refined*, *purged*, placed in *submission*, and *held down*. Not only is the Holy Spirit set against our bodily flesh, but the poem also implies that within oneself there is hostility between spirit and flesh. The senses rise up and rebel, and it is the duty of the heart, the soul, and the intellect to quell this insurgence. Heart, soul, and mind meanwhile are portrayed as allies of the Holy Spirit, joining battle against the insubordinate flesh.

Most of us will be familiar, at least at some level, with this way of describing the spiritual and virtuous life. It even has a kind of commonsense plausibility to it. "Spiritual" and "sensual" (i.e., "sense-ual") are often used as antonyms, as are "spirit" and "body." Even TV advertisements suggest that "indulging the senses" means moving away from a higher, nobler form of life: a chocolate dessert might be described as "decadent" or "sinfully delicious."

Perhaps, then (someone might suggest), the path to true spirituality is to move as far as possible from "dust"—from our senses or "earthy parts"—and to journey into the realm of pure, incorporeal spirit. Becoming "spiritual" on this account would mean becoming less and less "sensual," and the role of the Holy Spirit in our lives would be to purge and burn away body and senses. The ultimate healing and restoration of one's humanity would be the destruction of the malignant body.

In fact, a wise man once said just this. In the dialogue *Phaedo*, Plato describes the last moments of Socrates' life: "The coldness was spreading about as far as his waist when Socrates uncovered his face . . . and said—they were his last words—'Crito, we ought to offer a cock to Asclepius. See to it, and don't forget.' "[2] What does this cryptic saying mean? Asclepius is the god of healing. A cock is an offering of thanks. And the death of Socrates' own body, he suggests, is the ultimate healing. Another one of Plato's dialogues, the *Symposium*, offers a similar assessment of the body and, in light of this, outlines a program of spiritual advancement. This dialogue is also significant for our discussion because of the way it connects spiritual enlightenment with the experience of beauty.

A "symposium" is literally a drinking party, and Plato's dialogue describes an evening of drink and conversation. The friends determine to go in turn, each offering "a speech in praise of Love as he is capable of giving."[3] When it is finally Socrates' turn to speak, rather than offering his own opinion, he relates "the speech about Love I once heard from a woman of Mantinea, Diotima—a woman who was wise about many things besides this."[4] Diotima's speech describes not only "the wondrous vision which is the very soul of beauty," but also the journey by which one arrives at this vision.

> It is an everlasting loveliness which neither comes nor goes, which neither flowers nor fades, for such beauty is the same on every hand, the same then as now, here as there, this way as that way, the same to every worshiper as it is to every other.
>
> Nor will his vision of the beautiful take the form of a face or of hands, or of anything that is of the flesh . . . subsisting of itself and by itself in an eternal oneness, while every lovely thing partakes of it in such sort that, however much the parts may wax and wane, it will be neither more nor less, but still the same inviolable whole. . . .
>
> And this is the way, the only way, [one] must approach, or be led toward the sanctuary of Love. Starting from individual beauties, the quest for the universal beauty must find him ever mounting the heavenly ladder, stepping from rung to rung—that is, from one to two, and from two to every lovely body, from bodily beauty to the beauty of institutions, from institutions to learning, and from

2. Plato, *Phaedo*, 118, trans. Hugh Tredennick, in *The Collected Dialogues of Plato*, ed. Edith Hamilton and Huntington Cairns (Princeton: Princeton University Press, 1973), 98.

3. Plato, *Symposium*, 177d, trans. Alexander Nehamas and Paul Woodruff (Indianapolis: Hackett, 1989), 7.

4. Ibid., 201d, 45.

learning in general to the special lore that pertains to nothing but the beautiful itself—until at last he comes to know what beauty is.[5]

The Ladder of Beauty

Diotima describes a journey to the goal of loving, to Beauty itself. In our own idiom we might describe it as a journey to "spiritual enlightenment." In any case, according to Diotima, this journey begins with "beautiful things" and then leads on, step by step, until one finally encounters Beauty itself. Little "beauties" participate in Beauty. Every lovely thing, as Diotima says, "partakes" of transcendent Beauty, and this means that potentially any beautiful object can be the instrument of spiritual transformation. One may rise from beauties to eternal Beauty itself, climbing rung by rung.

It is a wonderful idea—the idea that in each flower, each face there glimmers a spark of the eternal Beauty. It seems to echo the declaration of Psalm 19:1: "The heavens are telling the glory of God; and the firmament proclaims his handiwork." Ultimately this idea of the Ladder of Beauty would become a regular theme of Christian theologians, particularly among medieval writers. Bonaventure writes that

> all the creatures of the sense world lead the mind of the contemplative and wise man to the eternal God. For these creatures are shadows, echoes and pictures of that first, most powerful, most wise and most perfect Principle, of that eternal Source, Light and Fulness, of that efficient exemplary and ordering Art. They are vestiges, representations, spectacles proposed to us and signs divinely given so that we can see God. These creatures, I say, are exemplars or rather exemplifications presented to souls still untrained and immersed in sensible things so that through sensible things which they see they will be carried over to intelligible things which they do not see as through signs to what is signified.[6]

Beautiful as this idea is, in another way it is a rather ambiguous assessment of beauty. The little beauties are signposts pointing onward to Beauty. The important function of a signpost, however, is to keep the traveler moving on her way. If instead she stops to enjoy the sign, it has become an obstacle rather than an aid. In the same way, for Plato the value of lower, temporal beauties depends entirely on our moving beyond them. Beauty becomes a way of moving beyond this world, and the spirituality of beauty is in its power to encourage the kind of purging and refining urged in "Veni Creator Spiritus." Beauty has the potential to lead us *beyond* the world of sense and experience, drawing the lover of beauty *up and out* of the material world into the realm of spirit.

5. Plato, *Symposium*, 211a–c, in *Plato: The Collected Dialogues*, ed. Edith Hamilton and Huntington Cairns, trans. Michael Joyce (Princeton: Princeton University Press, 1961), 562–63.

6. Bonaventure, *The Soul's Journey into God*, chap. 2, para. 11, as quoted in Gesa Elsbeth Thiessen, *Theological Aesthetics: A Reader* (Grand Rapids: Eerdmans, 2005), 86.

The negative side of Plato's theory of beauty is even more evident in his discussions of art. Plato characterizes art as *mimesis*—an imitation or representation. So, just as in *Symposium* particular beauties are said to echo transcendent Beauty, so Plato suggests that works of art echo more essential realities. Tolstoy described art as an expression of what is within; for Plato, on the other hand, art is an imitation of what is beyond. For Tolstoy, art moves from the depths of the artist out into the world; for Plato, art moves from the heights of reality down into the work of the artist. But for just this reason, the work of art is less reliable, and far less esteemed, than the realities it copies. So in the *Republic*, toward the end of a long discussion of art, Socrates will conclude: not only does painting—or rather representation in general—produce a product which is far from truth, but it also forms a close, warm, affectionate relationship with a part of us which is, in its turn, far from intelligence. And nothing healthy or authentic can emerge from this relationship."[7]

Taken together, this is a complex and ambivalent assessment of art and beauty. It certainly is not entirely negative. There is, in fact, an aesthetic moment, a surprising and overpowering encounter with beauty at the very beginning of the spiritual journey. It is an encounter so forceful that it sustains the beholder through all his long and demanding pursuit. The beautiful object or person meets us as a force outside of ourselves, and it has the power to lay hold of us. It stops us in our tracks and seizes our attention.

Moreover this encounter is *meaningful*. The aesthetic moment is not an infatuation or a delightful distraction. It is a transformative encounter. If we see something beautiful and truly *see* it, we are changed. Annie Dillard describes this kind of encounter with a backyard cedar that was suddenly revealed as "the tree with the lights in it."

> One day I was walking along Tinker Creek thinking of nothing at all and I saw the tree with the lights in it. I saw the backyard cedar where the mourning doves roost charged and transfigured, each cell buzzing with flame. I stood on the grass with the lights in it, grass that was wholly fire, utterly focused and utterly dreamed. It was less like seeing than like being for the first time seen, knocked breathless by a powerful glance. The flood of fire abated, but I'm still spending the power. . . . I was still ringing. I had been my whole life a bell, and never knew it until at that moment I was lifted up and struck.[8]

However, this transformational moment may also help us to understand Plato's ambivalence. "Gradually" Dillard writes, "the lights went out in the cedar, the colors died, the cells unflamed and disappeared."[9]

7. Plato, *Republic*, 603a–b, trans. Robin Waterfield (Oxford: Oxford University Press, 1993), 355–56.

8. Annie Dillard, *Pilgrim at Tinker Creek* (New York: Harper & Row, 1974), 33–34.

9. Ibid.

Dillard does not find this particularly problematic, but Plato would have. We might as well. We have a powerful, transformational, ecstatic encounter with a thing of beauty and then . . . we return to the seashore the next day, and the light isn't striking the sand at quite the same angle; we meet the face that several years earlier had held us transfixed and find that it has grown hard and haggard; we hear again the symphony that once had seemed like a revelation, but squeaking through the tinny speakers in our car it now sounds pompous and ridiculous. Most frustrating of all, we drag along a friend, hoping to show her the very beauty that left us "ringing like a bell" and—she doesn't see it at all ("What? Look at what? It's just a cedar tree!").

How can this be possible? If the truth we saw in that tree or heard in that music was really Truth—was really Beauty—then could it be so fragile as to disappear under a passing cloud or falter because of an inadequate speaker system? The changeableness, the transience, the frailty of material things, and the elusiveness, the unfixed and shifting character of physical beauty—this is what troubles Plato. If there is a transcendent good that we are encountering, then "it is not beautiful this way and ugly that way, nor beautiful at one time and ugly at another, nor beautiful in relation to one thing and ugly in relation to another; nor is it beautiful here but ugly there, as it would be if it were beautiful for some people and ugly for others."[10]

The easiest way out would be to say that we were simply mistaken, that we got caught up in the moment and mistook for transcendence something that was—no less than, but certainly, no more than—a marvelous sensation. The cognitive scientist Stephen Pinker (to take a contemporary example) speculates in this fashion concerning the power music exercises over us. "Perhaps [it is] a resonance in the brain between neurons firing in synchrony with a soundwave and a natural oscillation in the emotion circuits? An unused counterpart in the right hemisphere of the speech areas in the left? Some kind of spandrel or crawl space or short-circuit or coupling that came along as an accident of the way auditory, emotional, language, and motor circuits are packed together in the brain?"[11] This is the sort of attempt to explain (really, to *explain away*) beauty that would have sent Diotima running into the Aegean screaming.

Plato refuses to let go of the reality of the encounter. He will not dismiss the vision as a trick of the eye (or a trick of an "unused counterpart in the right hemisphere of the speech areas in the left"). But, Plato reasons, if there really was an encounter with Beauty, then the transcendent referent ("Beauty itself") must not—cannot—be the part of the experience that changes and wavers and decays over time; it could not possibly be the part that is threatened by a mere shifting of the light. Beauty itself must be something back behind—or beyond,

10. Plato, *Symposium*, 211a, trans. Nehamas and Woodruff (Indianapolis: Hackett Publishing, 1989), 58.

11. Stephen Pinker, *How the Mind Works* (London: Penguin, 1997), 538.

or above—the changeable aspect of the object encountered. It must be something that inhabits the object, something we can find in a purer and more concentrated form if we simply strip away the material husk enclosing it. This is the way to proceed, Plato says. As we do, he suggests, we will be led step by step, upward and beyond the beautiful object, first to beautiful ideas, and then to the Idea of the Beautiful, and then to Beauty itself. And at each step we will move further from the fickle and wavering world of the material. At each step we will journey deeper into the timeless and unchanging world of the immaterial transcendent.

Plato, in other words, recognizes both sides of the paradox we considered in the last chapter—we human beings, and all the created world along with us, are both frail and glorious. We are contingent and dependent, and yet made to receive the breath of God's Spirit. Plato's account of art and beauty recognizes both the great meaningfulness and the great fragility of the things we encounter in the world around us. Though we will ultimately disagree with Plato and part company with Diotima, this vision of beauty and enlightenment is itself a thing of great insight and beauty.

Kandinsky and the Kingdom of the Abstract

The power of Plato's vision is such that we encounter refractions of it throughout the Western tradition. These glimmers appear not only in theology and philosophy (such as in the medieval Ladder of Beauty), but in the arts as well. In fact, two of the most influential artistic movements of the twentieth century are driven by ideas that, while not derived directly from *Symposium*, are at least part of the same family tree.

Wassily Kandinsky (1866–1944) was born in Russia but spent much of his professional life in Germany and France. Although he did not actively pursue an artistic career until he was in his thirties, Kandinsky has come to be regarded as one of the most influential painters of the twentieth century. In particular, he was decisively important in the development of what has come to be known as "abstract art." "His role as the most significant founder of abstract art," says Jelena Hahl-Koch, "has been universally acknowledged."[12]

This artistic development, however, did not arise solely from aesthetic or formal considerations. Kandinsky was a man of mystical temperament, deeply influenced by theosophy,[13] a nineteenth-century religious movement that "harked back to Pythagoras and Plato" and "professed to be the rediscovery

12. Jelena Hahl-Koch, *Kandinsky* (New York: Rizzoli, 1993), 7. E. H. Gombrich observes that "it appears that the first artist to [exhibit a painting without any recognizable object] was the Russian painter Wassily Kandinsky. . . . [His efforts] really inaugurated what came to be known as 'abstract art'" (E. H. Gombrich, *The Story of Art*, 16th ed. [London: Phaidon, 1995], 570).

13. See Kandinsky's enthusiastic endorsement of theosophy in Wassily Kandinsky, *Concerning the Spiritual in Art*, trans. M. T. H. Sadler (New York: Dover, 1977), 13–14.

of ancient forms of wisdom that had been forgotten in the age of materialism and science."[14] Theosophy arose in response to the era of the machine, an age enthralled with the power of science and confident in the capacities of human reason. Along with other movements at the turn of the century, theosophy rejected modern reductionist accounts of the world and insisted instead on the primacy of mystery and spirit.[15] "On all sides," one art historian writes, "there was a resurgence of a pattern of ideas that contrasted the darkness of matter with the radiance of spirit."[16]

Kandinsky passionately articulates this contrast between matter and spirit in a short book titled *Concerning the Spiritual in Art*, first published in 1911. Whether or not Kandinsky read *Symposium*, his essay urges the same movement from the world of sense to the higher realm of immaterial Beauty. Unlike Plato, Kandinsky believes that art has a decisive role to play in this ascent. "Instead of reinforcing the false values of a materialistic society, art . . . would help people to recognize their own spiritual worlds."[17] Kandinsky believes that art and music may be the last bulwark against "the nightmare of materialism."[18]

Kandinsky argues that throughout history true artists have always "sought to express in their work *only internal truths*, renouncing in consequence all consideration of external form."[19] "Form," that is, the physical and sensual properties of art, should be recognized as merely "the outward expression of inner meaning."[20] The untrained or spiritually insensitive person may look at a painting and simply see an image, but "a more sensitive soul" perceives the "psychic effect" of shape and color. Kandinsky believes that the formal elements of art—shape, line, and particularly color—"produce a corresponding spiritual vibration, and *it is only as a step towards this spiritual vibration that the elementary physical impression is of importance*."[21] Like the beautiful boy in Diotima's speech, the sight of whom starts the seeker off toward transcendent beauty, the physical stuff of art properly points beyond itself. "The inner spirit of art," Kandinsky writes, "only uses the outer form of any particular period as a stepping-stone to further expression."[22]

Since the physical is only a stepping stone, Kandinsky believes that the spiritually sensitive artist will attempt to move further and further away from

14. Armin Zweite, "Free the Line for the Inner Sound," in *Kandinsky: Watercolors and Drawings*, ed. Vivian Endicott Barnett and Armin Zweite (Munich: Prestell, 1992), 14.

15. For a brief discussion of the variety of writings that influenced Kandinsky, see Hahl-Koch, *Kandinsky*, 190–95.

16. Zweite, "Free the Line," 14.

17. Norbert Lynton, "Expressionism," in *Concepts of Modern Art: From Fauvism to Postmodernism*, 3rd ed., ed. Nikos Stangos (London: Thames & Hudson, 1994), 43.

18. Kandinsky, *Concerning the Spiritual*, 2.

19. Ibid., 1, emphasis added.

20. Ibid., 29.

21. Ibid., 24, emphasis added.

22. Ibid., 34.

it, toward "dematerialized objects," advancing "deeper and more confidently . . . into the kingdom of the abstract."[23] If one wishes to know the "inner meaning" of things, then one will move away from externals—from the world of nature and physical objects. So, Kandinsky argues, "the forms, movement, and colours which we borrow from nature must produce no outward effect nor be associated with external objects. The more obvious is the separation from nature, the more likely is the inner meaning to be pure and unhampered."[24] Kandinsky's statements point toward a remarkable idea: one of the most notable developments in modern art—the emergence of nonfigurative, abstract art—arises in large part from Kandinsky's *theological* convictions. Because he has segregated the world of sense from the world of spirit, in his attempt to make spiritual art Kandinsky abandons the world of objects.[25] "He turned his back on the material world . . . committing art to the world of the spirit."[26]

If we consider two of Kandinsky's paintings from this period (fig. 3.1 and fig. 3.2), we can see his transition from the world of material things into the "kingdom of the abstract."

Both canvases are beautiful. We can see in them some similarities of brushwork, composition, and use of color. The former, however, is still a picture *of*—an image of this material world: "Winter Landscape." By 1913, Kandinsky had moved away from the world of objects into the realm of pure spirit. The development of abstraction in twentieth-century visual art, then, arises in large part from a desire to peel back the husk of materiality and find a moment of pure and spiritual enlightenment. The development of abstraction, one critic observes, "marks the conclusion of the painter's quest for a 'sound,' for a resonance purged of any material substrate, for a purely spiritual—and of course nameless—thing that would generate in the viewer the same psychic vibration that had filled the painter himself."[27]

This reference to "a sound" points us toward a parallel development in the world of twentieth-century music: the emergence of "serial" or "atonal" music. The composer chiefly associated with this development is Arnold Schoenberg. Schoenberg and Kandinsky were friends, in fact, and recognized one another as kindred spirits.

23. Ibid., 32.

24. Ibid., 50.

25. "Kandinsky views art as a pure spiritual medium and therefore increasingly turns away from representing the human figure and human actions in order to center his work around cosmic phenomena" (Hahl-Koch, *Kandinsky*, 152).

26. Lynton, "Expressionism," 43.

27. "It is thus evident—and this would seem to be particularly important—that pure abstraction, the production of paintings devoid of any reference to objective motifs, is not simply the outcome of a formal process of reduction" (Zweite, "Free the Line," 14). "Symbolism, with its systematic devaluation of concrete reality in favour of the transcendent, supersensible perception of a cosmic spiritual order, was undeniably an important factor in the development of Kandinsky's abstract art" (ibid., 11).

Fig. 3.1. *Winter Landscape I* 1909 by Wassily Kandinsky. (Erich Lessing, Art Resource, New York; © 2011 Artist Rights Society (ARS), New York/ADAGP, Paris)

Fig. 3.2. *Improvisation VII* 1913 by Wassily Kandinsky. (Erich Lessing, Art Resource, New York; © 2011 Artist Rights Society (ARS), New York/ADAGP, Paris)

Kandinsky believed that there was a profound link between music and painting.[28] He conceived of his own work in musical terms, describing the interaction of colors in terms of "harmony," "notes," "chords," and "vibrations."[29] Music seemed to him the least material and therefore the "most spiritual" of the arts. The painter who longs "to express his inner life," Kandinsky writes, "cannot but envy the ease with which music, the most non-material of the arts today, achieves this end."[30] And he notes with admiration that Schoenberg "has already discovered gold mines of new beauty in his search for spiritual harmony. His music leads us into a realm where musical experience is a matter *not of the ear* but of *the soul* alone."[31]

Schoenberg and "The Transparency of Clear-Cut Ideas"

In July 1921, Arnold Schoenberg told one of his music students, "Today I have discovered something which will assure the supremacy of German music for the next 100 years."[32] Schoenberg's breakthrough was the creation of a technique known as twelve-tone, or serial, composition. Over a decade earlier, Schoenberg had abandoned traditional musical tonality,[33] and in the years that followed, he struggled to find an alternate method of giving his compositions coherence. His solution was the "twelve-tone" system—a method of composition that organizes a piece of music according to a tone row or a "set" generated by the composer for that piece.

Schoenberg's innovations, like those of Kandinsky, represent a watershed moment in twentieth-century art. In the same way that Kandinsky moves away from "mere representation"—the mere depiction of objects from the world of sense—so Schoenberg moves away from mere "surface beauty"—sounds that merely please the ear. And, just as with Kandinsky, Schoenberg's new method is deeply connected to his philosophical convictions about spirit and matter. Boaz Tarsi observes that a Platonic dualism of the concrete (which includes the material and sensible) and the abstract (which includes "Idea" and the

28. Kandinsky, *Concerning the Spiritual*, 27.

29. See, for instance, ibid., 24–31.

30. Ibid., 19.

31. Ibid., 17, emphasis added.

32. Willi Reich, *Schoenberg: A Critical Biography*, trans. Leo Black (London: Longman, 1971), 130.

33. In *tonal* music, compositions are organized with reference to a particular key and to hierarchical relationships of consonance and dissonance. Different tones play different roles within the composition, representing different degrees of tension or resolution, activity or rest. In atonal music, on the other hand, these roles and relationships no longer structure the piece. In some sense all notes "are created equal." For a competent definition and discussion of "atonality" (a term Schoenberg disliked), see George Perle and Paul Lansky, "Twelve-Note Composition," and Paul Griffiths, "Serialism," both in *The New Grove Dictionary of Music and Musicians*, vols. 19 and 17, ed. Stanley Sadie (London: MacMillan, 1980).

spiritual) runs through both Schoenberg's music and his theoretical writings.[34] As Tarsi points out, this dualism is evident even in the title of Schoenberg's collection of essays, *Style and Idea*.[35]

For Schoenberg, the experience of beauty is not a matter of pleasing the eye or the ear, but rather "the relaxation which a satisfied listener experiences when he can follow *an idea*, its development, and the reasons for such development."[36] Beauty is perceived intellectually. It is an idea that shines through the superficial elements of harmony, melody, and rhythm. For this reason, Schoenberg insists, the ultimate aim of an artist is "to elaborate profoundly upon his *ideas*," and this aim "should not be condemned *even if the cerebral procedure causes loss of the surface beauty*."[37] What matters about a work of art is not what our senses perceive (the "surface beauty"). What matters is what our senses *cannot* perceive, the idea beneath the surface.

Schoenberg strove to apply these ideals to all the aspects of his compositional practice, including orchestration. In an essay on orchestral color (that is, the qualities and timbres of the various instruments in the orchestra), he writes, "The childish preference of the primitive ear for colours has kept a number of imperfect instruments in the orchestra, because of their individuality. More mature minds resist the temptation to become intoxicated by colours, and prefer to be coldly convinced by the transparency of clear-cut ideas."[38]

So, "more mature minds" should not be swept away by sensual beauty but should experience the sounding stuff of music as transparent. The material should draw no attention to itself but should allow the rationality of the idea *behind the matter* to shine through. For Schoenberg the deepest and truest beauty—the most profound and spiritually meaningful aspect of art—cannot be perceived by the crude apparatus of the senses. True beauty is the pure and immaterial idea.

Staying and Moving Beyond

And yet, "pure, immaterial idea" is not how we hear the music of Schoenberg, and it is not how we see works by Kandinsky. Schoenberg the philosopher is undermined by Schoenberg the composer, and Kandinsky the painter discredits Kandinsky the theologian. Their theological and philosophical commitments cannot accommodate our experience of their art.

Music theorist Fred Lerdahl and linguist Ray Jackendoff question whether it even would be possible (let alone natural or intuitive) for a listener to hear a piece

34. Boaz Tarsi, "Manifestations of Arnold Schoenberg's Abstract Versus Concrete Dichotomy," *Modern Judaism* 21, no. 3 (2001): 238–55. See esp. 239.

35. Arnold Schoenberg, *Style and Idea: Selected Writings of Arnold Schoenberg*, ed. Leonard Stein, with translations by Leo Black (London: Faber & Faber, 1975). See Tarsi, "Manifestations," 239.

36. Schoenberg, *Style and Idea*, 215, emphasis added.

37. Ibid., 55, emphasis added.

38. Ibid., 235.

in the way Schoenberg has composed it—in other words, to hear it as a complex structure organized according to a twelve-tone series and its permutations. "We find little reason to believe this possible," they conclude, "inasmuch as no serial composer has this ability beyond a very limited extent."[39] They cite further empirical studies that support this assessment. Schoenberg has organized his piece according to numerical structures of extraordinary complexity, but there is nothing to suggest that the listener is able to perceive these structures, let alone aspire to some abstract idea embodied in the music. When we hear Schoenberg, Roger Scruton writes, "we hear *against* the atonal order."[40]

Likewise, there is a telling passage in Kandinsky's *Concerning the Spiritual in Art*. He expresses frustration with the art-viewing public, many of whom, he observes, wander through a museum gallery, glancing absentmindedly at the works on display. They then "go away, neither richer nor poorer than when they came, and are absorbed at once in their business, which has nothing to do with art."[41] Still others, Kandinsky complains, approach a painting as simply a story in paint, or a record of a person or an event. They look at a painting simply as a means to the end of the storytelling and have no interest in its spiritual depths.

We may recall that Kandinsky the theologian believes that ideally the artwork is a stepping-stone. The crucial thing is that we move beyond the work itself, pushing past the outward appearance to the internal meaning of the art. Kandinsky the artist, however, expresses a different frustration with the insensitive viewers he describes. He does not fault them for becoming trapped at the level of the painting's materiality—its shapes, forms, colors, and textures. The first group of inadequate viewers, in fact, breeze right by these elements. They simply never bother to look very closely. As Kandinsky says (with more than a little condescension!), "the vulgar herd stroll through the rooms and pronounce the pictures 'nice' or 'splendid.' "[42] But we should note: the problem is not that they have failed to move *beyond* the painting. The problem, Kandinsky observes, is that they have failed to move *into* the painting.

Conversely, Kandinsky criticizes another group of viewers precisely because they *do* "move beyond" it. Some look at a painting and pass over its formal and aesthetic qualities in order to get to some story *behind* the painting. These are the viewers whom Kandinsky faults for being interested only in the "literary element" of the painting. They look at the canvas and think about the young soldier pictured sitting in the window. They wonder if he is

39. Fred Lerdahl and Ray Jackendoff, *A Generative Theory of Tonal Music* (Cambridge, MA: MIT Press, 1983), 299. See the discussion from 298–301.

40. Roger Scruton, *The Aesthetics of Music* (Oxford: Clarendon, 1997), 304. See the discussion from 295–304.

41. Kandinsky, *Concerning the Spiritual*, 3.

42. Ibid., 3.

frightened or merely pensive; they wonder if he is scanning the horizon for enemies or perhaps hoping for a visit from his beloved; they think about the grandness of the architecture surrounding him. They focus, in other words, on everything except the material qualities of the work of art itself. The bit of gold on the canvas is only appreciated as a button on the soldier's vest, rather than considered and appreciated for its very goldness.

Kandinsky explains that his abstract art intentionally strips away these literary elements. Likewise, he has deliberately defied standards of "conventional beauty," in order to deny the viewer these routes beyond the painting—to some casual assessment of its "prettiness" for instance, or to some reflection on the subject matter of the painting.

But what does that leave us? Instead we are left with only shape, color, geometry, and texture. Far from moving us beyond the material world, then, Kandinsky's paintings immerse us more deeply in it. We are thrown up against the redness of red and the roundness of round. We are offered blue and gold and straight lines, not as constituents of the dress jacket of a soldier, not as mere means to the end of visual representation, but as *blue* and *gold*—worthy in themselves of our attention and appreciation. Like Annie Dillard standing before her backyard cedar, Kandinsky presents us with the most basic furniture of our sensory experience and invites us to *wonder*—and to wonder that such things are capable of evoking wonder. Kandinsky is right to sense the meaningfulness of beauty, but we find this meaning, not by *moving beyond*, but by *staying*, *waiting*, and *looking*.

Altogether apart from any theological or philosophical assessment, then, the ideas set out by Schoenberg and Kandinsky fail as an account of what we experience in art, even as an account of what we experience in *their* art.

"That Which We Have Seen . . ."

If this conception is artistically problematic, then it is even more so theologically. At the heart of the Christian faith is the conviction that God has made himself known decisively by becoming flesh. We know the Word of God—the Way, the Truth, and the Life—not by moving beyond the veil of the physical into another higher world, but because the Word has taken humanity to himself and descended into ours.

"The Word became flesh and lived among us, and we have seen his glory, the glory as of a father's only son, full of grace and truth" (John 1:14). John is able to say what Plato cannot. The glory *is* seen, not simply shining somewhere back behind the material, but in the material presence of Immanuel. The opening of 1 John draws the worlds of sense and transcendence together even more closely. John is concerned with what "was from the beginning" and yet writes of "what we have heard, what we have seen with our eyes, what we have looked at and touched with our hands, concerning the word of life—this life was revealed, and we have seen it and testify to it" (1 John 1:1–2).

The emphatic declaration is that this transcendent glory—that which was from the beginning, the Word of life, the eternal life that was with the Father—has been revealed. Christ's appearance is not mere "appearance" but an unveiling. And those who have beheld his glory have done so not by ascending beyond the world of matter but by *hearing*, *seeing*, *looking*, and *touching*.

"Flesh" against "Spirit" in the Christian Scriptures

And yet—we began with the prayer "Veni Creator Spiritus," a prayer that, like Plato and Kandinsky, draws hard lines between the material and the spiritual. Clearly, across its history the Christian faith has had an ambivalent relationship with the body. Clearly, many forms of Christian spirituality have aspired to move beyond the material. Wuthnow refers to "the sharp distinction between body and spirit in much of Western culture. In this view, the body is mortal flesh, an organism or machine, and the source of temptation or evil, whereas the spirit connotes eternity and all that is godly, pure and uplifting."[43]

And indeed, when we turn to the Jewish and Christian Scriptures, at least in places there seems to be the same tendency to contrast flesh and spirit. Particularly in the writings of the apostle Paul, "flesh" and "spirit" are often set against one another. In Romans 8 Paul declares that those who belong to Christ

> do not walk according to the flesh but according to the Spirit. For those who are according to the flesh set their minds on the things of the flesh, but those who are according to the Spirit, the things of the Spirit. For the mind set on the flesh is death, but the mind set on the Spirit is life and peace, because the mind set on the flesh is hostile toward God; for it does not subject itself to the law of God, for it is not even able to do so, and those who are in the flesh cannot please God. However, you are not in the flesh but in the Spirit, if indeed the Spirit of God dwells in you.
>
> Romans 8:4–9 NASB

And again, perhaps even more forcefully: "But I say, walk by the Spirit, and you will not carry out the desire of the flesh. For the flesh sets its desire against the Spirit, and the Spirit against the flesh; for these are in opposition to one another" (Gal. 5:16–17 NASB). Elsewhere, Paul reproves the Christians in Corinth because though he had hoped to speak to them "as to spiritual men," he must still deal with them as "men of flesh" (1 Cor. 3:1 NASB).

43. Robert Wuthnow, *Creative Spirituality: The Way of the Artist* (Berkeley: University of California Press, 2001), 174–75.

A surface reading of these passages would suggest that the New Testament is very much in agreement with Kandinsky. These passages seem to reflect a deep and abiding suspicion of the body. What is more, this apparent hostility toward the body finds its focal point in the Spirit. In each of the passages we looked at, it is not just God, or the gospel generally, but the Spirit particularly that is said to be utterly opposed to the flesh. While this may appear to be the same dualism we encountered in Plato, in this case the appearance *is* merely an appearance. In fact, the biblical categories of "flesh" (*basar* in the Old Testament, and *sarx* in the New Testament), and "spirit" (*ruach* in the Old Testament, and *pneuma* in the New Testament) are significantly different from the Platonic categories of "body" and "soul."

In some places in Scripture, *flesh* does indeed refer to physical bodies; for example, "At twilight you shall eat meat [literally, "flesh"], and in the morning you shall have your fill of bread" (Exod. 16:12), and in the Pauline epistles, "Without any doubt, the mystery of our religion is great: He was revealed in flesh [*sarx*], vindicated in spirit, seen by angels, proclaimed among Gentiles, believed in throughout the world, taken up in glory" (1 Tim. 3:16).

Other times, *flesh* is extended metaphorically (or used metonymically), to mean something like "mortal/s." This is the case, for instance, in Genesis 6:12–13, where "flesh" clearly isn't interchangeable with "physical bodies": "And God saw that the earth was corrupt; for all flesh had corrupted its ways upon the earth. And God said to Noah, 'I have determined to make an end of all flesh.'" Similarly, Paul clearly has more than just bodies in mind when he writes: "by the works of the Law no flesh [*sarx*] will be justified" (Gal. 2:16 NASB). (So, the NRSV quite correctly translates this passage "*no one* will be justified by the works of the law.") In both of these instances—where the word *flesh* means "physical body," or where it means "human being"—*flesh* doesn't carry any negative connotation.

In other places, however, flesh is sharply contrasted with God's Spirit. In these places, *flesh* refers to humanity in a way that emphasizes its mortality, frailty, and transience.[44]

> Then the Lord said, "My spirit [*ruach*] shall not abide in mortals forever, for they are flesh [*basar*]; their days shall be one hundred twenty years."
>
> Genesis 6:3

> If he [the Almighty] should take back his spirit [*ruach*] to himself, and gather to himself his breath, all flesh [*basar*] would perish together, and all mortals return to dust.
>
> Job 34:15

44. Again, this is a kind of metonymic use of *flesh*.

> A voice says, "Call out." Then he answered, "What shall I call out?" All flesh [*basar*] is grass, and all its loveliness is like the flower of the field. The grass withers, the flower fades, When the breath [*ruach*] of the Lord blows upon it; surely the people are grass. The grass withers, the flower fades, but the word of our God stands forever.
>
> Isaiah 40:6–8 NASB

In each of these passages, *flesh* stands for humanity in its fragility and impermanence. It stands, in fact, for humanity apart from the sustaining breath of God's Spirit. For this reason, once again, the NRSV renders the last passage according to this less literal sense of *flesh*: "All *people* [rather than *flesh*] are grass, their *constancy* [rather than *loveliness*] is like the flower of the field." The writer is not specifically concerned in pointing out that human beings are material, but rather that they are passing, ephemeral, and without constancy. Flesh fades, like the flower of the field; it perishes and withers. Flesh is wholly dependent upon and at the mercy of the blowing, passing, and the coming and the going of *ruach*. This is the reason the prophet writes, "Thus says the Lord: Cursed are those who trust in mere mortals and make mere flesh [*basar*] their strength, whose hearts turn away from the Lord" (Jer. 17:5).

Human beings are not cursed for *having* flesh but for depending upon flesh, for depending upon what is limited, finite, and passing, rather than upon the Lord.[45] The flesh when it is contrasted with Spirit, then, stands for human ability independent of God. This is the sense in which it is strongly condemned by the apostle Paul. The one who lives "according to the flesh" lives by her own strength, abilities, and righteousness. Paul describes what it might mean for him to live by his "flesh":

> For it is we who are the circumcision, who worship in the Spirit of God and boast in Christ Jesus and have no confidence in the flesh [*sarx*]—even though I, too, have reason for confidence in the flesh [*sarx*]. If anyone else has reason to be confident in the flesh [*sarx*], I have more: circumcised on the eighth day, a member of the people of Israel, of the tribe of Benjamin, a Hebrew born of Hebrews; as to the law, a Pharisee; as to zeal, a persecutor of the church; as to

45. "In no case then is the spirit of man to be regarded as the higher, purer, or more ideal part of him, and his body as the sinful part. . . . 'Flesh' is as much God's gracious gift as the spirit. The only thing that is evil or sinful is man, who puts his trust in the 'flesh' alone instead of trusting in God" (Eduard Schweizer, *The Holy Spirit*, trans. Reginald H. and Ilse Fuller [London: SCM, 1980], 19). "It is probably always wrong to interpret such passages in terms merely of a contrast between the material and the immaterial, though this is what is most naturally suggested to a modern reader. . . . On the whole, the biblical writers had little room for a dualism of spirit over against matter. . . . But 'flesh' did stand, in the Old Testament as well as in the New, for what is frail, and transitory, and mortal" (C. F. D. Moule, *The Holy Spirit* [Grand Rapids: Eerdmans, 1978], 40).

> righteousness under the law, blameless. Yet whatever gains I had, these I have come to regard as loss because of Christ.
>
> Philippians 3:3–7

If Paul were to place his confidence in his flesh, he might appeal to many things, including his family heritage, his training in Torah ("a Pharisee"), his zealousness, or his flawless observance of the law. Most of these are not, strictly speaking, bodily or material. All of them, however, are flesh. Of course, if Paul were to place his confidence in his physical body, that would be flesh as well. The point is that flesh is a way of speaking about *all* of our humanity—both its material and immaterial aspects—in its natural capacities. The point is brought home in the next verses of Philippians 3:

> More than that, I regard everything as loss because of the surpassing value of knowing Christ Jesus my Lord. For his sake I have suffered the loss of all things, and I regard them as rubbish, in order that I may gain Christ and be found in him, not having *a righteousness of my own* that comes from the law, but *one that comes through faith in Christ*, the righteousness from God based on faith.
>
> Philippians 3:8–9, emphasis added

The one who believes he can have "a righteousness of his own"—achieving righteousness by his own strength and piety—is living according to the flesh. So in the Old and New Testament, when flesh is contrasted with spirit, it is not a contrast of material versus immaterial or bodily versus nonbodily. In these instances, the fragility and mortality of our physical flesh serves as a way of speaking of the limits and weakness of our humanity generally. *Flesh* can very well mean immaterial things (as in fact it often does in Paul's letters)—things like human ambition, pride, wrong attitudes, or self-righteousness.

The Embodying Work of the Spirit

All of this is simply to observe that Christianity, like Platonism, recognizes the mortality and transience of human beings. These two traditions offer different analyses of the dilemma, however, and propose radically different solutions.

The dilemma, from the perspective of the Platonic tradition, is that we are "spirits in the material world." We are most truly "souls," immaterial beings who have fallen into the world of sense and matter, change and motion, decay and mortality. In contrast to this, the biblical testimony never suggests that the material world is foreign to our humanity. Indeed, the creation accounts of Genesis 1 and 2 are structured in such a way as to emphasize that this earth is humanity's home. Days one, two, and three of creation move from the lights of the heavens to the terrestrial; from the sea to dry land—the creative movement culminating in a habitable place for human beings. In the same way, days four, five, and six build steadily toward the creation of humanity. This humanity is "placed" in the garden—it is humanity's place. The human is further commissioned with its care; tilling the soil is humanity's vocation. Earth and humanity are made for one another, a point underlined by the fact that the *adam* is created from the *adamah*. *Adam* is translated "human," but more than one commentator has observed that, given its etymology, it could be rendered "earthling." From a biblical perspective, then, our dilemma is not our materiality nor the material world in which we live.

A recognition of our mortality—our "fleshiness"—arises naturally from our belief in one God. Only God is God. There is no other Creator or Sustainer. There is no other source of life. Therefore, when creatures turn from God, they turn from life; when God withdraws from them, life is withdrawn, and they steadily return to the dust from which they were made.

Moving Beyond versus Indwelling

If the human dilemma is, as the Platonic tradition suggests, our situation within a material world, then the solution is to *move beyond* the material—to pierce the veil of appearances and move through into the world of true Being. The artist, Kandinsky writes, hopes ultimately to "break the bonds which bind us to nature."[46]

If, however, our dilemma is that we have been separated from the source of life, then the solution is not "moving beyond" but an "indwelling" of the material—that we would be filled with the *ruach* of God. And this, as we saw in the last chapter, is how the gospel accounts portray Jesus. He is the Messiah, powerfully indwelt by the Spirit of God and able to pour out the life-giving Spirit on all who belong to him (see, for instance, John 20:21–22; Acts 2:33). Once again, Athanasius articulates this logic: the Spirit gives life to Christ's humanity and then unites us to this transformed humanity of Jesus.

> [The Word of God] became for us a human being and became our brother through the likeness of the body, nevertheless, even in that regard, he is still said to be and is the "first." For while all humanity was perishing because of the transgression of Adam, his flesh was the first to be saved and freed, as being the body of the Word himself. From then on we are "incorporated" with his body and saved through our accord with it.[47]

> The Savior . . . being God, and forever ruling the kingdom of the Father, and being himself the supplier of the Spirit, is nevertheless now said to be anointed

46. Kandinsky, *Concerning the Spiritual*, 47.

47. Athanasius, *Orations against the Arians*, 2.61, in Khaled Anatolios, *Athanasius* (New York: Routledge, 2004), 155.

> by the Spirit, so that, being said to be anointed as a human being by the Spirit, he may provide us human beings with the indwelling and intimacy of the Holy Spirit, just as he provides us with exaltation and resurrection.[48]

God's desire, as expressed in both the Old and New Testament, is not so much to move us beyond this world, but for his presence—which is his Spirit, his shekinah glory—to dwell among us within it.

Ascending versus Inbreaking

There is also a difference in the metaphors used by the Platonic and biblical traditions to express the spiritual journey. The Platonic vision, as we have seen, uses the spatial metaphor of an "ascent." Kandinsky writes that even in the midst of the material world and its confusions, the spiritual visionary "slowly but surely, with irresistible strength, moves onwards and upwards."[49] As he ascends, so the artist aids others in their ascent. So, he says, "every man who steeps himself in the spiritual possibilities of his art is a valuable helper in the building of the spiritual pyramid which will one day reach to the heaven."[50]

The language of ascent, of course, suggests that the realm of Spirit/spirit is above and other than the realm in which we reside. The realm of true Being, the really Real, is not here, but "upwards" in "heaven" (in Kandinsky's words).

The Christian tradition, however, turns the contrast of "heaven above" and "earth below" on its side, speaking much more naturally of "this present age" and "the age to come"[51] (see, for instance, Mark 10:30; Gal. 1:4; Eph. 1:21; Titus 2:12). The Christian hope, strictly speaking, is not "going to heaven," but for a new creation and a new Jerusalem "*coming down* out of heaven from God" (Rev. 21:2, emphasis added). God's people, then, do not desire to *ascend* (to what is above) but long for God's reality to *arrive* (from the future). They do not aspire; they hope.

From this perspective, then, the glory that we perceive in the material world is not a signpost directing us to journey above or some dim participation in a heavenly reality. Rather, we see in the world around us intimations of its own transformed glory.[52] And we look with longing, not to some ideal realm beyond the skies, but for the inbreaking of God's promised future.

48. Ibid., 1.46, 103.

49. Kandinsky, *Concerning the Spiritual*, 8.

50. Ibid., 20.

51. This insight is from Trevor Hart, professor of divinity, University of St. Andrews.

52. Jürgen Moltmann, *God in Creation: An Ecological Doctrine of Creation*, trans. Margaret Kohl (London: SCM, 1985), 58–59, 63.

Mortification versus Resurrection

This biblical orientation toward the future points us to another contrast.

If the body is that which ties us to the world of sense and matter, and if spiritual enlightenment is about transcending the material world, then the body must be gotten out of the way—or expressed more forcefully, it must be *put to death*. In *Phaedo*, another dialogue of Plato, Socrates explains to Simmias why the philosopher (that is, the lover of wisdom) welcomes, even longs for, death:

> All experience shows that if we would have pure knowledge of anything we must be quit of the body, and the soul in herself must behold all things in themselves: then I suppose that we shall attain that which we desire, and of which we say that we are lovers, and that is wisdom, not while we live, but after death, as the argument shows; for if while in company with the body the soul cannot have pure knowledge, one of two things seems to follow—either knowledge is not to be attained at all, or, if at all, after death. For then, and not till then, the soul will be in herself alone and without the body. In this present life, I reckon that we make the nearest approach to knowledge when we have the least possible concern or interest in the body, and are not saturated with the bodily nature, but remain pure until the hour when God himself is pleased to release us. And then the foolishness of the body will be cleared away and we shall be pure and hold converse with other pure souls, and know of ourselves the clear light everywhere; and this is surely the light of truth.[53]

The spiritual life, then, is fundamentally a matter of mortification—a putting to death of the body.

For Christian spirituality, however, mortification is only half the story. There is indeed a dying with Christ, but we hope that we also with him will be "made alive by the Spirit" (1 Pet. 3:18 NIV). Ultimately the Christian hope is not that the body would be put to death but that it would be raised to life. And this re-creation of our bodies is, in the proper sense of the word, *spiritual*—the work of the Holy Spirit. "Creatures," Athanasius says, "are granted life through the Spirit."[54] In saying this, Athanasius is simply acknowledging the Spirit's involvement in God's larger work of remaking his creation. Near the beginning of *On the Incarnation of the Word*, Athanasius explains that "the first fact that you must grasp is this: *the renewal of creation has been wrought by the Self-same Word Who made it in the beginning*."[55] While Athanasius speaks here of the work of the Word in making and remaking creation, the larger

53. Plato, *Phaedo*, in *The Essential Plato*, trans. Benjamin Jowett (n.p.: The Softback Preview, 1999), 604.

54. Athanasius, *Letters to Serapion on the Holy Spirit*, 584B, in Anatolios, *Athanasius*, 222.

55. Athanasius, *On the Incarnation*, 1.1, trans. and ed. by A Religious of C. S. M. V. (Crestwood, NY: St. Vladimir's Seminary Press, 2003), 25, emphasis original in translation.

point is that God has not given up on the world he has created. The same God—Father, Son, and Spirit—who created, is now about the work of re-creating—and not, in other words, frantically trying to deliver us from his creation. The theologian Irenaeus (c. 130–200) makes this same point:

> For it is not one thing that dies and another that is made alive, just as it is not one thing that is lost and another that is found, but the Lord came to look for that very sheep that was lost (Matt. 18:11). What was dead? Evidently the substance of flesh, which had lost the breath of life and became without breath and dead. This is what the Lord came to make alive so that as we all die in Adam . . . we all live in Christ because [we have been made] spiritual, after having put off not the work shaped by God but the desires of the flesh, and put on the Holy Spirit.[56]

It is more fitting, then, that we characterize the work of the Spirit as *vivification* rather than mortification. The hope held out for our frail and failing flesh is not its dissolution, but its resurrection. Indeed, Irenaeus writes, "the fruit of the labor of the Spirit is the salvation of the flesh; for what could the visible fruit of the invisible Spirit be if not to make the flesh mature and receptive of imperishability."[57]

The Scriptures offer us several concrete instances of the Spirit at work, making the "flesh mature and receptive of imperishability."

Bearer of Life

In Luke's gospel, the Spirit is said to be at work in the incarnation of the Word (Luke 1:35) and then descends upon Jesus at his baptism (Luke 3:21–22). Jesus ("full of the Spirit," Luke 4:1) then endures a time of testing in the wilderness, before returning to Galilee. He is, the text says, "filled with the power of the Spirit" (Luke 4:14)—God's anointed one—and he identifies himself as such in this passage: "The Spirit of the Lord is upon me, because he has anointed me to bring good news to the poor. He has sent me to proclaim release to the captives and recovery of sight to the blind, to let the oppressed go free, to proclaim the year of the Lord's favor" (Luke 4:18–19).

It is *specifically as the bearer of God's Spirit* that Jesus undertakes the "salvation of flesh"—bringing good news to the poor, proclaiming release to captives, healing the blind, freeing the oppressed, and announcing the year of the Lord's favor. As bearer of the Spirit, Jesus is not (in Platonic fashion) raised up out of this world but rather immersed in it. It is the Spirit who empowers Jesus to get his hands dirty, as it were, with the very physical and bodily needs

56. Irenaeus, *Against Heresies*, 5.12.3, in Robert M. Grant, *Irenaeus of Lyon* (London/New York: Routledge, 1997), 166.

57. Ibid., 5.12.3, 166.

of men and women—blindness, poverty, imprisonment. Luke then draws us along through Jesus's ministry, pointing out all the ways Jesus is indeed the Spirit-anointed one spoken of in Isaiah. Simon's mother-in-law has a fever, but a word from Jesus and she is able to get up (4:39). Others bring their sick and Jesus heals them (4:40). He heals a leper and a paralytic; he likens himself to a physician come to make people well; he sits down to eat and drink with those who are excluded; he refuses to make his disciples fast (chapter 5). Jesus and his disciples pick and eat grain rather than follow a certain kind of strict piety; he cures the sick and demon possessed; he preaches good news to the poor (chapter 6). And so on.

If Luke (and the other gospel writers) believed that the task of the Spirit was to mortify the body, then we would expect to see this reflected in their depiction of Jesus (who, after all, they believed to be the anointed one—the bearer of the Spirit). In such a case, at every stage in Jesus's ministry the sick would come to recognize their bodily infirmities as illusory and of no significance. The disadvantaged would embrace their hunger and poverty as a means of purging the soul. In his movement throughout society Jesus would be the very picture of austerity, fasting rigorously and associating himself especially with those of similar temperament. The disciples would come to Jesus, pointing out that the five thousand who had followed him into the desert needed food, and Jesus would refuse to provide it—declaring that his followers attend to their souls rather than their mortal bodies. Jairus, the widow of Nain, and Mary and Martha would welcome their loved ones' physical deaths, recognizing that their immortal souls were now free of their bodily imprisonment. Above all, Jesus's *body* would not be raised from the dead. The disciples would foolishly try to touch him, and fail; they would offer this translated ghost of Jesus broiled fish and he would refuse, explaining that he has now ascended beyond materiality.

Of course, we see just the opposite taking place. Wherever Jesus, the bearer-of-the-Spirit goes, life breaks out, not some metaphorical, etherealized, "immaterial" sort of life, either, but real bodily vitality. The lame walk, the blind see, the dead are raised to life, the hungry are fed. Jesus is the one filled with the Spirit, and precisely as the Spirit-filled one Jesus brings life and healing to broken bodies.

A Heart of Flesh

If we acknowledge that the work of the Spirit is to remake broken bodies, then we also are able to offer a much more satisfying theological account of art and beauty. If the work of the Spirit is to bring life, vitality, and wholeness to bodies, then it is much easier to explain our intuition that there is something spiritual about the arts. In music, painting, and other arts, our senses are engaged and enlarged, our physical experience both refined and broadened. We attend carefully to both the world and to our own physical experience of it. We gain practice in those very capacities that together indicate life and health—sight, hearing, attention, and responsiveness to touch. We become, in a very real sense, more fully embodied, more fully incarnate.

In this regard, the arts mirror the work of the Spirit. The Spirit's work is to make us responsive. Conversely, those who are spiritually dead have quite literally lost their senses. The biblical descriptions of their condition are a litany of sensory deprivation. They are blind, deaf, and mute (Isa. 43:8; 56:10); they have eyes that do not see and ears that do not hear (Isa. 6:10; Ezek. 12:2; Matt. 13:15; Mark 8:18; Acts 28:27); they have become calloused (Matt. 13:15; Acts 28:27), hardened in their hearts (Eph. 4:18), and have "lost all sensitivity" (Eph. 4:19).

Charlemagne prayed: "Refine and purge our earthy parts, / But O, inflame and fire our hearts." But hearts are (or at least are meant to be) made of flesh, not *flesh* as in "frail and limited" but *flesh* as in human, responsive, *sense*-itive. This is the connotation of the word in Ezekiel 36, and the creation of this sort of heart, one that senses and responds, is in fact the work of the Spirit.

> A new heart I will give you, and a new spirit I will put within you; and I will remove from your body the heart of stone and give you a heart of flesh. I will put my spirit within you.
>
> Ezekiel 36:26–27

4

Remaking Community

Singing to One Another in Songs, Hymns, and Spiritual Songs

Many people who have never read Plato or Kandinsky, Tolstoy or Schleiermacher, nevertheless believe that there is some sort of connection between the arts and spirituality. Perhaps this is partly because philosophical ideas like those we've surveyed filter down to popular culture and enter into general circulation. But of course ideas and beliefs don't only "filter down" from academics and philosophers; they also (some would say primarily) "bubble up" from culture and society. This is certainly the case for the association between spirituality and the arts. The connection that many make between these two domains is not simply conceptual or philosophical, but historical and social. The association between art and spirituality is embedded in social practices.

In our culture and in cultures across time and history, people have celebrated their religious beliefs in dance, story, image, and song. The connection between religion and music is particularly strong. "Music," Paul Honigsheim writes, "is intertwined with religious elements."[1] Daniel Levitin summarizes anthropological studies of ritual, concluding that the religious rituals of the world's cultures "almost always involve music or rhythmic, pitch-intoned

---

Much of this material also appears in the service of a slightly different argument in Steven R. Guthrie, "The Wisdom of Song," in *Resonant Witness: Conversations between Music and Theology*, ed. Jeremy Bigbie and Steven R. Guthrie (Grand Rapids: Eerdmans, forthcoming).

1. Paul Honigsheim, "On Form of Music and Form of Society," in Carl Dalhuas and Ruth Katz, eds., *Contemplating Music: Source Readings in the Aesthetics of Music*, vol. 4, *Community of Discourse* (New York: Pendragon, 1993), 70.

chanting." This tendency to express religious belief musically can be found "in the religious ceremonies of Muslims, Hindus, Christians, Jews, Sikhs, Taoists, Buddhists, and Native Americans, as well as hundreds of ceremonies of preliterate and preindustrialized societies. . . . The story of ritual is intimately bound up with music—which almost always accompanies it."[2] Similarly, Oliver Sacks observes that "there is evidence that religious practices began with communal chanting and dancing."[3]

Certainly since its beginnings, Christianity has been a singing faith. Calvin Stapert reminds us that "the New Testament begins and ends with outbursts of song. The birth of Jesus brought about the first outburst—four songs recorded in the first two chapters of Luke. . . . The second outburst occurs in Revelation: there the song to the Lamb is picked up in ever-widening circles until the whole cosmos has joined in."[4] Paul urged Christians to sing to one another in "psalms and hymns and spiritual songs" (Eph. 5:19), a command the church has obeyed in all the centuries that have followed. "The testimony of history speaks so loudly here," says Nicholas Wolterstorff, "that belaboring it would be pointless and tedious. . . . The church has always felt that, in ways too mysterious to describe, music profoundly enhances its liturgy. The way to put the point is perhaps this: in its assemblies the church has always found itself *breaking out* into music, especially into song."[5] When we consider religion in general, then, and Christianity in particular, the association of art and spirituality is not merely an idea but a historical reality.

Identity in Community

This discussion of the role of art in religious rituals, societies, and communities reminds us of yet another dimension of our humanity. In the last chapter we saw that our humanity includes our physical bodies. We aren't just "souls" or "spirits in the material world." My human identity includes my body, as does yours. But this is not all. Our humanity is also bound up with communities and relationships, with traditions and social practices.

To take a simple and obvious example, an important part of my human identity is my name. Indeed, in some ways my name *is* my identity. In a noisy room, the sound of my name lays hold of me. I have been *summoned*.

2. Daniel J. Levitin, *The World in Six Songs: How the Musical Brain Created Human Nature* (New York: Dutton, 2008), 195.

3. Oliver Sacks, *Musicophilia: Tales of Music and the Brain*, rev. ed. (New York: Vintage, 2008), 267.

4. Calvin R. Stapert, *A New Song for an Old World: Musical Thought in the Early Church* (Grand Rapids: Eerdmans, 2007), 14.

5. Nicholas Wolterstorff, "Thinking about Church Music," in *Music in Christian Worship: At the Service of the Liturgy*, ed. Charlotte Kroeker (Collegeville, MN: Liturgical Press, 2005), 11, emphasis original.

And yet, my name is not located somewhere in my DNA, nor anywhere on my physical body. It was given to me by my parents. I call myself "Steve" because others first called me that and also because those who know me now continue to do so. I also have a middle name (Richard), which was given to me after my father, and a "family name," Guthrie. Again, these names are completely, profoundly "my own," but I do not and could not have them "on my own." They arise from and represent my connection to others. In the same way, my youngest daughter is Lucy—though she is only two months old, and it will be some time before she knows that she is "Lucy." When she does, it will be because for months her mother and I, along with her brothers, sister, and many others, have cooed, spoken, and sung her name over her.

And of course, much more than a name is given us by others. Those things we think of as making us "human" rather than beasts—speech and language, social institutions like marriage and family, cultural norms and practices, art, music, story and dance, religious ceremonies, technology, political structures—all of these are "our own" only because they are someone else's as well. *My* language, *my* culture, and *my* values are learned, received, and shared.

If the work of the Holy Spirit, then, is truly to perfect and complete our humanity, this perfecting work will inevitably have a social dimension. This idea is in fact borne out by Scripture. One way of describing the biblical story is as the story of the creation, loss, and restoration of community.

Communion Created and Lost

The creation story tells of a humanity intended for community and right relationship—right relationship with God and with one another. In Genesis 1 human beings are said to be created "in the image and likeness of God." This *imago Dei* has been variously understood by the theological tradition and has been associated with everything from the capacity for reason to an upright posture.[6] For now, we should simply notice that this passage suggests that our "likeness" to God is not simply an individual endowment or capacity. Rather, there is a sense in which we bear the image of God as *human beings in community*. "Let Us make man in Our image, according to Our likeness," God declares, "and let *them* rule. . . . God created man in His own image, in the image of God He created him; *male and female He created them*" (Gen. 1:26–27 NASB, emphasis added).[7] It is specifically as male and female—as a

6. See the discussion in Jürgen Moltmann, *God in Creation: An Ecological Doctrine of Creation*, trans. Margaret Kohl (London: SCM, 1985), 219–25, and in Gordon J. Wenham, *Word Biblical Commentary, Genesis 1—15* (Waco: Word, 1987), 29–32.

7. Moltmann reads Genesis 1 through the lens of Trinitarian theology: "These shifts between singular and plural at this particular point are important: 'Let *us* make human beings—*an*

community of persons in relationship—that humanity shows forth the image of God.[8]

The creation account in Genesis 2 also points to the social nature of our humanity, though in a different way. The garden in Eden is a well-watered, pleasant place (the word *Eden* means "delight"). It is filled with "every tree that is pleasant to the sight and good for food" (2:9) as well as gold and precious stones. But one thing is not good: the Lord says, "It is not good that the man should be alone; I will make him a helper as his partner" (2:18). "What is being said here," Claus Westermann writes, "is that a human being must be seen as one whose destiny it is to live in community."[9] Eden—the place of delight—is not complete; creation is not complete while the man is alone. So the Lord creates woman from the man's side, and Adam responds with the first bit of poetry in the Hebrew Bible: "This at last is bone of my bones and flesh of my flesh; this one shall be called Woman, for out of Man this one was taken" (2:23). Man and woman are made from and made for one another. Significantly, the last note in the song of paradise, the last view we have of an unspoiled Eden is this—"Therefore a man leaves his father and his mother and clings to his wife, and they become one flesh. And the man and his wife were both naked, and were not ashamed" (2:24–25). In God's good garden, man and woman are naked and unashamed.

Conversely, humanity's first act after the fall is to hide themselves—from one another and from God (Gen. 3:7, 10). Where there had been openness and mutuality, now there is secrecy, shame, and separation. And when the couple's disobedience is uncovered, Adam will defend his actions by a further betrayal of intimacy. He accuses God and blames Eve (3:12). The loss of Eden, then, is the loss of community.

In the chapters that follow, the author of Genesis illustrates the spread of sin by showing how community progressively gives way to its opposite, violence.

---

image that is like *us*.' That is to say, the image of God (singular) is supposed to correspond to the 'internal' plural of God, and yet be a *single* image. In the next verse the singular and plural are distributed in the opposite way: God (singular) created the human being (singular), as man and woman (plural) he created them (plural). Here the human plural is supposed to correspond to the divine singular. Whereas the self-resolving God is a plural in the singular, his image on earth—the human being—is apparently supposed to be a singular in the plural. The one God, who is differentiated in himself and is at one with himself, then finds his correspondence in a community of human beings, female and male, who unite with one another and are one" (Moltmann, *God in Creation*, 217–18).

8. "The 'sacred story' begins with God's eternal purpose for man. . . . His eternal purpose was that mankind should be 'one body', with the unity of a perfect organism: a higher kind of organism, indeed than any that we know . . . a free and harmonious fellowship of persons united in the love of God. . . . That is God's plan for mankind: that it should be 'one body' " (D. M. Baillie, *God Was in Christ: An Essay on Incarnation and Atonement* [London: Faber and Faber, 1948], 203).

9. Claus Westermann, *Genesis 1–11: A Continental Commentary*, trans. John J. Scullion (Minneapolis: Fortress, 1994), 160.

Cain—the first man born of man and woman—will raise his hand to kill his brother (4:8). This is followed by an exponential expansion of evil. In the seven generations that follow Adam, violence on the earth increases from sevenfold to seventy-sevenfold. We discover this from Lamech (4:19–24), who provides the second bit of poetry in Genesis. As Adam sang for Eve, so Lamech sings to his wives. His verse, however, is a horrible distortion of Adam's one-flesh love song. He declares, "Adah and Zillah, hear my voice; you wives of Lamech, listen to what I say: I have killed a man for wounding me, a young man for striking me. If Cain is avenged sevenfold, truly Lamech seventy-sevenfold" (4:23–24).

This generation-on-generation multiplication of violence continues until the author of Genesis offers the assessment: "The earth was corrupt in God's sight, and the earth was filled with violence" (6:11). Violence—the destruction of community—is in fact the reason given for the flood, the most famous instance of biblical judgment. God tells Noah, "I have determined to make an end of all flesh, for the earth is filled with violence because of them" (6:13). God's intention to create community has been undone, and so now, God will undo his creation.

Creation and fall, then, are in large part the story of right relationship given and lost. God desires human beings to enjoy communion with God and community with one another. And the most characteristic mark of sin in the early chapters of Genesis is the loss of this right relationship. Rather than a garden of delight, characterized by fellowship with God and openness to one another, the earth is corrupt and filled with violence.[10]

The Image Re-Created

If this is the story of our fall, and if the Word of God has come "to bring again the corruptible to incorruption" (so Athanasius, *On the Incarnation*), then the healing of our humanity will mean the restoration of community. Certainly it means the restoration of communion between humanity and God: "Through [Jesus] God reconciled everything to himself. He made peace with everything in heaven and on earth by means of Christ's blood on the cross. This includes you who were once far away from God. You were his enemies, separated from him by your evil thoughts and actions. Yet now he has reconciled you to himself through the death of Christ in his physical body" (Col. 1:20–22 NLT). But in addition to this, the remaking of our humanity also means the restoration of *human* community.

10. Donald Baillie continues with his summary of sin and the loss of community: "[This] is God's plan for mankind: that it should be 'one body'. But something has gone wrong. The organism has somehow failed to function as one body. It has come to be divided into countless little bits of life, each person trying to be a quite independent cell, a self-sufficient atom" (Baillie, *God Was in Christ*, 203–4). See footnote 8 above.

We see this with particular clarity in Ephesians, where Paul[11] characterizes the new community of the church as something of monumental, cosmic significance. In the church Paul sees nothing less than the completion of God's purpose in creating humanity. Here, every sort of social barrier is set aside as Jew and Gentile, male and female, rich and poor, are joined as one community, in Christ, through the Spirit. The church is nothing less than a divine act of re-creation. Here God puts to death divisions and hostility—the separation and violence that (as we saw in Gen. 3–6) has corrupted God's good creation. In place of this antagonism, God creates one new humanity.

> For he is our peace; in his flesh *he has made both groups* [that is, Jews and Gentiles] *into one* and has broken down the dividing wall, that is, the hostility between us. He has abolished the law with its commandments and ordinances, that *he might create* [*ktise*] in himself *one new humanity* in place of the two, thus making peace, and might reconcile both groups to God in one body through the cross, thus *putting to death that hostility* through it.
>
> Ephesians 2:14–16, emphasis added

In the church a new humanity is created, and this humanity once again occupies the honored place of image bearer, showing forth the likeness of God. So Paul writes, "You were taught . . . to be renewed in the spirit of your minds, and to clothe yourselves with *the new self, created* [*ktisanti*] *according to the likeness of God* in true righteousness and holiness" (Eph. 4:22–24, emphasis added).

I have highlighted the verb *ktiso*—to create—in the preceding passages to underscore Paul's portrayal of the church as a new creation, a restoration of humanity. This verb and its cognates occur fifteen times in the New Testament. They are only ever used of God—no one else "creates" in this sense—and in eleven of the fifteen instances, the word refers in some way to God's original act of creation in the beginning. Three other occurrences of the word are in Ephesians (2:10, 15; 4:24), and here, notably, the word is used not to describe God's original act of creation, but to the creation of the new humanity that is the church.[12]

By using the language of Genesis/creation, Paul makes clear that the birth of the church is an epoch-making event in the history of salvation. The cross

11. Whether Ephesians is Pauline or Pseudo-Pauline is not directly relevant to my argument. For the sake of convenience, I will refer to the author as Paul.

12. The remaining instance of the word is in Colossians 3, where Paul once again has the church in view (and once again speaks of the renewal of the image): "you have . . . clothed yourselves with *the new self*, which is being renewed in knowledge *according to the image* of its creator [*ktisantos*—literally, "creating-One"]. In that renewal there is no longer Greek and Jew, circumcised and uncircumcised, barbarian, Scythian, slave and free; but Christ is all and in all!" (Col. 3:10–11, emphasis added).

and blood of Christ have brought together Jew and Gentile, abolishing the hostility that existed, not only between them and God, but between one another. The creation of this new community is not an added side benefit of redemption, but is "in accordance with the eternal purpose that [God] has carried out in Christ Jesus" (Eph. 3:11). God's eternal plan to create humanity in his own image has now been realized. In the church, the image of God is again a declaration of God's character, wisdom, and power. Paul declares that the creation of this one body of Jews and Gentiles is nothing less than "the mystery hidden for ages" (3:9). Before, this mystery was not known to humanity, but now it has been revealed by the Spirit (3:5). The church makes known to the "powers and principalities"—the evil spirits arrayed against God and humanity—the victory of God, the accomplishment of his purposes. The New Living Translation does a good job of catching the sense of this in simple language:

> God's purpose was to show his wisdom in all its rich variety to all the rulers and authorities in the heavenly realms. They will see this when Jews and Gentiles are joined together in his church. This was his plan from all eternity, and it has now been carried out through Christ Jesus our Lord.
>
> Ephesians 3:10–11

Psalms, Hymns, and Spiritual Songs

The establishment of the multiethnic community of the church is a new creation, and as such, is part of God's remaking of humanity. This cosmic conception of the church as a new humanity in turn helps us to better understand a familiar command issued just a little further on in Ephesians: the command to sing.

> And do not get drunk with wine, for that is dissipation, but be filled with the Spirit, speaking to one another in psalms and hymns and spiritual songs, singing and making melody with your heart to the Lord; always giving thanks for all things in the name of our Lord Jesus Christ to God, even the Father; and be subject to one another in the fear of Christ.
>
> Ephesians 5:18–21 NASB

At first this command may seem to drop in at random. Paul is in the midst of a serious discussion of godliness, holiness, and being filled with the Spirit. Indeed, commentators often treat Paul's entreaty to sing as a bit of a throwaway comment. Singing, they suggest, is simply one ready-to-hand example of the sort of good thing that Spirit-filled Christians might do. Eric Routley, for instance, has this passage in view when he observes that the New Testament has relatively little to say about music—aside from "a stray remark in two of the Epistles about the singing of hymns and spiritual songs."[13] The structure of the passage, however, doesn't allow us to interpret this as an offhand comment.

"Be Filled with the Spirit"

Throughout the letter Paul wants to impress upon his audience their identity as "a holy temple in the Lord; in whom you also are built together spiritually into a dwelling place for God" (Eph. 2:21–22). As we saw in chapter 2, the temple (and before it, the tabernacle) is at the center of the Jewish universe, specifically because it is the place on earth where God makes his dwelling and manifests his glory.[14] In the gospels, Jesus makes the astonishing claim that his body is now the temple—the place on earth where God's presence and glory are made manifest (John 2:19–22). In Ephesians, Paul reminds his readers that this is still the case. The new temple is Christ's body—which by God's Spirit *is* the church: "Now you are the body of Christ, and each one of you is a part of it" (1 Cor. 12:27 NIV). The new community of Jew and Gentile is now the temple, the place of God's own dwelling. "In him [Jesus] *the whole structure is joined together* and grows into *a holy temple* in the Lord; in whom you also are *built together* spiritually [*en pneumati*—that is, "in the Spirit"] into a *dwelling place* for God" (Eph. 2:21–22, emphasis added).

Of course, if the temple is to be the dwelling place of God, it must not only be built, but filled—filled with the glory, the presence, the Spirit of God.[15] We should recall here the Old Testament scenes when the newly built tabernacle and temple were filled with God's radiant glory in dramatic fashion. The temple is filled with God's Spirit; it is the place of God's fullness. Paul's most fervent prayer for the church is that in this sense it would be the temple indeed—that it would be *filled* with God's Spirit. In his opening prayer he speaks of the church as the body of Christ, "the *fullness* of him who *fills* all in all" (Eph. 1:23, emphasis added). Again, in chapter 3 he prays for the church "so that you may be *filled* with all the *fullness of God*" (3:18–19, emphasis added).

So then, when in Ephesians 5:18 Paul urges the church to "be filled with the Spirit," this is not simply an exhortation to individual piety. It is a charge to be "joined together" (Eph. 2:21) as the people of God, and so, to be the temple. The command to be filled with the Spirit draws on all of the temple imagery we have surveyed. Here Paul says, in effect: be the gathered people of

13. Eric Routley, *Church Music and the Christian Faith* (London: Collins, 1980), 15. Routley is referring to this passage in Ephesians and the parallel passage in Colossians.

14. See for example, Exod. 29:42–43.

15. David Ford writes, "If I were choosing just one theme to emphasise about the God of Ephesians in relation to salvation it would be that of abundance—the pervasive sense of lavish generosity in blessing, loving, revealing and reconciling. . . . If in addition I had to choose just one characteristic term through which to focus this theme it would be *pleroma*, fulness" (*Self and Salvation: Being Transformed* [Cambridge: Cambridge University Press, 1999], 113).

God, in whose midst God dwells; be the new temple of God, the place where his presence is made manifest on earth; be the tabernacle of God, the place in the center of the community filled with the radiant glory of God's Spirit. The imperative command of verse 18 "is not just another in a long string; rather, it is the key to all the others."[16] Indeed, this command can be seen as the culmination of the entire book.

It is just at this point Paul urges the church to sing, and he does so in a way that excludes any characterization of this injunction as a "stray remark." Singing and the filling of the Holy Spirit are bound together grammatically. Ephesians 5:19–21 comprise a single grammatical unit, controlled by the main verb, "be filled" (*plērousthe*), from verse 18. This command is a passive imperative, followed by four subordinate participial clauses: (1) **speaking** (*lalountes*) to one another in songs, hymns, and spiritual songs; (2) **singing** (*adontes*) and **making music** (*psallontes*) in your hearts; (3) **giving thanks** (*eucharistountes*) to the Lord; and (4) **submitting** (*hupôtassomenoi*) to one another.[17] These five participles are grammatically dependent upon the verb. Conversely, the participles also support the verb, giving substance and content to the command to be filled with the Spirit.[18] Structurally, we might set out the passage in the following way:

Be filled with the Spirit:
speaking to one another in songs, hymns, and spiritual songs
singing
and
making music in your hearts
giving thanks to the Lord . . .
submitting to one another . . .

Five participles elaborate the command to be filled with the Holy Spirit. Three of these have to do with music: *speaking* to one another in songs, hymns, and spiritual songs; *singing*; and *making music*.

This strong connection between song and the filling of the Spirit is remarkable, and perhaps even puzzling, until we recall that the work of the

16. Gordon Fee, *God's Empowering Presence: The Holy Spirit in the Letters of Paul* (Peabody, MA: Hendrickson, 1994), 721.

17. See Timothy G. Gombis, "The Divine Warrior in Ephesians" (PhD diss., University of St. Andrews, 2005). The analysis in this essay has been guided by conversations with Tim and by his article, "Being the Fullness of God in Christ by the Spirit: Ephesians 5:18 in Its Epistolary Setting," *Tyndale Bulletin* 53.2 (2002): 259–72.

18. There is some disagreement whether these are participles of means (i.e., "be filled with the Spirit, *by means of* . . .") or effect (i.e., "be filled with the Spirit, *which will result in* . . ."). (For further discussion, see Gombis, "Being the Fullness.") In either case, we can say that Paul sees a close and vital relation between being filled with the Spirit and the actions mentioned in Eph. 5:19–21.

Spirit is to create a new human and that the creation of the new human means the restoration of peace and right relationship among human beings. We are made for community and sin is the destruction of community. Therefore, when God creates "new humanity" (Eph. 2:15) this also means remaking community—"making peace" and "putting to death [their] hostility" (Eph. 2:15–16). When the church sings together, it announces the new community the Spirit has created in Christ. But the church's singing not only announces this new community, it enacts it. When the church sings together, the creation of "one new humanity in place of the two" (Eph. 2:15) becomes an aural reality—something Paul's readers could hear with their own ears. When they sang together in songs, hymns, and spiritual songs, they would have heard one voice composed of many voices. They would have heard a single melody arising from the mouths of men and women, Jews and Greeks, slave and free. If the church is the new humanity, then here is its voice.

Singing is not the only way of enacting the new community. Another obvious example of this is the Lord's Supper. Paul says that the shared life of the church becomes an experienced reality at the communion table: "Because there is one bread, we who are many are one body, for we all partake of the one bread" (1 Cor. 10:17). Shared song, then, is yet another way that this common life becomes a part of lived experience. In song, the church shares not "one bread" but one voice. Speaking or singing with one voice is both an instance and an expression of the church's shared life. Paul brings these ideas of unity (or "harmony") and "one voice" together toward the end of Romans (in a passage that also refers to singing):

> May the God of steadfastness and encouragement grant you to live in harmony with one another, in accordance with Christ Jesus, so that together you may *with one voice* glorify the God and Father of our Lord Jesus Christ. Welcome one another, therefore, just as Christ has welcomed you, for the glory of God. For I tell you that Christ has become a servant of the circumcised on behalf of the truth of God in order that he might confirm the promises given to the patriarchs, and in order that the Gentiles might glorify God for his mercy. As it is written, "Therefore I will confess you among the Gentiles, and sing praises to your name"; and again he says, "Rejoice, O Gentiles, with his people"; and again, "Praise the Lord, all you Gentiles, and let all the peoples praise him."
>
> Romans 15:5–11, emphasis added

All the diverse members of the church are to live in "harmony," Paul writes—and in this instance, harmony becomes more than a metaphor.[19] The one voice they raise together is a sign that they have "welcome[d] one another,

19. "Whether or not this passage refers directly to liturgical song, as some commentators believe it does, it expresses two musical conceptions that become common in patristic literature: living in harmony and exclaiming in a single voice, the *una uoce dicentes* of the eucharistic prayer"

just as Christ has welcomed you." As they sing or speak "with one voice" they experience the reality of the church as a single organism of many members.[20]

Colossians 3 (where we find a parallel to Eph. 5) is yet another passage where Paul draws together the ideas of singing, unity (or "harmony"), and the church's life as *one body*.

> Above all, clothe yourselves with love, which binds everything together in perfect harmony. And let the peace of Christ rule in your hearts, to which indeed you were called in the *one body*. And be thankful. Let the word of Christ dwell in you richly; teach and admonish one another in all wisdom; and with gratitude in your hearts sing psalms, hymns, and spiritual songs to God.
>
> Colossians 3:14–16, emphasis added

For Paul, music is a way of *being* the body that is the church, while also (literally) giving voice to this new community. In song we are able to not just imagine but *hear* this restored humanity. "Songs, hymns, and spiritual songs," in other words, are both a way that people are incorporated into a community and, at the same time, an embodiment of that community.

As a freshman at the University of Michigan I sang the Michigan fight song along with my fellow students—at football games, in the student lounge watching basketball, at pep rallies on campus. Singing "Hail to the Victors valiant! / Hail to the conquering heroes!" I felt proud of my university and a sense of loyalty to it. I felt a profound camaraderie with my classmates, our institution, and its sports teams. And though I had no good reason whatever to dislike our school rivals, I was soon completely united with my peers in my antipathy toward Ohio State and Michigan State! Singing was not the sole reason that I came to feel a part of my university, but singing was a moment when my growing sense of inclusion in the university was focused and concentrated. At the same time, "Hail to the Victors" served as a kind of embodiment of the University of Michigan community for me. When I first heard the song sung in a stadium full of Michigan supporters, I felt I was "meeting" that extended community and joining in its character and identity. When I hear it now, it carries with it still some flavor of the place, those people, and my experience among them.

This is a trivial and in many ways unusual example; it is a single song that is sung on occasions of a special sort and is explicitly designated to represent an institution. Nevertheless, it illustrates on a superficial level the sort of thing that happens much more profoundly among a group of people—such as a church—who gather together regularly and sing. Songs are one way that

(James McKinnon, *Music in Early Christian Literature* [Cambridge: Cambridge University Press, 1987], 14).

20. "Unity was an important matter to the early Christians, and . . . almost from the beginning music was an expression of, a metaphor for, and a means toward unity" (Stapert, *New Song*, 26).

a community has its identity and one way that individuals find their identity within a community.

Philosophers and scholars from outside of Christianity and from many disciplines also have observed the role of music in forming and representing a community. Plato, for instance, speaks of both functions. Music forms community, and so "caution must be taken in adopting an unfamiliar type of music: it is an extremely risky venture, since any change in the musical modes affects the most important laws of a community."[21] Likewise, music gives us a sounding image of a certain sort of well-ordered society: "Self-discipline literally spans the whole octaval spread of the community, and makes the weakest, the strongest, and the ones in between all sing in unison. . . . We couldn't go wrong if we claimed that self-discipline was this unanimity, a harmony between the naturally worse and naturally better elements of society."[22]

In the twentieth century the philosopher and musicologist Theodore Adorno (1903–69) would argue that "musical composition was not merely analogous to social organisation. It was also a form of political action."[23] It is so by performing two cognitive functions. "The first of these was to portray the 'true' state of the subject, to provide that subject with a mirror of her relation to the social whole."[24] Music is a way of diagnosing, in other words, the structures and tendencies of society. The second cognitive function is "to exemplify: in and through the abstract procedures of its composition—the arrangement of material—music offered models of how part–whole relationships could be conceived and configured. In so doing it also showed how the subject (being) or material (nature) could stand in relation to the social and cognitive totality. Musical form thus served a didactic function."[25] Adorno believes that in this way music acts as a conceptual resource,[26] a way of imagining and investigating various forms of social organization.

Christian theologians are not alone, then, in recognizing the significance of communal song. They are, however, interested in speaking of a very particular sort of community.

Differentiated Unity

The new humanity is created in the image of God, and the God in whose image the new humanity is created exists eternally as Father, Son, and Holy Spirit.

21. Plato, *Republic*, 424c, trans. Robin Waterfield (Oxford: Oxford University Press, 1993), 128.

22. Ibid., 432a, 139.

23. Tia DeNora, *After Adorno: Rethinking Music Sociology* (Cambridge: Cambridge University Press, 2003), 11.

24. Ibid.

25. Ibid., 12.

26. Ibid.

Orthodox Christian belief recognizes distinction between these three persons while continuing to insist that there is but one God. While a complete statement of the doctrine of the Trinity would come later, Athanasius articulates the essential logic of Trinitarian theology when he speaks of Father, Son, and Spirit as *homoousios*.[27] At the Council of Nicea, the Christian church considered the teaching of Arius, who argued that Jesus Christ is a creature. Certainly, Arius insisted, Christ is an exalted creature, the firstborn of creation. Nevertheless, he is created, and so, other than God. The council would reject Arius's teaching and instead, with Athanasius, confess belief "in one Lord Jesus Christ . . . God of God, Light of Light, true God of true God, begotten not made, of one substance (*homoousios*) with the Father."[28] In his *Letters to Serapion* Athanasius extends this affirmation to the Spirit as well, writing that the Spirit "is not an angel, but rather is one and belongs to the one Word, and accordingly belongs to the one God and is of the same being (*homoousion*)."[29] In God there is distinction between persons of Father, Son, and Spirit: "Just as the Father could never be Son, so also the Son could never be Father. And just as the Father will never cease to be uniquely Father, so also the Son will never cease to be uniquely Son. . . . Neither is the Spirit called Son in the Scriptures."[30] Nevertheless the three persons of Father, Son, and Spirit are one God, wholly united and indivisible, "holy and perfect, confessed as God in Father, Son and Holy Spirit, having nothing foreign or extrinsic mingled with it, nor compounded of creator and created, but is wholly Creator and Maker. It is identical with itself and indivisible, and its activity is one."[31]

The unity of the Godhead does not arise through negating the distinction between Father, Son, and Spirit, but rather through the mutual indwelling of Father, Son, and Spirit. Father, Son, and Spirit act and have their being in and through one another. "The Father," Athanasius writes, "does all things through the Word and in the Holy Spirit. Thus the oneness of the Holy Trinity is preserved and thus is the one God 'who is over all and through all and in all' preached in the Church."[32] Basil the Great explains, "The Son is in the Father and the Father in the Son . . . such is the unity."[33]

The Son is in the Father and the Father in the Son. The Father does all things through the Word and in the Spirit. This is an extraordinary sort of

27. For this idea, see T. F. Torrance, *The Christian Doctrine of God: One Being, Three Persons* (Edinburgh: T&T Clark, 1996), 168–92.

28. "The Creed of Nicaea," in *Documents of the Christian Church*, new ed., ed. Henry Bettenson and Chris Maunder (Oxford: Oxford University Press, 1999), 27.

29. Athanasius, *Letters to Serapion on the Holy Spirit*, in Khaled Anatolios, *Athanasius* (New York: Routledge, 2004), 227.

30. Ibid., 215.

31. Ibid., 227.

32. Ibid.

33. St. Basil the Great, *On the Holy Spirit*, 18.45, trans. David Anderson (Crestwood, NY: St. Vladimir's Seminary Press, 1980), 72.

communion—clearly something other than the harmony of Plato's ideal society, where "harmony" of a sort is maintained only by keeping the lowest and least firmly in their place. Instead here we have a thoroughgoing sharing in the life of another, having one's being in another, acting through another and being acted through. Theologians describe this mutual indwelling or interpenetration of Father, Son, and Spirit by the Greek term *perichoresis*, or the Latin term *circumincessio*. And as we consider this perichoretic life of God we may come to recognize that the doctrine of the Trinity, far from being (as it is sometimes popularly caricatured) the most abstract and irrelevant of doctrines, is actually something vital and beautiful. It tells us that at the heart of God and at the heart of all reality is self-giving community. The architectonic center of the cosmos is not power or might or truth—though all of these may be ascribed to God. At the center of all things is love. "Do you believe in God the Father, the Son, the Holy Spirit?" asks Hans Urs von Balthasar. "But these three phrases, too, are an expression—and Jesus Christ provides the proof of this—of the fact that the one God is, in his essence, love and surrender. . . . Herein lies the most unfathomable aspect of the Mystery of God: that what is absolutely primal is no statically self-contained and comprehensible reality, but one that exists solely in dispensing itself."[34] The being of God is the eternal communion, the eternal offering of one to another of Father, Son, and Spirit.[35] This is a truth that is not only beautiful but which is also immediately relevant to our own lives. The image God intends humanity to reflect is the *perichoresis* of Father, Son, and Spirit, in their eternal community of self-giving—"the eternal movement of Love or the Communion of Love which the Holy Trinity ever is within himself."[36]

If our thinking about the church is formed and informed by trinitarian theology, Miroslav Volf suggests, it will guard the integrity and importance of both the individual person and the community. The individual Christian will not be anonymously absorbed into some monolithic church collective. At the same time, the self in Christian community will be "a self that is always 'inhabited' or 'indwelled' by others."[37] St. Theophilus writes that "God created Adam and Eve that there may be great love between them, reflecting the mystery of Divine unity." [38] The two are created out of one,[39] yet without a loss of unity. There is a similar echo of the trinitarian life and its perichoresis when,

34. Hans Urs von Balthasar, *Credo: Meditations on the Apostles' Creed*, trans. David Kipp (Edinburgh: T&T Clark, 1990), 29, 30.

35. On this conception of the being of God, see Torrance, *Christian Doctrine of God*, 171–80, 185–92.

36. Ibid., 171.

37. Miroslav Volf, *After Our Likeness: The Church as the Image of the Trinity* (Grand Rapids: Eerdmans, 1997), 3.

38. Quoted in *Pope John Paul II's Theology of the Body in Simple Language*, adapted into everyday English by Sam Torode (n.p.: Philokalia Books, 2008), epigraph.

39. See Gen. 2:21–24.

in Jesus Christ, God creates a new humanity. In this instance the one is created out of two (Jew and Gentile)[40] yet without loss of distinction. The unity in Christ does not swallow up the unique identity of its members. "Interpersonal communion is an image of the Trinitarian communion and a participation in it," says Dumitru Staniloae. "Hence the divine image in the human person is an image of the Trinity and reveals itself in human communion."[41]

Paul tells the Ephesians to "make every effort to keep the unity of the Spirit through the bond of peace," for "there is one body and one Spirit" (Eph. 4:3–4 NIV). He continues, however: "But to each one of us grace has been given as Christ apportioned it. . . . It was he who gave some to be apostles, some to be prophets, some to be evangelists, and some to be pastors and teachers" (Eph. 4:7, 11 NIV). The new human being is "one body," but this one body maintains, insists, and depends upon the distinctiveness of its members.

Music, particularly shared song, seems to provide a powerful sounding image of the kind of community life we have been describing—one where there is distinction without the loss of unity, where there is unity without the removal of individuality, where the members of the community have their life in and through one another.

When we sing together we hear "*simultaneous voices which are nevertheless also one voice*."[42] We might say equally: when we sing together we hear one voice which is nevertheless the voice of many. Music enacts and makes sensible, as few other activities can, a self that is " 'inhabited' or 'indwelled by others.' " When I sing among others, I hear a voice that is both mine and not mine, a voice that is both in and outside of me. I hear my voice and your voice, and this third thing: our voices together, a sound that has properties that belong neither to your voice nor to my voice alone, but one that is nevertheless shaped and takes its substance from the individual voices comprising it. The church's song is a sound its participants indwell even as it indwells them.

This would have been so even though the early church's song would have been mostly sung in unison. Even when two or more singers share the same melody, their individual voices are not lost in the confluence. This has been impressed upon me on various occasions when I have recorded vocal tracks in a recording studio. There is a striking difference—immediately discernible—between the sound of (say) three or four vocalists all singing the same melody in unison and the sound of just one voice, recorded three or four times over and stacked on top of itself to produce a "chorus." Individual differences in tone, timbre, inflection, and pronunciation continue to sound out even in the midst of a "unison." In the early church, the unison singing would have been

40. See Eph. 2:15.

41. Dumitru Staniloae, *The Experience of God: Orthodox Dogmatic Theology,* vol. 2, *The World: Creation and Deification*, trans. Ioan Ionita and Robert Barringer (Brookline, MA: Holy Cross Orthodox Press, 2005), 99.

42. Roger Scruton, *The Aesthetics of Music* (Oxford: Clarendon, 1997), 339, emphasis added.

even less uniform than four studio vocalists sharing a melody. One would have heard male and female voices singing in different octaves; one would have heard quavering voices of the elderly and the confident voices of the young; one would have heard the differences in pronunciation, reflecting different geographical and ethnic backgrounds, different social classes, and different education. And, there would have been more than a little "incidental harmony"—just as there is in church singing today—as some of the congregation landed on the correct pitches and others landed some distance away! All of this is simply to say, one need not have a sixteen-voice polyphony or an eight-voice fugue to experience the many-yet-one-ness of community singing.

Roger Scruton observes that many activities—dancing, sport—embody orderly and aesthetically pleasing social interaction. Music, however, is distinctive in the kind of society it is able to enact: "The concerted movements of a dance troupe are embodied in separate performers. Each dancer occupies his own space: the harmony between dancers does not cancel their separation. In music however, movements coalesce and flow together in a single stream. The phenomenal space of music contains no places that are 'occupied,' or from which competing gestures are excluded. Moreover, the aural world is transparent: nothing that occurs in it is blocked from view, and all that flows through it is revealed to the ear as flowing."

Scruton goes on to ask:

> Why should this confluence contain so great an appeal for us? Here is a suggestion: the coordination of movement in dancing and marching grants a vision of social order. But the movements here combined are seen as apart from one another, each occupying its exclusive space and expressing its distinct agenda. In music, however, all distance between movements is abolished, and we confront a single process in which multiplicity is simultaneously preserved and overridden. No musical event excludes any other, but all coexist in a placeless self-presentation. . . . It is as though these many currents flowed together in a single life, at one with itself.[43]

Perhaps one reason Ephesians binds together singing and the filling of the Spirit is singing's unique capacity to show us this sort of communal life. Namely, singing enacts a way of life in which union is not unanimity, nor multiplicity a cacophony. In this way, it reflects the reality of a God whose unity does not abolish the reality of Father, Son, and Spirit and whose being as Trinity does not encroach upon the unity of the Godhead.

Freedom in Submission

It also is significant that the commands to sing are followed by a section on right relationships in the church, home, and workplace. We have already seen

43. Ibid., 338–39.

that the command "be filled with the Holy Spirit" is joined to five dependent participles. The first three have to do with singing and making music. The fifth and last is "submitting to one another in the fear of Christ" (Eph. 5:21 HCSB).

The section that follows (5:22–6:9) considers how this "submitting to one another" is to work itself out—in relationships between wives and husbands, parents and children, slaves and masters.[44] We should not miss the fact, however, that *singing* to one another, *giving* thanks to God, and *submitting* to one another are all part of the same command. All of these together fill out the dimensions of the imperative "be filled with the Spirit."[45] Those who are filled with the Spirit both sing to one another and submit to one another.[46] Both singing and mutual submission enact and make manifest the new humanity in Christ.[47] The command to submit to one another, David Ford suggests, "can appropriately be given a musical meaning."[48] If these two activities are drawn up to one another side by side—as they are in Ephesians 5, if they are allowed to shape and inform one another, then both our singing and our submitting will be enriched. Mutual submission tells us something about what it means to sing together well, and music, as "a way of happening *par excellence*"[49] reveals something about how the "happening" of mutual submission may occur. "Submit in this way," the singers say by their singing, and "sing in this way," say the husbands, wives, masters, and slaves by their living together in community. "We are to imagine," Ford writes, "singing husbands and wives, singing parents and children, singing masters and slaves."[50]

> The specific contribution of music to this building up of community in worship includes its encouragement of alertness to others, immediate responsiveness to

44. "Paul urges the Christians 'to be filled with the Spirit' (v. 18) . . . they need to be full of the Spirit for their corporate worship (vv. 19–20) . . . [and] they need to be full of the Spirit in order to maintain the 'unity of the Spirit' in their several relationships in a believing household (v. 21), which are then spelled out in detail in 5:22–6:9" (Fee, *God's Empowering Presence*, 719).

45. "All of verses 19–21 take the form of a series of participles that modify the primary imperative in verse 18" (ibid.).

46. Unfortunately verse 21 is often treated as the point at which Paul concludes the preceding material and turns to a new theme. The New International Version, along with some other modern translations, actually breaks up the five participles that are grammatically dependent on verse 17 and inserts a paragraph break between verse 20 and 21.

47. See, for example, Eph. 5:28–32 (NIV), in which the marriage relationship enacts the new humanity: "In this same way, husbands ought to love their wives as their own bodies. He who loves his wife loves himself. After all, no one ever hated his own body, but he feeds and cares for it, just as Christ does the church—for we are members of his body. 'For this reason a man will leave his father and mother and be united to his wife, and the two will become one flesh.' This is a profound mystery—but I am talking about Christ and the church."

48. Ford, *Self and Salvation*, 122.

49. Tia DeNora, *Music in Everyday Life* (Cambridge: Cambridge University Press, 2000), 158.

50. Ford, *Self and Salvation*, 122.

> changes in tone, tune and rhythm, and sharing in the confidence that can come from joint singing. Singing together embodies joint responsibility in which each singer waits on the others, is attentive with the intention of serving the common harmony.[51]

If we are to sing well, we must be aware of and responsive to those with whom we are singing. If the character of sin is that it is *incurvatus in se*—turned in upon itself—then the character of good musicianship is that it is turned attentively toward others. Paul writes that those in darkness are characterized—ironically—by both sensuality and a lack of sensitivity. They are separated from God and lost in ignorance "due to the hardening of their hearts" (Eph. 4:18 NIV). "Having lost all sensitivity," he continues, "they have given themselves over to sensuality" (Eph. 4:19 NIV). Young's Literal Translation renders the verse: "who, *having ceased to feel*, themselves did give up to lasciviousness." Indeed, Fee observes that in the chapters of Ephesians that follow, "most of the sins mentioned express the self-centeredness that contradicts love and disrupts the unity of the body."[52] Those in darkness attend and respond to only their own desires, "gratifying the cravings of [their] sinful nature and following its desires and thoughts" (Eph. 2:3 NIV). Those filled with the Spirit, however, listen and respond to one another in songs, hymns, and spiritual songs. As they sing, they gain experience in hearing one another; they learn to move in time and in harmony with those around them. They are reminded that the new humanity in Christ includes voices other than their own—voices of different quality, timbre, and register, to which they must tune their own song.

Shared song also qualifies our understanding of "submission." Singing together necessarily involves something that might be described as "mutual submission" as singers yield to a tempo, a melody, a rhythm, and a whole host of other constraints. They surrender the freedom to sing whatever notes they choose, at whatever speed, in whatever order, and so on. These limits, however, are not oppressive. They do not frustrate but instead facilitate the participants' intention to sing. If their mutual submission entails the loss of one sort of freedom (the freedom to sing whatever notes one wants, in whatever way one chooses), it also enables freedom of another sort—the freedom to join the community in song, the freedom to be part of a chorus.

At the same time, this chorus is a society whose life depends upon its members contributing their voices. The "submission" vital to music-making cannot mean silencing individual voices—or else the music will simply stop. Each member must contribute her voice, and each member must "make room" for other voices. The submission required for choral song cannot be imposed on the group by some of its members. If one voice persistently "enforces the rules"—insisting upon a particular tempo by drowning out the others, for

51. Ibid.

52. Fee, *God's Empowering Presence*, 709.

instance—then there is a loss of ensemble. This personal insensitivity manifests itself in an ugliness that is both moral and aesthetic.

In song we learn and enact a kind of mutual submission in which we do not lose, but discover, our voices. This is a submission that is creative, that does not eliminate but opens up opportunities. Moreover, music manifests a mutual submission that is winsome and appealing rather than dull, oppressive, and burdensome.

What Unity?

Organists, choir directors, worship leaders, ministers of music, and church music volunteers everywhere are forgiven for any bitter laughs or cynical sneers while reading this material about the unity that comes about through the music of the church. "Differentiated unity nurtured through music" sounds like a beautiful idea, but in practice, music more often seems to be a source of contention and bitterness. The last few decades of the twentieth century saw many North American churches locked in angry battles over "contemporary worship" versus "traditional worship." These debates are often collectively referred to—and with only little exaggeration—as "The Worship Wars." Many individuals have left churches because of music; in other instances, whole congregations have been split by disagreements over the singing of contemporary worship choruses, or the singing of hymns, or the use of guitars in worship, or the use of an organ. Even in churches where there is relative unanimity of musical taste, there are regular conflicts and disagreements about music. Ministers of music spend nearly as much time dealing with bruised egos and hurt feelings as they do choosing music and leading rehearsals.

If music is one way that people are gathered into community, then why in practice has church music so often disrupted community?

Sadly, this is not a problem unique to music. The central celebration of the church's unity is the Eucharist. Paul reminds the Corinthians: "Because there is one bread, we who are many are one body, for we all partake of the one bread" (1 Cor. 10:17). Just a little later, however, it becomes plain that among the Corinthians this powerful enactment of the church's unity has instead reinforced divisions within the church: "When you come together as a church, I hear that there are divisions among you. . . . When you come together, it is not really to eat the Lord's supper. For when the time comes to eat, each of you goes ahead with your own supper, and one goes hungry and another becomes drunk. . . . Do you show contempt for the church of God and humiliate those who have nothing?" (1 Cor. 11:18, 20–22). And of course, historically, Communion has been anything but a point of theological "communion." The meaning of this celebration has been a point of bitter and sometimes violent disagreement, between Protestants and Catholics, and among the various wings of the Protestant Reformation.

Shared table fellowship between Jews and Gentiles was likewise a powerful mark of the new community and one way of actually bringing this new community to lived experience (see, for instance, Acts 10 and the significant meal Peter shares with the centurion Cornelius). Table fellowship was also, however, a practice that continued to generate angry quarrels and disputes in the apostolic church—not least between the apostles Peter and Paul (Gal. 2:11–14; see also Acts 15 for the account of the church council which gathered to address this crisis).

Baptism, the other central sacrament of the Christian faith, also speaks of the church's unity. Just after his discussion of the Lord's Supper, Paul tells the Corinthians: "For in the one Spirit we were all baptized into one body—Jews or Greeks, slaves or free—and we were all made to drink of one Spirit" (1 Cor. 12:13). Yet again, this mark of unity has historically led to a good deal of discord within the church. The practice of believer's baptism by immersion cost some Anabaptists their lives. Today, there are still family relationships strained by a couple's decision to baptize, or not baptize, their infant. Those in other families are similarly wounded by the decision of an adult, baptized as an infant, to be baptized again by immersion.

Similar comments could be made about sexual relations. As we have already seen, the sexual union of man and woman is both a mark and a means of a more far-reaching union. The two become "one flesh" (Gen. 2:24; see also 1 Cor. 6:16) both in and through sexual union. Moreover, it is a creaturely echo of the relationship of Father, Son, and Spirit. But again, even when practiced within a committed marriage relationship, sex has often been the focal point for discord, tension, and heartache. Poor communication, wrong expectations, insecurities, insensitivity, misunderstanding, and the persistence of old wounds can transform this act of union into a wedge that drives two people further and further apart.

In each case, discord and acrimony of a particularly bitter sort find fertile soil around the roots of some supposedly unifying practice. Why should this be so? Perhaps the fact that we can so easily produce examples of this sort suggests that these practices wound and cause division not *despite* but *because* of their power to create community. Bread and water, song, and physical intimacy bind us to one another, but they bind us together in all of our woundedness and in all of our power to wound.

Moreover, it is because these acts and practices so effectively mark out the dimensions of our communities, our families, and even our own identity, that we care about them passionately. Who will and will not be included in our family, what kind of community we will live in—these things obviously, and rightly, matter a great deal to us. Debates about church music, then, are rarely debates about church *music* properly speaking. They are disagreements over the shape and identity of a community. They are impassioned both because they touch deep relationships and because they do so in ways that are difficult to articulate. Songs like "The Old Rugged Cross," "Great Is Thy Faithfulness," and "Blessed Assurance," for instance, embody the church, the community, and the culture of my childhood in more ways than I could possibly put into words. If I have strong feelings—positive or negative—toward that church, community, or culture, I will probably have correspondingly strong feelings—positive or negative—about those songs.

Beyond this, the fact that music often brings division reminds us that *music* does not create the new human, God does—in Jesus Christ and through the Holy Spirit. It is the Spirit, Paul says, who brings about oneness: "In the one Spirit we were all baptized into one body—Jews or Greeks, slaves or free—and we were all made to drink of one Spirit" (1 Cor. 12:13; cf. Eph. 4:1–6). Music cannot summon up from within itself the power to "break down the dividing walls" and "abolish the hostility between us" (see Eph. 2:14). This is the work of God. Nevertheless, as with bread and wine, as with the waters of baptism, or as with sexual intimacy, music is one means by which God may teach us community and make it a lived reality among us. Sometimes music does not testify to the church's unity but rather testifies against it. The function of music in these cases may be, as Adorno suggests, "to remind the subject of what, in other realms, had been lost."[53] Even where the church fails to act as the church—even in fact well outside the boundaries of the church—music may be the means by which God begins to draw us toward community with others, while speaking to us of the fullness of community he intends.

An Incarnation of Community

A recent radio documentary by Michelle Mercer offers a testimony to this experience of community in song. Mercer reports that she had in the past year joined a community chorus. She was excited about the opportunity to sing but at first was a bit unsettled by the enthusiasm and almost cultlike camaraderie of her fellow choristers. "I had joined the church of happy harmonizers," she muses. In time, however, Mercer discovers that this sense of blissful communion is not just an odd eccentricity of the group. Rather, the experience of community is profoundly connected to the act of music-making. One of the members of the choir explains that at times singing seems to take one to "a place that is in some peculiar way out in the middle of the air halfway between where the chorus is standing and where the audience is sitting." That experience, he says, "is what we're all after. We want to get up and out of ourselves and collectively occupy that space." It was only some

53. DeNora, *After Adorno*, 12.

time later, Mercer reports, during her first performance with the choir, when she understood what her colleague had meant. "I finally got it. When you submit to an ensemble, streamlining your own voice to the mass of sound around you, you lose your ego and your sense of separation from others. That's singing's deepest, most convincing happiness, I think, the real reason choristers keep coming back for more. And as long as there's music I'm glad to be one of them."[54]

Music, as we saw at the outset of this chapter, is a way of gathering the community. More than that, it is a way of manifesting the community. When people gather together for worship and religious celebration, they chant, sing, and dance. The Christian account of the world is able to make good sense of these human practices—as well as experiences like my singing "Hail to the Victors" or Michelle Mercer's experience in a community chorus. Christians can recognize these sorts of experiences as theologically significant (as opposed to only sociologically or psychologically significant). If the work of the Spirit is in large part the restoration of our humanity, and if the restoration of our humanity includes the remaking of human community, then it is right that we would sense that there is something profoundly spiritual—and yes, again, *Spirit*-ual—about singing together. If the Christian story is true, then singing together *should be* moving and meaningful. In song, community is both incarnated and announced. Song is a shared and participatory experience that in turn gives rise to a sounding emblem of the community. And those who worship the God who is Father, Son, and Spirit confess that community is at the heart of all things.

54. Michelle Mercer, "Community Choruses: Singing and Happiness," *All Things Considered*, National Public Radio, January 16, 2006. Transcript available at http://www.npr.org/templates/story/story.php?storyId=5159728.

PART 2

The Spirit's Making and Ours

5

Ionized Inspiration

Can a Human Voice Be Heard?

I believe that all we create is sent from somewhere. It is as if our ideas already exist, and pass through us in order to be seen. What is up in the air comes down and comes through you.

Ang Lee, film director[1]

The whole idea for [the art exhibition] Rings just came to me. I do not take any credit for it. Only the good Lord knows where this idea, this inspiration came to me from.

J. Carter Brown, former director of the National Gallery of Art[2]

Sometimes I wake up in the morning and I can just hear melodies and little themes, and I know that it's directly from God because it's pure, it's good, it just came through me.

Wynton Marsalis, trumpeter and composer[3]

What happens when an artist creates? What does that process look like? Natural ability, training, and hard work all seem to be involved. But is there, in addition

1. Joanna Laufer and Kenneth S. Lewis, *Inspired: The Breath of God* (New York: Doubleday, 1998), 108.

2. Ibid., 117.

3. Ibid., 122.

to these, some "creative spark" that needs to be accounted for? Is the artist somehow in contact with a creative source outside of herself? The preceding quotations all suggest at some level that the artist is God's mouthpiece, a channel for divine creativity. The artist doesn't create so much as re-create. The divine Spirit moves, and the artist simply passes along what has been given. When she speaks, or plays, or writes, what comes out is not her own but a gift from some higher realm.

These quotations are from relatively recent interviews, but the idea they express is very ancient. Moreover, it is an idea that suggests yet another connection between art and spirituality. The experience of artistic creation is characterized as one of *inspiration*—being *en-spirited* or *breathed into*. The real author of the artwork—the true Artist—is God (or the Muse, the universal life force, or some other transcendent source). The human artist, on the other hand, is the instrument, the means by which the divine Creator realizes his artistic vision. And moving from God's lips through the passive human instrument is the divine Spirit-Breath. Clearly this is a way of connecting art and spirituality that depends on a very particular understanding of not only art but of the Spirit and the way the Spirit acts on human beings.

The imagery of inspiration is used powerfully in Peter Shaffer's play, *Amadeus*. Antonio Salieri—the jealous, older composer who is the play's narrator—accompanies Mozart to the premiere of his opera, *The Magic Flute*. Salieri listens to the work in agonized amazement. It is brilliant, breathtaking, flawless. Where could such music come from? How did Mozart—*Mozart! this silly, vulgar youth!*—arrive at these impossibly beautiful harmonies, melodies, and textures? He turns to look at Mozart, and realizes:

> *There* was the Magic Flute—*there beside me*! (He points to MOZART. . . .) Mozart the flute, and God the relentless player.[4]

Mozart is an instrument in both senses of the word. He is a tool in the hand of God, and a flute, on which God's Spirit-Breath plays these miraculous melodies. Mozart and all true artists, on this account, occupy a position that is both humble and exalted. On the one hand, Mozart is only a vessel (to change the metaphor); on the other hand, this vessel carries a cargo that is not only precious, but divine.

Inspiration in the *Ion*

Once again, we find an early presentation of this idea in Plato, this time in his dialogue *Ion*. As the dialogue begins, Socrates meets up with Ion, who is returning from the festival of Asclepius. Ion is a rhapsode—something

4. Peter Shaffer, *Amadeus* (New York: Samuel French & Co., 2003), 107.

halfway between an actor and a singer, whose business is giving public recitations of poetry. Socrates has encountered Ion in good spirits; it turns out that his performance at the festival has just won him first prize. So Socrates congratulates him and—being Socrates—begins to question Ion about his art. For what sort of achievement, Socrates wonders, has Ion been honored? Just what sort of competence are we praising in a prize-winning rhapsode? And when a rhapsode does his job well and moves his audience, what sort of skill and what kind of power is he displaying?

The Passive Poet

Plato's dialogue offers some surprising answers to these questions. Put in the most basic terms, *Ion* claims that creativity arises from receptivity. At the point of origin of the creative act there is an encounter with and surrender to something outside oneself. For this reason Socrates suggests that the rhapsode is not really who (or what) we are hearing when we listen to the performance. Ironically, Ion the singer—the professional speaker—never really speaks with his own voice.

First of all, Socrates points out, Ion certainly does not present *his own* words to the audience. Someone else—Homer in this instance—places the words in Ion's mouth. The rhapsode cannot claim to be anything more than the transmitter through which the poet's utterances are broadcast. What is more, these utterances lead us away from the rhapsode himself. When Ion stands on stage, he speaks as a general, a doctor, a fisherman, a charioteer, and so on, though of course he is none of these. So when we hear Ion speaking at the festival, it is not Ion we hear but "a soldier" or "a goddess" or "a prince."

There is, however, an even more fundamental reason to deny Ion the credit for his performance. The Odyssey begins, "*Sing in me*, Muse, and *through me* tell the story."[5] If Homer's prayer is answered, then not even Homer (much less Ion) can claim ownership of his words. When Homer opens his mouth, the voice singing in him is that of the Muse. And when Ion's listeners respond to his recitation, it is the power of the Muse that moves them. The whole process is like a magnetic current that runs through one bit of metal and then another and then another, says Socrates. Whatever power passes through the metal belongs to the magnet. Really, what can the metal claim for itself? Only that some other power has passed through it. "That's not a subject you've mastered—speaking well about Homer," Socrates tells Ion. "It's a divine power that moves you, as a 'Magnetic' stone moves iron rings . . . and the power in all of them depends on this stone. In the same way, the Muse makes some people inspired herself, and then through those who are inspired a chain of

5. Homer, *The Odyssey*, 1.1, trans. Robert Fitzgerald (New York: Vintage Classics, 1961), 1, emphasis added.

other enthusiasts is suspended. You know, none of the epic poets, if they're good, are masters of their subject; they are inspired, possessed, and that is how they utter all of those beautiful poems."[6]

The human artist's business, then, is not *spiration*—breathing forth, but in-*spiration*—being breathed into. The poem itself, along with any power it carries, originates somewhere behind the performer, behind the poet, and moves through him. In fact, if this is the case, Socrates points out, then any active contribution on the part of the human artist is not only unnecessary, it actually *jeopardizes* the work of art. To be effective, the Muse's *activity* must be matched by the artist's *passivity*. "That's why the god takes [the poets'] intellect away from them when he uses them as his servants, as he does prophets and godly diviners," Socrates explains. Why? "So that we who hear should know that *they are not the ones who speak those verses* that are of such high value, for their intellect is not in them."[7]

The rhapsode speaks, but he does not speak. Homer's words are heard, but it is not Homer that we hear. Through Socrates' relentless questioning, even Ion finally must admit this:

> Ion: "I do think it's by a divine gift that good poets are able to present these poems to us from the gods."
>
> Socrates: "And you rhapsodes in turn present what the poets say."
>
> Ion: "That's true too."[8]

So—listen to a good rhapsode; what you are really hearing is a good poet. Listen to a good poet; what you are really hearing is the voice of a god. Neither Ion nor Homer speaks for himself; both poet and rhapsode have lost their voices.[9]

Nonrational

If the artist does not generate his own speech, then this suggests a second feature of the creative process: namely, it is nonrational. "Their intellect," Socrates observes of poets and performers, "is not in them." Socrates asks his friend, "Well Ion, should we say this man is in his right mind at times like these: when he's at festivals or celebrations, all dressed up in fancy clothes, with

6. Plato, *Ion*, 533d–534a, trans. Paul Woodruff, in *Two Comic Dialogues: Ion and Hippias Major* (Indianapolis: Hackett, 1983), 25. Unless otherwise indicated, all references to Plato's *Ion* are from this edition.

7. Ibid., 534d, 26, emphasis added.

8. Ibid., 535a, 27.

9. The issue here is not whether Socrates (or indeed Plato) believes that Ion is *really* possessed by the divine Muse. In fact, it seems that Socrates' exchanges with Ion are richly ironic. Socrates, as usual, does not proclaim his own beliefs but questions those of others. Whatever Socrates' own view on the matter, in the dialogue he is concerned with drawing out the uncomfortable implications of *Ion's belief* that he is inspired.

golden crowns, and he weeps, though he's lost none of his finery—or when he's standing among millions of friendly people and he's frightened though no one is undressing him or doing him any harm? Is he in his right mind then?"

Poor Ion replies, "Lord no, Socrates. Not at all, to tell you the truth."[10]

Picture the rhapsode on the stage, playing his part. He screams in terror, though there is no immediate danger. He sobs piteously though he has not experienced any loss. The rhapsode acts without reason. (He has no reason to weep, tremble, rage, and laugh the way he does in performance, and this is just one further indication that his activity is not guided by his faculty of reason.) The script says "Cry out!" and so he does. Because he does not speak with his own voice, he cannot trace his actions to some rational process of his own. It is not reason, intellect, or sober reflection that leads him to act this way. From Socrates' perspective, creative artistry clearly is not rational.

Not Knowledge Bearing

Finally, we learn that not only does poetry not *arise* from knowledge, it does not *result* in knowledge. Socrates' interrogation leads Ion to confess that the words of the poet do not communicate understanding; they do not educate or enlighten. Nicholas Wolterstorff writes that "Plato's aim in the *Ion* was to show that the making of poetry is not a craft, not a *techne*. . . . Hence poetry-making does not incorporate true knowledge."[11]

To get at this point Socrates draws Ion's attention to a passage he has performed many times—a passage from Homer in which Nestor advises his son Antilochus how to negotiate a difficult turn in a chariot race. Ion, the accomplished rhapsode, is able to recite these lines powerfully, beautifully, convincingly.

Socrates: "Then who will know better whether Homer speaks beautifully or not in the lines you quoted? You or a charioteer?"

(We can hear the dead pause as the point dawns on poor Ion.)

Ion: "A charioteer."
Socrates: "That's because you're a rhapsode, of course, and not a charioteer."
Ion: "Yes."[12]

Mercilessly, Socrates moves through one topic after another—topics of which Homer writes and rhapsodes speak.

10. Plato, *Ion*, 535d, 27.

11. Nicholas Wolterstorff, "The Work of Making a Work of Music," in Philip Alperson, ed., *What Is Music? An Introduction to the Philosophy of Music* (State College, PA: Pennsylvania State University Press, 1996), 104.

12. Plato, *Ion*, 538b, 30.

Fishing

Socrates: "Should we say it's for a fisherman's profession or a rhapsode's to tell whether or not [Homer] describes this [fishing expedition] beautifully?"

Ion: "That's obvious, Socrates. It's for a fisherman's."[13]

Medicine

Socrates: "Would a fine diagnosis here come from a doctor's profession or a rhapsode's?"

Ion: "A doctor's."[14]

Socrates certainly seems to have a point. Remember the old line made famous in TV commercials: "I'm not a doctor, but I play one on TV." Who would you prefer to perform brain surgery on you? The actor or someone who's been to medical school?

Homer speaks about fishing, and Ion repeats Homer's speech about fishing, but all this fish-talk does not extend the knowledge of either Homer or Ion. Since neither one is really the *author* of his words, neither one can speak with any *author*-ity. The one who is inspired does not by virtue of that inspiration become knowledgeable.

One suspects that Ion would have come away from his conversation with Socrates feeling more than a little deflated. Despite the laurel he has just won, he cannot claim to have achieved much by his art. In fact, he has no art, no *techne*, to speak of. He is the passive conduit for the activity of another. His participation in this transmission is not rational, nor does he gain any knowledge or understanding from it. All in all, it is hardly the sort of discussion that would make one want to run off and join the theater.

Ion's Pneumatology

Plato's dialogue advances both a vision of artistic creativity and a pneumatology. Socrates' exchange with the poet suggests that *this* is what it looks like when the divine spirit acts on human beings; this is the relationship between divine and human activity.

In particular, according to *Ion*, if the divine spirit is active, then we must be passive; if the divine voice is to be heard, then we must be silent; where there is divine wisdom, we remain ignorant. The Muse "takes possession" of the poet and "robs him of his intellect." In picturing *Ion*'s inspired artist, we wouldn't be far off the mark to imagine a soothsayer at a séance: the eyes roll back in the head, the face goes blank, and a foreign voice "from beyond"

13. Ibid., 538d, 31.
14. Ibid., 538c, 31.

emerges eerily from the mouth of the medium. The perfect vehicle for this spirit is an empty shell, a wholly inert lump of clay.

The ending of *Ion* is incredibly poignant. Ion is vain and a fool, but he is also pitiable. Here is a man whose identity and livelihood is bound up with speaking; and now, in a relatively brief exchange, he has been exposed—to us, and perhaps, to himself—as a man with no voice at all. And with the loss of his voice has come the loss of his identity. Near the end of the dialogue, Socrates complains that he can't tell who or what Ion is. Like Proteus, the rhapsode is forever changing shape. Now he is a general, now a doctor, now a fisherman. "Like Proteus [he has] become all manner of people at once" so that "at last [he] slip[s] away."[15] Socrates wonders aloud: who then is Ion truly? Either he is a liar and a fraud, pretending to be many things he is not, or he really is possessed by a god, a neutral and malleable medium, able to be shaped into many forms. Socrates presents Ion with a stark *choice*: "So choose, how do you want us to think of you—as a man who does wrong, or as someone divine?" (*hêmôn adikos anêr einai ê theios*). Faced with this dilemma, Ion replies, "It's much lovelier to be thought divine."[16]

Inspiration costs Ion his identity, and ultimately, his humanity.

Art in Society

We began this chapter by asking: What happens when an artist creates? What is the process and what is the source that lies behind the works of art? *Ion* suggests an answer that is, to contemporary ears, distinctly odd and yet in some respects accords remarkably well with the quotations set out at the beginning of this chapter. Whatever we think of *Ion* as a theology, it seems to provide us with something like a phenomenology of the arts. For at least some artists, at least some of the time (and of course, these two qualifications are important), this is what it *feels like* to create. The source of this work is somewhere outside of me (the idea already exists, somewhere up in the air). My role in creating is passive as much as it is *active* (the music just comes through me). The work didn't arise from my conscious knowledge and understanding (only the good Lord knows where the idea came from). Though it is in some respects far removed from our way of thinking and speaking, in other ways Ion does a good job of articulating one dimension of the artist's experience.

On the other hand, *Ion*'s account of creation is sharply at odds with our discussion in the last chapter. According to Plato's dialogue, divine inspiration means human passivity. We are not really hearing Homer, and we are not really hearing Ion. And if the work of art has a transcendent source, then

15. *Ion*, 541e, in *The Essential Plato*, trans. Benjamin Jowett (n.p.: The Softback Review, 1999), 1139.

16. Plato, *Ion*, 542a–b, Woodruff translation, 35.

we are not really hearing a product from Homer's (or Ion's) time and culture either. The Homeric poem Ion recites did not originate in Homer's Greece (according to Plato's account); it comes from another realm altogether. It is not the work of human hands, and, therefore, when we examine it, we should not expect to find any human or cultural "fingerprints." The artwork is altogether unmediated, untouched—a little piece of eternal beauty drifted to earth. In the last chapter we saw the many ways in which works of art emerge from and reflect particular communities and cultures. If the *Ion* is to be believed, however, works of art do not arise from a culture but descend upon it. In focusing on divine involvement, then, the dialogue seems to deny the social (indeed, the human) dimension of artistic creation.

In the face of this, however, the arts would seem to be "paradigmatic examples of social practices."[17] An aspiring artist in any genre enters into a tradition and a culture—through taking courses, enduring music lessons, undertaking apprenticeship, and so on.[18] Through these means and others, the young artist learns the techniques of performance. She learns the culturally agreed-upon canon of that particular art form—the recognized "great works" that set the standards of excellence. She also learns the criteria for judging between good and bad examples of the art form, successful and unsuccessful performances. The artistic culture also bequeaths to her an understanding of what sort of people are (or are not) "artists," what social standing artists have, what function art works serve, on what occasion and in what places art works are presented, and so on. This established tradition will likewise set out the tools and materials for her art—the particular sort of canvas or instrument or stone that she will use (and along with this, all the possibilities and limitations of those tools). The musicologist Christopher Small underlines this point with a couple of notable artistic examples:

> It may seem too obvious to mention, but all those who engage in the practice of musical performance, famous and unknown, amateur and professional, skilled and unskilled, work always from a base in the firmly known sets of musical relationships we call a tradition, or a style. . . . Even the revolutionary Beethoven was firmly rooted in the European traditions of the eighteenth century, and throughout his life he remained at a very deep level faithful to their conventions, while Charlie Parker's innovative improvised performances, which seemed so incomprehensible to many of his contemporaries, were equally firmly rooted in traditional blues and black folk song.[19]

17. Wolterstorff, "The Work of Making," 112.

18. The following paragraph follows the description of an artistic culture given in Wolterstorff, "The Work of Making."

19. Christopher Small, *Musicking: The Meanings of Performing and Listening* (Middletown, CT: Wesleyan University Press, 1998), 216.

Musicology "from Above" and "from Below"

So we have two very different accounts of artistic creation. In one, works of art are cultural artifacts, bearing the clear imprint of the societies in which they arise. In the other, works of art drift earthward from the heavens, altogether untouched by human hands. We might (with a nod toward discussions of theological method) describe these contrasting approaches as artistry "from below" and artistry "from above." The musicologist Susan McClary describes these as two opposing poles in the critical understanding of art. "From very early times up to and including the present," she writes, "there has been a strain of Western culture that accounts for music in non-social, implicitly metaphysical terms. But parallel with that strain . . . is another which regards music as essentially a human, socially grounded, socially alterable construct. Most polemical battles in the history of music theory and criticism involve the irreconcilable confrontation of these two positions."[20]

If *Ion* conceives of art "from above," the contemporary theoretical study of art has been dominated by the approach "from below." Over the last few decades art theory and criticism generally have given more and more attention to the way cultural forces shape artistic practice and aesthetic norms.[21] Influenced by developments in critical theory as well as poststructuralist and postmodern philosophy, art theorists have focused attention on the social and historical "location" of works of art. These theorists emphasize the ways in which artistic "texts" and practices "encode" a society's norms of gender, class, and relationships of power. In the field of music scholarship these ideas have been the principal concern of the so-called New Musicology. *Constructing Musicology*[22]—the title of a recent survey of this movement—reflects the movement's central theme. New Musicology draws attention to the ways in which musical norms and practices are socially and historically "constructed." Artistic practices emerge from and embody the values and interests of their society.[23]

20. Susan McClary, "The Blasphemy of Talking Politics during Bach Year," in *Music and Society: The Politics of Composition, Performance and Reception*, ed. Richard Leppert and Susan McClary (Cambridge: Cambridge University Press, 1987), 15.

21. It was nearly twenty years ago when a musicologist wrote: "The notion that Art—at least Great Art—transcends the social, the political and the everyday has been under attack for fifteen years or so, in a concerted development of work across a number of disciplines" (Janet Woolf, "The Ideology of Autonomous Art" in Leppert and McClary, eds., *Music and Society*, 1).

22. Alastair Williams, *Constructing Musicology* (Aldershot, England: Ashgate, 2001).

23. "I want to explore in music history the kinds of processes Raymond Williams calls 'structures of feeling', Fredric Jameson the 'political unconscious' . . . or Ross Chambers simply the 'social contracts' that establish the conditions of the production and reception of artworks. Whatever we label these structures, they are intensely ideological formations: whether noticed or not, they are the assumptions that allow cultural activities to 'make sense'. . . . And I want to examine the values they represent, the interests they reinforce, the activities they enable, the possibilities they exclude and their histories within the contested field that music inevitably is"

Art That Is "Located"

This affirmation includes a denial. In saying that a particular piece of music is constructed by cultural practices and social norms, New Musicology is equally concerned to deny that it springs from some divine spirit—or any transcendent source for that matter, whether it be "Eternal Principals of Beauty," the cosmic Music of the Spheres, or the fundamental mathematical order of the universe. The New Musicology argues that music articulates and transmits "nothing less than the premises of an age, the cultural arrangements that enable communication, co-existence, and self-awareness," while at the same time insisting that "none of these counts as anything more than artificial constructs human beings have invented and agreed to maintain—in particular contexts, for particular reasons, to satisfy particular needs and desires."[24] Music is full of meaning, but "not, to be sure . . . transcendental meaning."[25] Rather in music we encounter "human meanings, grounded in the historical contexts in which they performed—and in many cases, *still* perform—crucial social functions."[26]

Susan McClary draws particular attention to the music of Bach—a composer who has often been praised by Christians for his piety and the theological depth of his work. But if we recognize the human and social dimension of music, McClary writes, then the suggestion that Bach's music (or any other for that matter) is "divinely inspired" will begin to appear "bizarre."[27] Instead, we must recognize the works of Bach, Mozart, and other composers for what they are: "*human* constructs, created in particular social contexts and for particular ideological interests."[28] "The claim to transcendental truth that attaches to Bach and Mozart," she writes, "will continue to undercut our efforts until we can begin to define all these various kinds of artistic production as social practice."[29]

Art and Ideology

This mention of "ideological interests" signals another important theme in the New Musicology. If art arises from and reflects the values of a particular society, then the idea of divine inspiration is not only bizarre, but politically dangerous. It encourages us to regard particular and contingent artistic norms

(Susan McClary, *Conventional Wisdom: The Content of Musical Form* [Berkeley: University of California Press, 2000], 5).

24. Ibid., 6.
25. Ibid., 8.
26. Ibid., 8–9.
27. McClary, "Talking Politics during Bach Year," 57.
28. Ibid., 60, emphasis added.
29. Ibid.

as universal and absolute. The idea of "inspiration" takes one, very human way of looking at the world and places a stamp of divine approval upon it. So (for example) if someone suggests that Bach's music is divinely inspired, or that it reflects some absolute standard of Beauty (with a capital B), or that it somehow arises from the natural order of things—in any one of these cases, McClary might say—we are potentially blinded to the ways in which Bach's music arises from and reflects the perspectives, values, and prejudices of his own culture. As one text summarizes this objection: "Discourses about truth, knowledge, justice and beauty are really about political power and control."[30]

The New Musicology (again, taking its cue from developments in postmodern critical theory[31]) sets out to demonstrate that the supposedly transcendent standards of truth, goodness, and artistic beauty are really "stories carefully designed to sustain dominant social order and power structures."[32] Artistic practices themselves, such as the practice of music, function "as a means of social definition and self-definition. . . . Each musical performance articulates the values of a specific social group, large or small, powerful or powerless, rich or poor, at a specific point in its history."[33]

New Musicologists argue that the classical repertory in particular "is and has always been cultivated by the holders of power, first in Europe and later in its colonies and outposts. . . . The acts of composing, performing, and listening to these works have reflected and shaped the perceptions of those who have held power."[34]

Language and song, gesture and image—these are the tools by which we engage our world and one another. But these tools, the contemporary theorist insists, have been fashioned by our society, and are necessarily bound up with the (often oppressive) ideologies of our society. Our songs, poems, stories, and images are not clear windows but lenses, manufactured by our culture and shaped to admit certain vistas and to exclude others.[35] Our art "encodes"

30. Wayne D. Bowman, *Philosophical Perspectives on Music* (New York: Oxford University Press, 1998), 395.

31. "As even readers with little investment in what is called 'postmodernism' have already no doubt discerned, my project shares many of the deconstructive assumptions animating much of the current work in literary criticism and film studies" (McClary, *Conventional Wisdom*, 7). See also Lawrence Kramer: "The best means to do this [i.e., to pursue the agenda of the New Musicology] . . . lie in the conceptual and rhetorical world of postmodernism" (*Classical Music and Postmodern Knowledge* [Berkeley: University of California Press, 1995], 3).

32. Bowman, *Philosophical Perspectives*, 395. See also Cynthia Freeland, *Art Theory: A Very Short Introduction* (Oxford: Oxford University Press, 2001), 90: The Western canons of "great art" are " 'ideologies' or belief systems that falsely pretend to objectivity when they actually reflect power and dominance relations."

33. Small, *Musicking*, 133.

34. Ibid., 220.

35. The analogy used here is due to Belsey: "Poststructuralism proposes that the distinctions we make are not necessarily given by the world around us, but are instead produced by the symbolizing systems we learn. . . . But we learn our native tongue at such an early age that it

certain ideologies in ways of which we are for the most part unaware. Again, McClary writes that the structures by which artists make meaning "are intensely ideological formations: *whether noticed or not*, they are the assumptions that allow cultural activities to 'make sense.' Indeed, *they succeed best when least apparent, least deliberate, most automatic*." Artistic forms and practices are "conventions that so permeate human transactions that *we usually fail to notice their influence*."[36]

Ion suggests that art descends from the heavens. Postmodern art theory and the New Musicology, on the other hand, insist that art is profoundly situated within particular cultures. *Ion* suggests that works of art stand altogether outside of human culture and history, when in fact, the New Musicologists insist, works of art are one of the principal ways that a culture preserves and articulates its identity.

The Secret Knowledge

Nevertheless, ironically, the postmodern critique urges us toward a similar assessment of the artist as the one we find in *Ion*. In both cases the creative process is irrational. In both cases the artist is ignorant of her art's true content. Whether in *Ion* or in postmodern art theory, the artist literally doesn't know what she is talking about. In Plato's dialogue, the artist's intellect is disengaged as the god speaks through him. The rhapsode Ion is exposed as a fraud. He speaks beautifully about charioteering, but he doesn't know a thing about it. He offers marvelous speeches about fishing and medicine, but at the end of these speeches, neither Ion nor his listeners truly know any more about these subjects.

Similarly, in postmodern critical theory, the artist is for the most part unaware of what he is saying—or at least unaware of what he is *really* saying. Likewise, those listening come away without realizing what they have *really* heard. The composer thinks she is merely writing a minuet; in fact, she is reinforcing the power structures of patriarchal bourgeois society. The audience believes they are hearing a love sonnet. In fact, they are being indoctrinated as the poetry advances its hidden ideological agenda. This language of deception, obfuscation, and ignorance runs through McClary's analysis of Bach. Bach "*concealed* his political agenda" by "*seeming* just to be writing notes."[37]

seems transparent, a window onto a world of things, even if some of those things are in practice imaginary, no more than ideas of things, derived from children's stories. Are ideas the source of meaning, then? That was once the conventional view, but our ideas are not, poststructuralists believe, the origin of the language we speak. Indeed, the reverse is the case. Ideas are the effect of the meanings we learn and reproduce" (Catherine Belsey, *Poststructuralism: A Very Short Introduction* [Oxford: Oxford University Press, 2002], 7).

36. McClary, *Conventional Wisdom*, 5, emphasis added.

37. McClary, "Talking Politics during Bach Year," 56, emphasis added.

Eighteenth-century music generally "*hides* its social agenda inside *what appear to be* pure, self-contained patterns of notes."[38] Bach's music "shapes itself in terms of bourgeois ideology," but at the same time it also "*cloaks* that ideology."[39] Bach "gives the impression that *our* way of representing the world musically is God-given," and he makes this impression convincingly through compositional "sleight of hand."[40] And we, the listeners, are complicit in this cover up: "The tonal procedures developed by the emerging bourgeoisies to articulate their sense of the world here becomes presented as what we, in fact, want to believe they are: eternal universal truths."[41] McClary believes that "texts" such as Bach's music "powerfully articulated the social values of the emergent bourgeoisie *under the guise* of universal rationality, objectivity, truth."[42] Moreover, these musical works continue to shape our view of reality, carrying within their musical structure "hidden ideological underpinnings."[43]

Despite its vehement rejection of Platonic idealism, then, the postmodern critique repeats one of the principal themes of *Ion*. Artistic creation neither arises from nor results in knowledge. The artwork purports to be about one thing (fishing, patterns of notes) but is in fact about another (an artistic performance, a social ideology). In the same way, those encountering the artwork do not gain knowledge as a result. Ion's listeners do not learn how to fish; Bach's listeners remain deaf to the ideological dimensions of the work. Like Ion, Bach does not know what he is really talking about. He is the unwitting host-carrier for the virus of bourgeois ideology. And like Ion's audience, we the listeners fail to recognize the real content of Bach's music. We *want to believe* that the notes are just notes. Truly, *they seem to be* just notes—this is their power—but they conceal a hidden agenda: the ideology of the emerging bourgeoisie. At the end of the day, then, the composer rarely knows what he's *really* writing, and you and I, the art-loving public, rarely know what we're *really* hearing.

The Muse and the Big Other

There is another similarity between *Ion* and the New Musicology; namely, in both Plato and the postmodern account, the artist loses his voice. Of course, Ion has a voice in the most literal sense. He is a rhapsode; he has just won a garland for his performance of Homer. Homer too is able to speak. He is commended by Socrates as the most sublime of all poets. But as we saw earlier, in the course of Plato's dialogue the Muse is revealed to be the vital source of

38. Ibid., 57, emphasis added.
39. Ibid., 58, emphasis added.
40. Ibid., emphasis original.
41. Ibid.
42. Ibid., 60, emphasis added.
43. Ibid.

both Homer's stanzas and Ion's performance. The most fundamental note is sounded by the god. "We who hear," says Socrates, "should know that they [that is, the poets and the rhapsodes] are not the ones who speak those verses that are of such high value."[44]

Postmodern critics likewise acknowledge that singers sing, writers write, composers compose, and so on. Of course they do. But, says McClary, whereas "the traditional methods of hermeneutics often focus on explicating deliberate meanings . . . my project also factors in these seemingly automatic dimensions—which I take to be *the most crucial because the most fundamental*."[45] McClary acknowledges, then, that the artist speaks and will have things she wants to communicate ("explicit deliberate meanings"). But "the most crucial" and "the most fundamental" meaning, McClary argues, arises from factors that are at work "automatically." These include the voice of the "political unconscious," for instance, the silent "Speaker" whose words are "least apparent, least deliberate, most automatic."[46] On this account, even as the artist speaks there is a much more essential and powerful text at work, far beneath her words. This fundamental text is not one the artist has composed, but instead, one she has received. In a very real sense, the artist is not responsible for the artwork. We find an example of this idea in Catherine Belsey's analysis of George Eliot's novel, *Adam Bede*. Belsey exposes the offensive and oppressive ideologies contained in the novel and then asks, "Does this mean that George Eliot should be roundly condemned for colluding with exploitation?" Belsey's answer is surprising. "Of course not," she writes. Eliot should not be condemned because "George Eliot is not the origin or the explanation of the cultural convictions her novel reproduces. . . . The text is an effect of the meanings and values in circulation at its own historical moment. Adam Bede (who does not exist), George Eliot (who is not Adam Bede's origin) and the unsuspecting reader (the one who has not carried out a semiological analysis) participate in a shared practice which reproduces the ruling ideology."[47]

Our intuition is that Homer is responsible for his work, but in fact, Socrates claims, another is speaking. "The god takes [the poets'] intellect away from them when he uses them as his servants." Similarly, our persistent intuition is that words and creative acts of "signification" (such as *Adam Bede* or a Bach cantata) arise from the consciousness of their creators. According to Belsey, however, poststructuralism "questions the view that consciousness is an origin, treating it rather as an effect of signification: *I owe to the big Other the meanings and differences that permit me to think at all*."[48] So when the pretense of surface intentions is stripped away, the voice we finally hear is that

44. Plato, *Ion*, 534d, 26.
45. McClary, *Conventional Wisdom*, 6, emphasis added.
46. Ibid., 5.
47. Belsey, *Poststructuralism*, 37.
48. Ibid., 66, emphasis added.

of "the big Other" (Belsey's remarkable term); that is, we hear the cultural and historical location in which the artist is embedded. Plato robs the artist of his voice by placing the artwork completely *outside* his social location. Postmodern criticism robs the artist of her voice by completely *identifying* the artwork with the artist's social location.[49]

In fact, the postmodern eliminates the artist's voice even more completely than the Platonist. If one comes to recognize that artists (like all of us) are unwitting carriers of oppressive ideologies, then some sort of strategy must be devised to resist these ideologies. If artists are the unsuspecting hosts of oppressive ideologies, then perhaps the appropriate response is to pull apart the Trojan horse, plank by plank, joint by joint, and expose its fatal cargo. Better still, one might take the resulting pile of lumber and use it to enclose a different and opposing agenda. In just this way, McClary advocates a radical approach to Bach's music, in which critics, performers, and listeners undertake "deconstruction as a political act."[50]

First, she advises, one must recognize and acknowledge the ideologies in Bach's music.[51] Second, one must "perform Bach's music such that it speaks its

49. Some within the New Musicology camp recognize and reject this implication of the position. McClary writes, "This is not to suggest that music is nothing but an epiphenomenon that can be explained by way of social determinism. Music and other discourses do not simply reflect a social reality that exists immutably on the outside; rather social reality itself is constituted within such discursive practices. . . . It is also within the arena of these discourses that alternative models of organizing the social world are submitted and negotiated. That is where the ongoing work of social formation occurs" (Susan McClary, *Feminine Endings: Music, Gender and Sexuality* [Minneapolis: University of Minnesota Press, 1991], 21). Christopher Small makes a similar point: "Reality may be socially constructed, but no individual is bound to accept unquestioningly the way it is constructed. Musicking, being exploration as well as affirmation and celebration, is one way in which the question can be asked" (Small, *Musicking*, 134). Again, in the discussion of Adam Bede we considered a moment ago, Belsey writes, "The unsuspecting reader (the one who has not carried out a semiological analysis) participate[s] in a shared practice which reproduces the ruling ideology" (Belsey, *Poststructuralism*, 37). The *unsuspecting reader* reproduces ideology. The reader who knows how to subject the text to semiological analysis, however, apparently may avoid doing so.

None of this, however, seems very convincing. It is not at all clear why the postmodern critic, or the practice of semiology, or the application of musicology, or any other academic discipline might prove immune to this same encoding of ideology found in artworks. If all words and thought structures are embedded in the power structures of society, then the semiologist and the New Musicologist do not occupy a position any more privileged than that of the "innocent listener." Similarly, if ways of thinking and acting reflect political ideologies and agendas, then this applies to ways of thinking such as sociology, musicology, and poststructuralism. These socially constructed systems must also be suspected of harboring ideology and political agendas. If George Eliot is unaware of the ideology concealed within her novel, why should we expect that Small, Belsey, or McClary are aware of the ideology concealed within their disciplinary methodologies? And if this is the case, we must ask, why should we prefer *their* ideology to any other?

50. McClary, "Talking Politics during Bach Year," 60.

51. Ibid.

encoded story of order and noise."[52] The socially constructed agendas of Bach's music are exposed, in other words, in a performance that dares to "articulate audibly the violent dimensions of [the] music."[53] "Finally," McClary says, "I would propose the age-old strategy of rewriting the tradition in such a way as to appropriate Bach to our own political ends."[54] McClary concludes that "each group since the early nineteenth century has found it necessary to kidnap Bach from the immediately preceding generation and to demonstrate [Bach's] affinity with the emerging sensibility."[55] Seeing this, we too (like previous generations of kidnappers) should go about the task of "actively reclaiming Bach and the canon in order to put them to our own uses."[56]

Here, as I've said, we move well beyond *Ion*. As in Plato's dialogue, the postmodern artist has no voice at the point of origin. Instead, she is the unwitting mouthpiece of a massive social and political agenda. What is more (and what takes us well beyond Plato), here the composer has no voice at the point of *reception*, either. In fact, simply to say that she has "no voice" is to put it rather blandly. Following McClary's more colorful imagery of abduction we might say the composer is bound and gagged. She is "kidnapped," and her music is employed to advance "our own political ends," "our own uses"—the political and social agenda of the listener.

The Competitive Self

The work of art neither arises from nor communicates reliable knowledge. The artist is essentially passive, bearing a message that originates outside of herself. And finally, the artist is exposed as lacking any voice of her own. In all of these ways, surprisingly, artistic Platonism and postmodern criticism turn out to be mirror images of one another. The image may be reversed, but it is the same face staring out through the glass. In fact, the similarities arise from a common theological stance, one which sets both the postmodern and the Platonic accounts of artistry at odds with the pneumatology we have outlined to this point. McClary claims that the history of music criticism can be described as an "irreconcilable confrontation" between those who account for music in "metaphysical terms" and those who regard music as a "human, socially grounded"[57] activity. In other words, music may be "essentially" a human, social activity, or it may be essentially the product of some transcendent source, but it cannot be both. It is a dilemma that echoes the moving conclusion

52. Ibid., 61.
53. Ibid.
54. Ibid.
55. Ibid., 61–62.
56. Ibid., 62.
57. Ibid., 15.

of *Ion*: "So choose, how do you want us to think of you—as a man who does wrong, or as someone divine?"

This is the common ground between the Platonic and postmodern accounts we have considered: both present a fundamentally competitive "theology" with respect to human action. Where the transcendent is active, the human artist is inactive. Where the human is at work, the transcendent cannot be expressed. For Plato, this expresses itself in a competitive model of divine–human interaction. God can only speak when the artist is silent. For God to be heard, we must lose our own voices. "That's why the god takes their intellect away from them when he uses them as his servants, as he does prophets and godly diviners, so that we who hear should know that they are not the ones who speak those verses that are of such high value, for their intellect is not in them."[58]

For both the Platonist and the postmodern, humanity and God (or the transcendent) cannot occupy the same space. In fact, postmodernism extends this competitive theology into a competitive anthropology and sociology as well. Not only the transcendent–human relation but also the relationship between self and others is conceived in competitive terms. We know that consciousness cannot be an origin, it is claimed, *because* we have discerned "the big Other" at work. The implication is that if the self is to speak, the Other must be silent—and vice versa. If we recognize that cultural agendas and political ideologies are at work, then it is necessarily the case that individual agency is a fiction. If others are active, then I am passive. "Constructed to a high degree by the big Other, subjected to meanings outside its control and even its consciousness . . . the subject of poststructuralism is neither unified nor an origin."[59] Here self and identity are understood in terms of *control* and *domination*. If I am "subjected to meanings outside [my] control," then I am no longer an "I."

The two accounts share an essentially competitive vision of relation. For this reason, Plato's dialogue cannot acknowledge both human activity and divine influence, and for this reason the postmodern account struggles to acknowledge the full reality of both individual activity and social influence.

The Dehumanizing Spirit

> The poem is more something we find than something we make.
>
> Mark Doty, poet[60]

> I am just a medium, man. The shit's coming from somewhere. I don't sit down and really think! I just get in this mode and I do what I do. That's why I hate

58. Plato, *Ion*, 534b, 26.
59. Belsey, *Poststructuralism*, 65.
60. Laufer and Lewis, *Inspired*, 105.

> doing interviews, because people ask me, "How do you do what you do?" I don't know!
>
> Eddie Van Halen, guitarist[61]

> It still seems at times as if the creation of the work just happens. Sometimes my hand is moving with the spirit of the project, and hopefully, God is moving my hand.
>
> Faith Ringgold, painter, sculptor, and writer[62]

What happens when an artist creates? What sort of process is at work? Fundamentally, both *Ion* and the New Musicology believe that we must reach beyond the individual artist herself to give a complete account of any creative act. In this way, they help us make some sense of the kind of artist statements listed above and at the start of this chapter—the sense that the work of art is given to the artist from outside himself. Both *Ion* and the New Musicology affirm this intuition. The artwork does indeed arise from outside the artist. Along the way *Ion* reminds us that the source of our creativity remains mysterious, and not only to an audience or a group of admirers, but even—maybe *especially*—to the artist. McClary and others remind us of the profoundly social character of artistic creation. Works of art are not sealed off from gender, politics, ideologies, and all the other dimensions of a culture. Indeed, they are one way these dimensions are expressed and enacted.

But *Ion* and postmodern critical theory explain the artist's experience of "inspiration" at a considerable cost. Each strains against some of our deepest intuitions about creativity. For instance, each rules out the intuition that we explored in our discussion of John Coltrane: our sense that in at least some significant measure the artwork arises from and reflects the distinctive voice of the artist. What is far more troubling is that, by stripping the artist of her voice, both *Ion* and postmodern critical theory offer an account of the arts that is ultimately dehumanizing.

As we observed earlier, any account of the spirituality of the arts assumes both an understanding of art and an understanding of Spirit/spirit. And so, in assessing the experience of inspiration (which is in the first instance a theological term), *Ion* and the New Musicology advance not only an account of human creativity but a particular theological vision. *Ion* does this by describing what it looks like when the divine spirit acts on a human being. The New Musicology does this by rejecting the very possibility of a transcendent source of art—although interestingly, it rejects this possibility because it basically agrees with *Ion*: if the transcendent is active, then humanity must be passive.

61. Eddie Van Halen, quoted in Matt Resnikoff, "Jamming with Edward," *Musician Magazine*, May 1991.

62. Laufer and Lewis, *Inspired*, 120.

In either case, we end up with a very different theology and a very different pneumatology than that developed in the previous chapters. I have argued that the activity of God's Spirit secures, rather than threatens, our humanity. It is by this breath—this in-*spiration*—that dust becomes a human being. Likewise, I have contended that it is only as we share life with others that we fully realize our calling as human beings—to reflect the glory of God. The life of the community is a tuneful chorus in which I find my own voice rather than a big Other who keeps me from ever really being an "I." In the next chapter we will return to the pneumatology set out in earlier chapters and will consider what it might mean for the issue of artistic inspiration.

6

The Gift-Giving Spirit

De-Ionized Inspiration

The Christian doctrine of the Holy Spirit is not only *other* than the vision of both *Ion* and the postmodern, it is the *antidote* to *Ion* and the postmodern. Paul tells us that "where the Spirit of the Lord is, there is freedom" (2 Cor. 3:17). In the next chapter we will consider the ways in which the Spirit of freedom liberates men and women from the tyranny of "the Big Other" and releases them from "the prison house of language."[1] In this chapter, however, we will attempt to console the dehumanized rhapsode left crestfallen at the end of Plato's dialogue. Socrates' pneumatology of *possession* is healed by a biblical pneumatology of *gift*.

The God Who Is Gift

St. Augustine famously suggested that "Gift" is one of the names of the Holy Spirit. It is a fitting title, he reasoned, since the Spirit is both the gift of God and the God of gifts. "Through the gift which the Holy Spirit is in common for all the members of Christ, many gifts which are proper to them severally

1. Fredric Jameson, *The Prison House of Language: A Critical Account of Structuralism and Russian Formalism* (Princeton: Princeton University Press, 1975).

are divided among them."[2] In speaking of the Spirit as "gift" Augustine is simply developing the language of the New Testament:

> Repent, and be baptized every one of you in the name of Jesus Christ so that your sins may be forgiven; and you will receive the gift of the Holy Spirit.
>
> Acts 2:38[3]

> Now there are varieties of gifts, but the same Spirit. . . . To one is given through the Spirit the utterance of wisdom, to another the utterance of knowledge according to the same Spirit, to another faith by the same Spirit, to another gifts of healing by the one Spirit.
>
> 1 Cor. 12:4, 8–9

These biblical texts imagine the divine–human relation in a very different way from *Ion*. Here the divine Spirit is "gift" and "giver." And in the instance of the Holy Spirit, by God's free choice a human being comes to enjoy something that belongs to God (wisdom, knowledge, God's own Spirit). In *Ion*, on the other hand, the Muse lays hold of something that belonged to the human being (mind, use of one's own voice, command of one's own responses). Socrates declares that a poet "is not able to make poetry until he becomes inspired and goes out of his mind and his intellect is no longer in him. As long as a human being has his intellect in his possession he will always lack the power to make poetry or sing prophecy. . . . The god takes their intellect away from them when he uses them as his servants, as he does prophets and godly diviners."[4] The activity of the Muse is that of "taking away," emptying out the human.

The story of Bezalel from the book of Exodus provides a striking contrast to this and does a good job of illustrating the difference between the "possession" of *Ion*'s Muse and the giving of God's Holy Spirit. Bezalel appears at one of the crucial moments of the Old Testament story. The book of Exodus recounts the defining event of Israel's history: her deliverance from slavery in Egypt. But the climax of the Exodus story is not Israel's escape. God has brought this people out of slavery "that I might dwell among them" (Exod. 29:46). The movement of the book of Exodus is from slavery to worship, and the culmination of the Exodus story is the creation of a place where God's people will gather in his presence.[5] Bezalel (along with Oholiab and other

2. Augustine, *De Trinitate*, Book 15, trans. Edmund Hill, *The Trinity* (Brooklyn, NY: New City, 1991), 422–23.

3. See also John 14:16; 20:22; Acts 2:33.

4. Plato, *Ion*, 534d, trans. Paul Woodruff, in *Two Comic Dialogues: Ion and Hippias Major* (Indianapolis: Hackett, 1983), 26.

5. Though it may seem somewhat anticlimactic to a modern reader, the narrative structure of Exodus reflects the theological conviction that Israel has been delivered *from* slavery *for* worship. Chapters 1–15 recount the deliverance from Egypt, chapters 16–25 describe the journey

artists and craftsmen) is enlisted and empowered by the Spirit for the vital task of constructing and adorning the tabernacle.

> Then Moses said to the Israelites: See, the LORD has called by name Bezalel son of Uri son of Hur, of the tribe of Judah; he has filled him with divine spirit [*ruach Elohim*], with skill, intelligence, and knowledge in every kind of craft, to devise artistic designs, to work in gold, silver, and bronze, in cutting stones for setting, and in carving wood, in every kind of craft. And he has inspired him [literally, "put in the heart of him"] to teach, both him and Oholiab son of Ahisamach, of the tribe of Dan. He has filled them with skill to do every kind of work done by an artisan or by a designer or by an embroiderer in blue, purple, and crimson yarns, and in fine linen, or by a weaver—by any sort of artisan or skilled designer.
>
> Bezalel and Oholiab and every skillful one to whom the LORD has given skill and understanding to know how to do any work in the construction of the sanctuary shall work in accordance with all that the LORD has commanded. Moses then called Bezalel and Oholiab and every skillful one to whom the LORD had given skill, everyone whose heart was stirred to come to do the work.
>
> Exodus 35:30–36:2

Unlike the spirit who "takes away their intellect," the inspiration of Bezalel and the other workers results in "skill," "intelligence," and "knowledge" (35:31); in the power to "devise" and "work" (35:32); in "understanding" and "know how" (36:1); and in the ability to "teach" (35:34). (Nor should we automatically assume that this sort of teaching was of a lower order than other sorts of instruction and proclamation. The same word translated "teach" occurs again in Leviticus 10:11, where the Lord commissions Aaron and his sons as Israel's priests: "you must *teach* the Israelites all the decrees the LORD has given them through Moses.") Spirit-possession does not enrich Ion as a person. He is a passive conduit, a piece of magnetized metal through which divine current flows. Bezalel and his workers, on the other hand, *become* "skilled one[s]" (36:2); they are those to whom "the Lord *had given* skill" (36:2). The difference between Ion's encounter with the divine Spirit and Bezalel's is the difference between the prepositions "away from" and "into." It is the difference between *possession* and *gift*.

The New Testament also speaks of the Spirit as one who bestows *charisms*, or gifts. In *Ion*, when the divine spirit encounters humanity, the result is a loss of mind. If Christians held to a similar vision, then Scripture might describe spiritual progress as a progressive numbing of the mind, until one attains the ultimate goal of complete intellectual barrenness. Maturity would be measured on a scale of mental vacuity. We may have encountered Christians who seem to

---

to Sinai and the receiving of the law, and chapters 26–40 are for the most part concerned with the construction of the tabernacle and instructions for priests.

embody this spiritual ideal, but this is not the biblical vision of the Spirit-life. Paul, in his letter to the church at Corinth, also acknowledges that there are some who by God's Spirit speak without understanding: "Those who speak in a tongue do not speak to other people but to God; for nobody understands them" (1 Cor. 14:2). Paul doesn't deny that there may be some value to this sort of speech. But while *Ion* suggests that speech without understanding is the quintessential trait of spirit-filling, Paul insists that of all the gifts of the Spirit, the highest are those that lead to wisdom and knowledge (1 Cor. 12:31; 14:1). From Paul's perspective, the goal of the Spirit-life is not a neutralized intellect but a mind fully engaged in the praise of God and the encouragement of others (1 Cor. 14:14–15, 18–19).[6]

Christianity and Heteronomy

Not everyone would agree with this characterization. Some have argued that the dehumanizing account presented in *Ion* is *precisely* what we find in Christianity. *Ion* claims that creativity arises from receptivity, with surrender to something outside of oneself. Does not Christianity say more or less the same thing concerning the origin of the Spirit-life? And what about *Ion*'s portrayal of human passivity before the divine and the surrendering of one's own self? Is *Ion* all that far removed from the language of Christian piety at this point? Christian hymn texts bear titles such as "I Surrender All" and "Take My Life and Let it Be." There is John the Baptist's declaration that "he must increase, but I must decrease" (John 3:30) and the apostle Paul's claim, "I no longer live but Christ lives in me" (Gal. 2:20 NIV). Jesus likewise urges his followers to deny *themselves* and follow *him*. Is not all of this human passivity and a surrender of oneself to another's control? Someone might argue, then, that when Christians ask the Holy Spirit to fill them, they are aspiring to the same sort of divine ventriloquism found in *Ion*.

This is one of the charges of the post-Christian theologian Daphne Hampson. Hampson believes that the fundamental problem with Christianity is that it encourages "heteronomy" rather than "autonomy." Christians, in other words, set out to live by another (*heteros*) law (*nomos*), external to themselves, rather than living according to their own true nature and being.[7]

6. Even this prayer without knowledge—the prayer in tongues—is distinct from what is described in *Ion*. Though the person praying in tongues may not understand her prayer with her "mind," nevertheless she is actively praying with *her* "spirit." Not even here do we find the kind of complete passivity that is suggested in *Ion*. See also Richard Bauckham, *The Climax of Prophecy: Studies on the Book of Revelation* (Edinburgh: T&T Clark, 1993), 150–55. Bauckham draws a clear contrast between John's experience of being "in the Spirit" (Rev. 1:10, 4:2) with "those pagan prophets of antiquity who became in a trance the wholly passive mouthpieces of the god" (152).

7. Hampson approvingly relates a conversation that a friend of hers once had with a Christian bishop. "I have some problems with Jesus Christ," the woman told the bishop. "What sort

Ion suggests that divine inspiration means personal annihilation. Hampson and other critics believe that the same is true of Christianity. By urging people to give themselves over to some divine being, Christianity teaches individuals to disown their selves, to abandon their identity, and to despise their own humanity. By ceding control to the Holy Spirit, Christians refuse both the delight and the responsibility of being who they are.[8] Wouldn't it be better, Hampson asks, to encourage people to take mature responsibility for their own lives and actions? Rather than advising people to become the marionettes of a divine puppeteer, would it not be healthier spiritually to teach them to be fully human, fully faithful to their own unique selves? "Our goal," Hampson writes, "must be that persons are centred in themselves and open to one another."[9] So, she writes, "I wish an ethical position in which I do not give over my being to any person or to any God who lies outside myself."[10]

We have described the Spirit of God as the *humanizing* Spirit. But Hampson would say that to surrender oneself to the Spirit—to imagine oneself as utterly dependent upon the Spirit, to think of oneself as dust animated by the breath of God—is to be less than fully human. And, she might well point to *Ion* in support of her claims. Ion is inspired by the Muse and ceases to be Ion. To answer these charges we need to recall Augustine's suggestion that the name of the Spirit is "Gift."

God's Giving and Ours

It certainly is the case that Scripture speaks about personal surrender and giving oneself over to God. This language, however, stands alongside statements about the Spirit being *given to us*. If human beings are called to pour themselves out (Phil. 2:7), then they are also promised that God's Spirit will be poured out on them (Acts 2:33; Joel 2:28). Christians, then, want to say two things that, at least at first, may seem to be at odds with one another: (1) We are called to give ourselves to God; and (2) God relates to humanity as One who gives. A few observations may help us think through the relationship between our giving and God's.[11]

---

of problems?" the bishop asked. "Well, for example," the woman replied, "[Jesus] had said 'Follow me', whereas I do not think that one should follow anyone!" (Daphne Hampson, *After Christianity* [London: SCM, 1996], 76).

8. See, for instance, ibid., 76–77, and chapter 6.

9. Daphne Hampson, ed., *Swallowing a Fishbone? Feminist Theologians Debate Christianity* (London: SPCK, 1996), 122.

10. Hampson, *After Christianity*, 38.

11. Throughout this discussion of gift I am indebted to Dumitru Staniloae, *The Experience of God: Orthodox Dogmatic Theology*, vol. 2, *Creation and Deification*, trans. Ioan Ionita and Robert Barringer (Brookline, MA: Holy Cross Orthodox Press, 2005), esp. chapter 2, "The World as Gift and Word." I am also following Miroslav Volf's rich and thoughtful reflection in *Free*

God's Giving Precedes and Exceeds Our Own

God initiates and sustains this relationship of giving. All that has life and being has its life and being by the breath of God:

> If he should take back his spirit (*ruach*) to himself,
> and gather to himself his breath,
> all flesh would perish together,
> and all mortals return to dust.
>
> Job 34:14–15

So, it is not as if *this* bit of creation over *here* receives its life from God, while *that* bit over *there* has life through its own internal resources. Only God has life in himself, and this means, necessarily, that all that is not God has been *given* its being *by* God.

This, in part, is what theologians are getting at when they speak of *creatio ex nihilo*—creation out of nothing. In the work of creation God was not compelled by either external conditions or internal deficiency. God did not create out of molten lava or preexisting dark matter; nor did God create out of loneliness, creative angst, boredom, or desperation. Needing nothing, God made everything. Karl Barth writes, "Creation is grace: a statement at which we should like best to pause in reverence, fear and gratitude. . . . That there is a world is the most unheard-of thing, the miracle of the grace of God."[12] In the relationship between God and humanity, then, God's giving necessarily precedes ours. "What do you have that you did not receive?" Paul asks the Corinthians (1 Cor. 4:7).

Moreover, God's giving *exceeds* ours, and this is so also as a matter of logical necessity. We have said that needing nothing, God made everything. God's gifts, then, are *wholly* gift, *wholly* gracious. God's gifts do not provide God with any benefit he had lacked, and, in this regard, God's giving exceeds ours. You and I may give generously and sacrificially, but we do not—we cannot—give as God does. I give gifts to my children because I love them—but also because I want them to love me, because it makes me feel good about myself, because I want to have a certain kind of family, because I want other people to think that I'm a good father, and so on. As finite beings, we are inevitably motivated by our own needs—at least in part. Each thing I do arises from a mixture of motives: good and bad, noble and shameful, selfless and selfish. God, however, has no insecurities to be eased by praise, no deep-seated desires for personal significance, no deficits he requires us to fill. God and God alone is "the One Who loves in freedom" (once again to borrow a phrase from Barth).

---

of Charge: Giving and Forgiving in a Culture Stripped of Grace (Grand Rapids: Zondervan, 2005), esp. 63–70.

12. Karl Barth, *Dogmatics in Outline*, trans. G. T. Thompson (New York: Harper & Row, 1959), 54.

God's Own Life Is One of Gift

The second point to note is that while the act of creation may show us God's character as giver, it is not the moment when God *becomes* a giver. Just as God is love before there are creatures to be loved, so God is giver before there is a world to receive his gifts. As we saw in our discussion of *perichoresis*, from all eternity, Father, Son, and Spirit give themselves to one another in love.

The eternal relationship of giving between Father, Son, and Spirit is revealed to our view as it is played out throughout Jesus's life and ministry. The gospel story begins with the Father giving the Spirit for the benefit of the Son. The angel Gabriel tells Mary: "The Holy Spirit will come upon you, and the power of the Most High will overshadow you; therefore the child to be born will be holy; he will be called Son of God" (Luke 1:35). Again at Jesus's baptism, the Father gives the Spirit, anointing the Son for ministry (Matt. 3:16–17; Mark 1:9–11; Luke 3:21–22; John 1:32–33). Finally, through the power of the Holy Spirit, the Father gives life to the crucified Jesus, raising him from the dead and to the place of power and glory (Rom. 1:4; 8:11; Acts 2:33).

The Son is also a giver—even as he receives life and power through Father and Spirit. Following his baptism Jesus surrenders himself to the leading of the Holy Spirit, "and the Spirit immediately drove him out into the wilderness" (Mark 1:12; cf. Luke 4:1). His is a life yielded to the Father, a giving over of himself that culminates on the cross, where once again, in the Spirit, he offers up his life: "Then he bowed his head and gave up his spirit" (*paredôken to pneuma*; John 19:30). Jesus's life reveals to us a constant movement of offer, surrender, receptivity, and response among Father, Son, and Spirit. The Father through the Spirit gives himself to the Son; the Son through the Spirit gives himself to the Father. Moreover, the Spirit, in his being sent, gives himself to Father and Son.

God's own life, then, is one of gift. "God gives continually and unfailingly," Miroslav Volf writes, "because God *is* essentially a giver just as God *is* love."[13] God is a giver, not only in relation to us but eternally, unchangeably, in God's own being.

God Gives Us the Gift of Being Givers

We asked: how can we say *both* that God calls us to surrender our lives *and* that the work of the Holy Spirit is to complete and perfect our humanity? The answer should now be clear. God calls us to surrender our lives *because* the work of the Holy Spirit is to complete and perfect our humanity. Humanity was created in God's image, to reflect God's character and glory. And God, as we have seen, is fundamentally a giver—a God who from all eternity has his being in pouring himself out. The work of the Spirit, then, is to restore us to our true humanity, to make us once again image bearers. He does this, as we

13. Volf, *Free of Charge*, 69.

have seen, by refashioning us in the image of the True Human, Jesus Christ. This will mean, however, remaking us in the image of the one who emptied and humbled himself (Phil. 2:7–8), whose food was to do the will of the one who sent him (John 4:34), who said: "The Son of Man came not to be served but to serve, and to give his life a ransom for many" (Mark 10:45). To be made fully human is to be made like Jesus. To be made like Jesus is to be made a giver.

As we've already pointed out, this is not how we are by nature. The character of our sinful condition is not to give but to shore up our own resources. This is the testimony of not only theologians but also evolutionary biologists and classical economists: whether in the wild or in the marketplace, we persistently—even violently—seek our own competitive advantage. This tendency can be described more theologically as *incurvatus in se*—being turned in upon ourselves. Martin Luther famously characterized sin in these terms:

> Due to original sin, our nature is so curved in upon itself at its deepest levels that it not only bends the best gifts of God toward itself in order to enjoy them . . . nay, rather, [it] "uses" God in order to obtain them, but it does not even know that, in this wicked, twisted, crooked way, it seeks everything, including God, only for itself.[14]

Our priority is not the good of others but our own good, says Luther, and all we can lay hold of we twist and bend toward ourselves.

The Spirit's gift is freedom from this prison of inwardness. By the Spirit we are enabled, first of all, to give ourselves to God. "No one can say 'Jesus is Lord,'" Paul declares, "except by the Holy Spirit" (1 Cor. 12:3). The Spirit enables us to do what we could not do otherwise, namely, surrender ourselves to God. But—again—according to the logic of the biblical narrative, this does not mean the loss of our humanity; it means the completion of it. Humanity is made to reflect the image and glory of the God who lives in an eternal movement of self-surrender. And by the Spirit, we are remade in the image of Jesus Christ, whose life "provides the proof . . . of the fact that the one God is, in his essence, love and surrender."[15]

The Spirit enables us to give, not only to God, but to others as well. This is another way in which the Spirit restores the image of God in us. We are made like God, who knows how to give good gifts abundantly to his children (Matt. 7:11). So, by the Spirit, *we* are made able to give good gifts to others. The Spirit gives gifts (*charisms*) to each, Paul says, not simply for our individual enjoyment, but "for the common good" (1 Cor. 12:7).

This is another significant departure from *Ion*. Nowhere does the dialogue suggest that the Muse hopes to enrich Ion's audience through him. For his

14. Martin Luther, "Romans, Chapter Five," in *Luther: Lectures on Romans*, ed. and trans. Wilhelm Pauck (Philadelphia: Westminster, 1961), 159.

15. Hans Urs von Balthasar, *Credo: Meditations on the Apostles' Creed*, trans. David Kipp (Edinburgh: T&T Clark, 1990), 29.

part, Ion seems equally uninterested in serving those who hear his recitations. Though he may be artistically "gifted," Ion clearly does not view his abilities as "gifts" to be given to others. They are assets to be exploited, a means of enriching himself with the applause and prizes he craves. ("Really, Socrates, it's worth hearing how well I've got Homer dressed up. I think I'm worthy to be crowned by the Sons of Homer with a golden crown."[16])

In this sense at least, *Ion* is not far removed from the way our culture typically thinks of artistic ability. Those who are artistically "gifted" are admired, revered, and praised. If their gift is widely recognized, then they occupy a privileged position in society, winning wealth and celebrity through their abilities. Those who are judged most gifted are profiled in the media and celebrated at red carpet awards ceremonies. In the world of the "high arts" the gifted person is the diva, the virtuoso, the master thespian, or the literary genius. In the world of the popular arts this person is the Hollywood celebrity, the rock star, the American Idol. The gifted person stands spotlit in center stage, while the anonymous crowd roars its adulation. There is very little sense that such a person has *received a gift*—in other words, has been freely entrusted with something precious, for which the most appropriate response is humility and gratitude. Nor is there typically the sense that the "gifted" person is a *gift-bearer*, one whose calling is to give to and enrich others.

The *charisms* of the Spirit, however, are gifts in both of these senses. They are gifts *from* and gifts *for*. Moltmann observes that even those extraordinary Spirit-anointed figures of the Old Testament—judges, prophets, and kings—are empowered *to serve*. "These . . . spontaneous and temporally limited gifts [are] conferred on individuals *for* the whole people."[17] In the same way, the Spirit gives gifts to the church in such a way that we are made able to give to others: "every generous act of giving, with every perfect gift, is from above" (James 1:17). As we give generously, we become more and more like God, the Supreme Giver, and we enter more and more fully into our lofty human calling, to be God's image bearers.

"The Love Which Is from God and Which Is God"

A pneumatology of gift, then, is set firmly against the competitive theology of *Ion* and the postmodern. Where *Ion* speaks in terms of confiscation (the god takes away their intellect) and the postmodern speaks in terms of domination (artists are subjected to meanings outside their control), Augustine describes the work of the Spirit in terms of *charity*: "The love which is from God and is God is distinctively the Holy Spirit; through him the charity of God is poured

16. Plato, *Ion*, in *The Philosophy of Art: Readings Ancient and Modern*, ed. Alex Neill and Aaron Ridley (New York: McGraw-Hill, 1985), 7.

17. Jürgen Moltmann, *The Spirit of Life: A Universal Affirmation*, trans. Margaret Kohl (Minneapolis: Fortress, 2001), 43, emphasis original.

out in our hearts, and through it the whole triad dwells in us. This is the reason why it is most apposite that the Holy Spirit, while being God, should also be called the gift of God."[18]

Ultimately what the Spirit makes manifest in the believer is not an ideology or an agenda but God's own person—the eternal community of Father, Son, and Spirit, in communion with a human being. In this relationship of shared life, the language of domination and exclusion no longer makes sense, nor does any opposition between outer forces and inner being. Richard Bauckham writes that

> the mystery of the Spirit's activity is that this divine presence at the center of human personhood does not reduce personal freedom but enables the free spontaneity of those who embrace God's will as their own. . . . It is the activity of the Spirit that transcends the alternative of autonomy and heteronomy by actualizing in our personal existence the truth that God's law is not the will of another, in the ordinary sense in which this would be true of the will of another creature, but, as the law of the Creator and his creation, also the law of our own being, in conforming to which we become most truly ourselves.[19]

And just as the Holy Spirit gives birth to community between God and humanity, the Holy Spirit also gives birth to human community (as we saw in chapter 4). The character of this human community—like that established between God and humanity—is fundamentally noncompetitive. The "new humanity" (Eph. 2:15) is no "big Other," annihilating the individual subject. In fact, as we saw, the very thing that distinguishes this new humanity is the diversity of its members, that *the different members* are *heirs together* and sharers of the promise: "This mystery is that through the gospel the Gentiles are *heirs together* with Israel, members together of one body, and sharers together in the promise in Christ Jesus" (Eph. 3:6 NIV, emphasis added).

The community of believers is not a threat to individuality but the place where one discovers it. It is as a member of "one body" that each one lives out her own distinctive gift and calling—some apostles, some prophets, and so on (Eph. 4:3–16). Conversely, the individuality of the members is not a threat to community. The unity of the whole arises from the *differentiated* activity of its members, each contributing something distinctive but necessary for the life of the entire body. "The whole body, joined and held together by every supporting ligament, grows and builds itself up in love, *as each part does its work*" (Eph. 4:16 NIV, emphasis added). The letter to the Ephesians speaks of a human community that is not driven by ideology nor which sets out to impose its will and agenda but one which "grows and builds itself up *in love*"

18. Augustine, *De Trinitate*, Book 15, 421.

19. Richard Bauckham, *God and the Crisis of Freedom: Biblical and Contemporary Perspectives* (Louisville: Westminster John Knox, 2002), 208.

(4:16 NIV, emphasis added) and which keeps unity, not through the suppression of others, but "through *the bond of peace*" (4:3 NIV, emphasis added).

The End of Giving

One way of answering the concerns and objections raised by Daphne Hampson is by looking at the character of the Spirit. The Spirit is gift and giver. Another way of answering these concerns and objections is by looking at Jesus Christ. We have been asking, what does it look like when God's Spirit acts on a human being? Plato's dialogue answers this question by looking at the example of Ion the rhapsode. Christians answer this question by looking at Jesus Christ. Jesus is the True Human, the pioneer and paradigm of restored humanity. He is the perfect picture, then, of divine–human interaction. Moreover, Jesus is both Messiah—the bearer of the Spirit—and the one who gives the Spirit to his disciples (John 20:22). We receive the Spirit because Jesus received and pours out the Spirit (Acts 2:33), and the Spirit we receive is the Spirit of Jesus Christ. Athanasius makes this point in his *Orations against the Arians*:

> The descent of the Spirit upon him in the Jordan was a descent upon us, because of our body which he carried. . . . For when the Lord was washed in the Jordan, it was we who were washed in him and by him. And when he received the Spirit, it was we who were made recipients of the Spirit by him.[20]

> The Savior . . . being himself the supplier of the Spirit, is nevertheless now said to be anointed by the Spirit, so that, being said to be anointed as a human being by the Spirit, he may provide us human beings with the indwelling and intimacy of the Holy Spirit, just as he provides us with exaltation and resurrection.[21]

What does it look like when the Spirit of God "descends and remains" (see John 1:33) on a human being? Jesus, the bearer of the Spirit, certainly did deny himself. He lived, not to be served, but to serve (Mark 10:45) and resolved that the Father's will, not his own, would be done in his life (Matt. 26:39). Paul urges the Philippians to follow this example of self-surrender:

> Though he was in the form of God [he] did not regard equality with God as something to be exploited, but emptied himself, taking the form of a slave, being born in human likeness, and being found in human form, he humbled himself and became obedient to the point of death—even death on a cross.
>
> Philippians 2:6–8

20. Athanasius, *Orations against the Arians*, 1:47, in Khaled Anatolios, *Athanasius* (New York: Routledge, 2004), 104.
21. Ibid., 1:46, 103.

It is this encouragement to empty oneself (often referred to as "kenosis," from the Greek verb here translated "emptied") that Hampson finds particularly problematic. Perhaps, she acknowledges, "humbling oneself" is a useful spiritual aspiration for those in power. But there are all sorts of people in the world who have already been humbled, and that against their will; they have been humiliated and enslaved by others. For these, Hampson says, Christ's example of self-surrender is far from being good news.

> Kenosis is indeed a critique of patriarchy. That it should have featured prominently in Christian thought is perhaps an indication of the fact that men have understood what the male problem, in thinking in terms of hierarchy and domination, has been. It may well be a model which men need to appropriate and which may helpfully be built into the male understanding of God. But . . . for women, the theme of self-emptying and self-abnegation is far from helpful as a paradigm.[22]

This is an important complaint and one the Christian tradition needs to hear. The New Testament message of humility and self-surrender has at times been misunderstood as a command to *shut-up and stay in your place*. Where this has happened, the church must respond with repentance. What this understanding of *kenosis*—and what Hampson—misses, however, is the towering "therefore" of Philippians 2:9. Jesus emptied himself, humbled himself, and became obedient to death. "*Therefore*," Paul continues, "God also highly exalted him and gave him the name that is above every name, so that at the name of Jesus every knee should bend, in heaven and on earth and under the earth" (Phil. 2:9–10).

The One to whom Jesus gives himself in obedience—and the One to whom Christians are called to surrender—is himself a giver, indeed, the Great Giver. Just as Jesus does not "exploit" or (as in other translations) "grasp" equality with God, neither does the Father exploit or grasp the life surrendered to him. Father, Son, and Spirit, we have said, exist in an eternal dance of giving and self-surrender, and we see this pattern of gift responding to gift in Jesus's life, death, and resurrection. In the Spirit, the Son gives himself up to the Father, and the Father, by the Spirit, gives life to the Son, exalting him to the highest place.

Paul traces this same trajectory for Jesus's followers. This after all was his starting point: "Your attitude should be the same as that of Jesus Christ" (Phil. 2:5 NIV). This is the answer to the concerns raised by Hampson. The Spirit who fills us is the Spirit of Jesus Christ, and in him we see the shape of this Spirit-life. Tom Smail writes (making the same point articulated by Athanasius centuries earlier), "What [the Spirit] does in us is always the same as what he did in Christ: he regenerates, he anoints, he transforms. What happens to us in the Spirit is totally dependent on what first happened to him."[23] And what we see in Jesus

22. Daphne Hampson, *Theology and Feminism* (Oxford: Basil Blackwell, 1990), 155.

23. Tom Smail, *The Giving Gift: The Holy Spirit in Person* (London: Darton, Longman & Todd, 1994), 107–8.

is that the life of the Spirit does not end at the cross but with resurrection, not with death but new life, not with humiliation but with glorification. So, while Philippians 2 begins with a call to "consider others better than yourselves" (2:3 NIV), it leads to Paul's hope that the Philippians will "shine like stars in the world" (2:15). Paul himself says that he wants to share in the sufferings and death of Christ (3:10) but not out of self-hatred or a desire for personal annihilation. His hope, he says, is "that I may attain the resurrection from the dead" (3:11).

God does not cease to be a giver once we have given ourselves to him. The Spirit may speak through us, he may pray through us, but, Yves Congar writes, "this is not a case of God *replacing* us. . . . God's substance does not take the place of our substance. . . . We continue to act."[24] By the Spirit we are welcomed into the circle of giving that moves through Father, Son, and Spirit, a movement in which we both give and receive. "Truly, I tell you," Jesus says, "there is no one who has left house or brothers or sisters or mother or father or children or fields, for my sake and for the sake of the good news, who will not receive a hundredfold now in this age—houses, brothers and sisters, mothers and children, and fields, with persecutions—and in the age to come eternal life. But many who are first will be last, and the last will be first" (Mark 10:29–31).

Of course, the words here about persecution and being "the last" should make clear that this circle of giving is not a divine pyramid scheme. The Spirit life is not an investment strategy—the sort of thing suggested by late night cable television preachers: "If you send me a gift of $100 today, God is gonna turn that around and give you a hundredfold return on that investment!" The cross is a real surrender, a real death. But if Jesus shows us a life filled with God's Holy Spirit, then we must also say that the end—the *telos*—of a life lived by the Spirit is not the loss of the self but the completion and even (in the most fully theological sense of the word) the *glorification* of the self. One could not find a clearer statement of this paradox than in Jesus's own words: "Whoever wants to save his life will lose it, but whoever loses his life for me and for the gospel will save it" (Mark 8:35 NIV).

A Creative Submission

Ion's pneumatology of possession could have no conception of this paradox, but it might have been suggested to him by his experience as an artist. The experienced artist already knows that the one who wants to save her creative life will lose it, but whoever loses her creative life will find it. Musicians, dancers, visual artists, actors, and writers will testify that artistry does not begin with self-expression but with active submission. This is true in two senses.

First, creative artistry includes receptivity to one's materials. One of my first composition classes as a music student included a string of guest

24. Yves Congar, *I Believe in the Holy Spirit*, vol. 1, *The Holy Spirit in the "Economy": Revelation and the Experience of the Holy Spirit*, trans. Geoffrey Chapman (New York: Crossroads, 2003), 32.

appearances by various instrumentalists. Percussionists and string, wind, and brass players of various sorts visited the class. "Play an ascending scale, please," the professor would ask. "Play a lyrical, melodic passage." "Play something very loud." "Play a fast, percussive passage." "Play a single, long, sustained note." In this way, the professor would direct the instrumentalist through a range of musical situations. Our job as students was—very simply—to listen and learn what sounds these instruments make. The starting point for our work as composers was to get to know the *sound* of sound. If we were to be workers in sound, then we needed to learn well the possibilities and limits of our material.[25]

This is not unique to music. Experienced novelists encourage beginning writers to eavesdrop on conversations—to learn how language works, to learn what people say to one another and the rhythm of dialogue. Poets attend patiently and carefully to the tone and cadence of words and phrases. Michelangelo famously described the process of sculpting as freeing the form hidden within the stone.[26] "It's easy," writes Nicholas Wolterstorff, "to think that the artist has in mind a clear image of what he or she wants and then, having acquired an assortment of skills, deftly imposes that image on the material. Most of the time the truth is far other. The work of art emerges from a *dialogue* between artist and material."[27]

Creativity, then, includes an act of humility and self-abnegation. The artist does not begin by speaking but by listening, attending, and learning. This much *Ion* knows. This act of surrender, however, is not the termination of one's own artistic voice but its necessary condition.

Second, creative artistry includes submission to the craft of one's art and, most likely, to a teacher. The would-be artist who insists on beginning with "autonomy" or "not following anyone" will not get very far. Artists may aspire to some sort of "self-expression," but they do not begin there. We begin by learning what others have said, repeating their words and movements. But the artistic process itself suggests that this submission is ultimately creative. Artistry involves a giving over of oneself that, again, paradoxically, opens up the possibility of self-expression.

The novelist Donald Ray Pollock described a striking instance of this kind of productive surrender in a recent radio interview with Scott Simon. Early in his writing career, Pollock explains, he was unsure of himself as an author and unsure of how to do the work of a writer.

25. Nicholas Wolterstorff contends that "the fundamental fact about the artist is that he or she is a worker in stone, in bronze, in clay, in paint, in acid and plates, in words, in sounds and instruments, in states of affairs" (*Art in Action: Toward a Christian Aesthetic* [Grand Rapids: Eerdmans, 1980], 91).

26. See, for instance, the discussion in Chandler B. Beall, "The Literary Figure of Michelangelo," *Italica* 41, no. 3 (September 1964): esp. 245–46.

27. Wolterstorff, *Art in Action*, 94–95, emphasis original.

POLLOCK: And so when I started out I also didn't know too much about how to begin, and so I would type out stories that I liked on a typewriter.

SIMON: You mean type other stories out?

POLLOCK: Yes, type other writers' stories. You know, I'd never been in a writing workshop or anything and I—you know, it just seemed to be a way to get closer to figuring out how other writers did what they did. So I did that quite a bit.

SIMON: What stories, do you remember?

POLLOCK: Several from Dennis Johnson's *Jesus' Son*, quite a few were Hemmingway stories, some Flannery O'Connor, Barry Hannah stories, John Schafer, Richard Yates, I tried quite a few different writers.

SIMON: What would you learn by typing?

POLLOCK: I think one of the principal things I learned from typing the stories out was how dialog works. Also just, you know things about structure and you know, I could read a story, but I really wouldn't see how it worked until I got closer to it.[28]

Pollock developed his own authorial voice by transcribing, repeating, inhabiting the voices of other authors. We can also see this principle at work in the musical development of John Coltrane.

Coltrane's devotion to his instrument has become proverbial among jazz musicians. From the time he was a young teenager Coltrane maintained an intense practice regime, playing for hours each day and, when neighbors complained, silently fingering the keys of his saxophone late into the night. His first wife, Naima, referred to Coltrane as "ninety-percent saxophone." She related stories of regular, twenty-four-hour practicing binges, and of a musician who often fell asleep holding his tenor sax.[29] Coltrane took classes at various music institutes and conservatories and pored over practice books such as Slonimsky's *Thesaurus of Scales and Patterns*.

Coltrane's is one of the most distinctive and recognizable instrumental voices in jazz. For decades, however, Coltrane dedicated himself to learning and internalizing the styles of older and established jazz musicians. For nine years, from 1946 to 1955, Coltrane was "an anonymous journeyman,"[30] working as a supporting musician in the bands of more established musicians. An older generation of sax players, such as Lester Young, Coleman Hawkins, and Dexter Gordon, served as models. Contemporaries such as Dizzy Gillespie, Johnny Hodges, Miles Davis, and Thelonious Monk served as instructors. In an interview Coltrane described how his time in Monk's band became an opportunity for intensive one-on-one tutorials:

28. Transcript of Scott Simon's interview with Donald Pollock, " 'Knockemstiff' Writer Pulls No Punches," *Weekend Edition Saturday*, broadcast April 12, 2008, National Public Radio.

29. Ashley Kahn, *A Love Supreme: The Making of John Coltrane's Classic Album* (London: Granta Books, 2002), 28.

30. Ibid., 10.

> I'd go by his apartment, and get him out of bed [laughs]—he'd wake up and roll over to the piano and start playing . . . I'd get my horn and start trying to find what he was playing . . . he'd tend to play it over and over and over . . . he would stop and show me some parts that were pretty difficult, and if I had a *lot* of trouble, well, he'd get his portfolio out show me the music . . . he's got all of it written and I'd read it and learn it . . . when I almost had the tune down, then he would leave me to practice it. . . . [When] I had it pretty well, then I'd call him and we'd play it down together. And sometimes, we'd get just one tune a day, maybe.[31]

Coltrane developed his own voice by surrendering it to another. Before he could speak on his own, he first gave himself to repeating again and again the things Monk had said. "He'd play it over and over and over." The paradox of artistry is that loss of the self is the prerequisite for self-expression. And, conversely, the object of mastering another's voice is finding one's own. Receptivity and creativity stand in a complementary relationship to one another—the former establishing the conditions for the latter, the latter providing the *telos* of the former.

The call to follow Christ, as we've said, does involve a *kenosis*, a self-emptying, a surrender of one's own way to follow the way of another. For Hampson this is a bleak and oppressive vision of the spiritual life; Christians, however, believe that this path of self-renunciation is also the way of life. Of course, Coltrane's music can't settle the difference between these two conceptions of spirituality—but it does lend plausibility to the Christian claim that self-surrender may be ultimately creative. His example also indicates that yielding oneself—setting aside one's own way and taking up the way of another—need not be construed in terms of power and oppression. At least in the domain of artistry, self-denial is the ground and the necessary condition for self-realization and self-expression. The Christian story is able to make sense of Coltrane's creative experience, and in fact offers a more satisfying account of that experience than some of its philosophical competitors.

We might say that in his description of artistry, Ion got the story half right. The half he got wrong corresponds to a deficiency in his pneumatology. In the human engagement with God's Spirit there is encounter, there is receptivity; we might even say that there is a loss of self. But the one to whom we surrender ourselves is a Giver, not a Possessor. In surrender to the gift-giving Spirit, one receives life in return, healed and whole.[32]

31. Ibid., 30.

32. "A non-competitive relation between creatures and God means that the creature does not decrease so that God may increase. The glorification of God does not come at the expense of creatures. The more full the creature is with gifts the more the creature should look in gratitude to the fullness of the gift-giver. The fuller the giver the greater the bounty to others" (Kathryn Tanner, *Jesus, Humanity and the Trinity: A Brief Systematic Theology* [Minneapolis: Fortress, 2001], 2–3).

7

Finding Our Voices

The Spirit of Freedom

In *Ion*, inspiration costs the artist his voice. For the postmodern, on the other hand, the artist has no voice to lose. Roland Barthes considers a sentence composed by the French author Balzac and concludes that "no one, no 'person', says it: its source, its voice is not the true place of the writing."[1] Rather than originating from a single authorial voice, a text is a "multi-dimensional space in which a variety of writings, none of them original, blend and clash. The text is a tissue of quotations drawn from the innumerable centres of culture."[2] The author can do no more than "mix writings."[3] Indeed, however much the writer may wish to "express himself," his sense of "self" is an illusion. The meaning the artist wishes to convey, Barthes says, is drawn from "a ready-formed dictionary."[4] He may choose to shift words around this way or that, but he is powerless to offer anything original. "Postmodern artists," a textbook explains, "abandoned the belief in a self, author, and creative genius. The artist is no longer the originary and unique self who produced the new in an

1. Roland Barthes, "The Death of the Author," in *Image-Music-Text*, trans. Stephen Heath (New York: Hill and Wang, 1977), 147.
2. Ibid., 146.
3. Ibid.
4. Ibid.

authentic vision." Rather than giving voice to her own vision, the artist merely "rearranges the debris of the cultural past."[5]

Recall for a moment Catherine Belsey's discussion of author George Eliot. Eliot, Belsey argues, is not to be faulted for the bourgeois ideology of *Adam Bede*. Why not? Because she is not the creator of this ideology, only its unwitting host.[6] We do not create our own language, much less our own voice. We are doomed to inherit our forms of thought and systems of symbols from our culture, and it is these that carry ideology and structures of power, which allow or exclude voices. In the last chapter we asked whether submitting oneself to the Holy Spirit must mean losing one's own voice. According to the postmodern this is a misguided question. There is no self, no "one's own voice." The idea that we could retain or surrender these is an illusion. "For the postmodernist, then, nothing we can do or say is truly 'original', for our thoughts are constructed from our experience of a lifetime of representation, so it is naïve to imagine a work's author inventing its forms or controlling its meaning."[7] Because there is no transcendent source of meaning—whether the Muse or the Holy Spirit—there is no way to rise above and see beyond the network of socially constructed meanings we inhabit. We may sincerely wish to resist oppressive ideologies—as perhaps George Eliot did. We may "make every effort" to keep "the bond of peace" with others (Eph. 4:3 NIV). But we are ourselves bound, incarcerated, in "the prison house of language."[8] Moreover, because our words, thoughts, and images are all inherited from our culture, all that we do is "implicated in the ideologies"[9] of that culture.

Both *Ion* and the postmodern, then, deny individual creativity in any rich sense. For *Ion*, it is not the artist but the Muse who creates. For Barthes as well, the author is not the author of a work, but merely someone who tinkers (a "*bricoleur*," Barthes says) with the meanings already given by language and society. In the last chapter we responded to Ion, whose intellect and voice had been taken from him, with a pneumatology of *gift*. In this chapter we will address the postmodern, locked within the prison house of language, with a pneumatology of *freedom*.

5. Steven Best and Douglas Kellner, *The Postmodern Turn* (New York: Guilford, 1997), 133.

6. Catherine Belsey, *Poststructuralism: A Very Short Introduction* (Oxford: Oxford University Press, 2002), 37.

7. Christopher Reed, "Postmodernism and the Art of Identity," in *Concepts of Modern Art: From Fauvism to Postmodernism*, 3rd ed., ed. Nikos Stangos (London: Thames and Hudson, 1994), 272.

8. Fredric Jameson, *The Prison-House of Language: A Critical Account of Structuralism and Russian Formalism* (Princeton: Princeton University Press, 1972). Jameson cites the following aphorism from Nietzsche as the epigraph to his text: "We have to cease to think if we refuse to do it in the prison-house of language; for we cannot reach further than the doubt which asks whether the limit we see is really a limit."

9. Reed, "Postmodernism," 272.

Sight and Freedom

In much the same way that the Spirit is both Gift and Giver, the Holy Spirit is both *free* and the *bringer of freedom*. The Spirit "blows where it chooses" (John 3:8), and none can chart its course or prevent its going this way or that. At the same time, Paul writes that "where the Spirit of the Lord is there is freedom" (2 Cor. 3:17). And Jesus (quoting Isaiah) says that he is empowered by the Spirit "to proclaim release to the captives and recovery of sight to the blind, to let the oppressed go free" (Luke 4:18). It is a declaration that highlights the important connection between the work of the Spirit and freedom.

Jesus's words underline another important connection, one made in the postmodern critique in fact, that is: the connection between *captivity* and *blindness*. The oppressive ideologies of our society are hidden, encoded, the postmodern complains. We are not free to choose how we think or who we are; instead "the subject [is] only a product of language and thought."[10] The source of our thoughts and actions is hidden from us. Likewise, social ideals such as beauty and justice contribute to our blindness and our captivity. These supposed commitments are in fact only an ornately crafted façade that hides self-interest, power, and privilege. The connection between blindness and captivity is also reflected in Belsey's analysis of *Adam Bede*. George Eliot can describe an eighteenth-century carpenter's shop, thinking that she is merely painting a "realistic" picture of things. She is blind to the oppressive class system she is tacitly endorsing through her narrative. Bach can compose cadences and melodic gestures without hearing the social subtext being sounded out. And this blindness (at least while it remains) means that they are powerless to alter the oppressive ideologies they have received and are passing along.

Where the postmodern advances these claims she does not dispute but rather endorses the judgments of Scripture. The postmodern critique highlights our need for the Spirit's work of liberation. *Yes*, Scripture replies in one of the most regularly repeated formulas in the Bible: *we have eyes but do not see, ears but do not hear*.[11] Isaiah says, "[My servant] sees many things, but does not observe them; his ears are open, but he does not hear. . . . This is a people robbed and plundered, all of them are trapped in holes and hidden in prisons; they have become a prey with no one to rescue" (Isa. 42:20, 22). Those who cannot see truly are trapped and imprisoned.

For her part, Susan McClary holds out the hope that in some instances the artist may rise above his own blindness and act "prophetically." She hopes to

10. Steven Best and Douglas Kellner, *Postmodern Theory: Critical Interrogations* (New York: Guilford, 1991), 22.

11. See, for instance, Ezek. 12:2; Isa. 6:9; 42:19; 43:8; Matt. 13:13–14; Mark 4:12; 8:18; Luke 8:10; John 9:39–41; 12:40; Acts 28:26; and Rom. 11:8.

inspire just this sort of artistry.[12] *Prophetically* certainly is the right word to use here. In the biblical text the prophets are those who expose what is hidden, who see what others are blind to, who recognize corrupt systems of thought and speak out against unjust power. This is how Abraham Heschel describes a prophet. Ordinary men and women have eyes but fail to see. "Our eyes," Heschel writes, "are witness to the callousness and cruelty of man, but our heart tries to obliterate the memories, to calm the nerves, and to silence our conscience."[13] The prophet, however, "is bowed and stunned at man's fierce greed. . . . Prophecy is the voice that God has lent to the silent agony, a voice to the plundered poor, to the profaned riches of the world."[14] Through the prophet the Spirit gives sight to blinded eyes, and through this restored vision the Spirit brings freedom. But—we cannot overlook—all of this is the work of the *Spirit*. The prophet is not simply a perceptive and morally sensitive individual but one who speaks by the Spirit of the Lord. ("We believe in the Holy Spirit," the Nicene Creed declares, "who has spoken through the prophets.") In the ministry of the prophets, we see the work of the Spirit and some of the things most characteristic of the Spirit's liberating work.

The Ministry of Reimagination

First, we see the Spirit bringing freedom by bringing sight. As we've already suggested, this means not just "seeing" but seeing differently. The people already have eyes, but they do not see. What is needed is a radically new perspective on familiar realities, a point of view that reframes existing certainties. This *reseeing* strips away pretense and duplicity; it exposes oppressive institutions, corrupt political ambitions, and manipulative ideologies. And this reseeing is possible because the prophet does not bear his own message but "the word of the Lord"—God's vision of the world. The prophet offers a view starkly at odds with human vision and, through his proclamation, urges people to see again, to see differently, and to see truly.

Richard Bauckham, for instance, describes the prophetic-apocalyptic writing of the book of Revelation. According to Bauckham, John's visions are not intended to portray a *different* world but, rather, *this world*, "see[n] from the heavenly perspective."[15] John's record "enables its readers to see their situation with prophetic insight into God's purpose . . . by disclosing the content of a vision in which John is taken, as it were, out of this world

12. Susan McClary, *Conventional Wisdom: The Content of Musical Form* (Berkeley: University of California Press, 2000), 128.

13. Abraham J. Heschel, *The Prophets* (New York: HarperCollins, 1962), 5.

14. Ibid., 5–6.

15. Richard Bauckham, *The Theology of the Book of Revelation* (Cambridge: Cambridge University Press, 1993), 7.

in order to see it differently."[16] In describing the world according to God's purposes, John "counter[s] the Roman imperial view of the world, which was the dominant ideological perception . . . that John's readers naturally tended to share. Revelation counters that false view of reality by opening the world to divine transcendence."[17] The prophet, speaking by the Spirit, exposes blindness, unveils structures of power and vested interests, and enables his listeners to see outside of and around the pervasive ideologies of their culture. "The task of the prophetic ministry," Walter Brueggemann writes, "is to nurture, nourish, and evoke a consciousness and perception alternative to the consciousness and perception of the dominant culture around us."[18]

So, where the world sees strength and glory in the established structures of power, the prophet speaks of transience and arrogance. In Isaiah 40, for instance, the prophet invites us to reimagine, to resee nations, wealth, rulers, and human strength.

> A voice says, "Call out." Then he answered, "What shall I call out?" All flesh is grass, and all its loveliness is like the flower of the field. The grass withers, the flower fades, when the breath of the LORD blows upon it; surely the people are grass.
>
> Behold, the nations are like a drop from a bucket, and are regarded as a speck of dust on the scales; behold, He lifts up the islands like fine dust. Even Lebanon is not enough to burn, nor its beasts enough for a burnt offering. All the nations are as nothing before Him, they are regarded by Him as less than nothing and meaningless.
>
> It is He who sits above the circle of the earth, and its inhabitants are like grasshoppers, who stretches out the heavens like a curtain and spreads them out like a tent to dwell in. He it is who reduces rulers to nothing, who makes the judges of the earth meaningless.
>
> Isaiah 40:6–7, 15–17, 22–23 NASB

Isaiah looks at the same reality as everyone else, but by the Spirit he is enabled to see it differently, to reimagine it, and so, to see it truly. Similarly, where the world sees only the powerlessness of the disenfranchised, the prophet holds out a vision of promise, God's future dawning on the horizon:

> This is what the LORD of Heaven's Armies says: Once again old men and women will walk Jerusalem's streets with their canes and will sit together in the city squares. And the streets of the city will be filled with boys and girls at play.

16. Ibid., emphasis added.

17. Ibid., 8.

18. Walter Brueggemann, *The Prophetic Imagination*, 2nd ed. (Minneapolis: Fortress, 2001), 3, original in italics.

> This is what the Lord of Heaven's Armies says: *All this may seem impossible to you now*, a small remnant of God's people. But is it impossible for me? says the Lord of Heaven's Armies.
>
> This is what the Lord of Heaven's Armies says: You can be sure that I will rescue my people from the east and from the west. I will bring them home again to live safely in Jerusalem. They will be my people, and I will be faithful and just toward them as their God.
>
> Zechariah 8:4–8 NLT

All this seems impossible to those hearing Zechariah's message, and this is why he brings the message.

Again, where the world perceives only the affluence and influence of those who control the market, the prophet speaks of moral compromise and a prosperity that is both fragile and treacherous.

> Woe to those who are at ease in Zion and to those who feel secure in the mountain of Samaria, the distinguished men of the foremost of nations, to whom the house of Israel comes.
>
> Those who recline on beds of ivory and sprawl on their couches, and eat lambs from the flock and calves from the midst of the stall, who improvise to the sound of the harp, and like David have composed songs for themselves, who drink wine from sacrificial bowls while they anoint themselves with the finest of oils, yet they have not grieved over the ruin of Joseph. Therefore, they will now go into exile at the head of the exiles, and the sprawlers' banqueting will pass away. The Lord God has sworn by Himself, the Lord God of hosts has declared: "I loathe the arrogance of Jacob, and detest his citadels; therefore I will deliver up the city and all it contains."
>
> And it will be, if ten men are left in one house, they will die.
>
> Amos 6:1, 4–9 NASB

The Spirit empowers the prophet to speak precisely in order to free people from the "totalizing" vision of those in authority: priests, kings, judges, and the wealthy, those who define and protect the prevailing reality. The biblical texts recognize the blindness and deception that pervades human society, human language, and human institutions. It is the role of the prophet, speaking by the Spirit, to bring sight to the blind and hearing to the deaf. The Spirit exposes the illusions and pretensions of society and frees us from its deception.

Sovereign Dynamism

The prophetic ministry also highlights the freedom of the Spirit. It is because the Spirit is free that he can bring freedom. The name *ruach/pneuma* draws attention to the freedom and mobility of the Spirit, and in the ministry of the biblical prophets we discover that the Spirit cannot be claimed as the possession of any particular class, office, or nationality. Divine authority does not automatically attend the speech of one political post or social group, nor does the Spirit hover approvingly over a given cultural ideology. The Spirit is free and the Spirit *moves*.

At times, particularly in the early part of Israel's history, the one who speaks by the Spirit is also the *leader* of Israel. So Moses is not only a prophet but also Israel's political and military head. The same could be said of Deborah, for instance, or Samuel. Later in Israel's history, however, the prophet will no longer be Israel's leader but rather (like Samuel later in his career or Nathan) will act as *counselor and advisor to* Israel's leaders. Finally, we encounter prophets, such as Amos and Joel, who will speak *in opposition to* Israel's leaders. So, at various points in history, the one who speaks by God's Spirit stands in the place of power, then stands to assist and correct those in power, and then stands against those in power. Indeed, "the variety of prophetic roles within Israel's culture has complicated attempts to fit the prophets into any category that would limit their activity to one institution, method, or message."[19] The prophets ministered in different regions and social contexts and arose from a variety of different backgrounds. "Some were priests as well as prophets; others appeared before the royal court and gave advice to the king but had no official responsibilities in the temple. A few wrote structured literary pieces in magnificent style while others seemed to behave like madmen."[20]

The biblical narrative, in other words, does not associate the presence and empowerment of the Spirit with any particular class, geographical region, political position, or family lineage. The authority of Spirit-speech is not socially but theologically determined. "A wide range of persons with diverse associations were called prophets because each in some way claimed to be communicating a divine message."[21] Of course, some may falsely claim Spirit authority for their visions, and there may be competing versions of the word of the Lord. Long before Nietzsche would make a similar critique, Scripture draws attention to and exposes the possibility of "the holy lie":

> "For both prophet and priest are polluted; even in My house I have found their wickedness," declares the Lord. "Therefore their way will be like slippery paths to them, they will be driven away into the gloom and fall down in it; for I will bring calamity upon them, the year of their punishment," declares the Lord. . . .
>
> Thus says the Lord of hosts, "Do not listen to the words of the prophets who are prophesying to you. They are leading you into futility; they speak a vision of their own imagination, not from the mouth of the Lord. "They keep

19. G. V. Smith, "Prophet," in *The International Standard Bible Encyclopedia*, vol. 3, *K–P*, rev. ed., ed. Geoffrey W. Bromiley (Grand Rapids: Eerdmans, 1982), 992.

20. Ibid.

21. Ibid., 986.

> saying to those who despise Me, 'The Lord has said, "You will have peace"'; and as for everyone who walks in the stubbornness of his own heart, They say, 'Calamity will not come upon you.'"
>
> Jeremiah 23:16–17 NASB

Not only, in other words, does the prophet critique priest and king. The prophet himself may be subject to critique. The text of Scripture does not award unconditional authority to even the office of prophet, nor to the claim to inspired speech. Neither office ("prophet and priest"), nor institution ("even in My house"), nor the social appeal of their message ("You will have peace") confer authority. The prophet's authority comes from the Spirit, and the Spirit is not limited to any office, class, or social institution. Because the Spirit is not bound to any group, family, or class, the Spirit can and does speak from outside their interests and limited perspective.

They Will All Know Me

Finally, as the preceding discussion suggests, the scriptural texts do not guard the Spirit as the unique and private possession of the prophets. In fact, the hope that one day the Spirit will be poured out on all flesh is embedded in the very message of the prophets.

Since the Enlightenment, a common accusation advanced against Christianity has been that "revelation" (meaning knowledge arising from inspiration) is simply a cynical means of safeguarding clerical power, a velvet rope marking off the territory of the priestly class. It is in the interests of the priests to enforce "mysteries." The priests are charged with administering the secrets of God. Since these secrets are beyond human understanding, any rational challenge can be dismissed. Nietzsche called the claim of inspiration "the holy lie." We should beware, he says, anytime we hear that the priest or the prophet is the mouthpiece of God. "The right to lie and the shrewdness of 'revelation' belong to the priestly type. . . . The 'law,' the 'will of God,' the 'holy book,' and 'inspiration'—All these are just words for the conditions under which priests come to power and maintain their power,—these concepts can be found at the bottom of all priestly organizations, all structures of priestly or philosophical-priestly control."[22] On this account the one who claims to speak by God's Spirit aims to enforce rather than dispel human blindness. The things of God, the prophet insists, cannot be understood by human minds. The simple believer must submissively entrust himself to the prophet, therefore, and to the words delivered from on high.

22. Friedrich Nietzsche, *The Anti-Christ, Ecce Homo, Twilight of the Idols, and Other Writings*, ed. Aaron Ridley and Judith Norman (Cambridge: Cambridge University Press, 2005), 56.

The trajectory of biblical pneumatology moves in the opposite direction, however. We see the desire for the universal giving of the Spirit at the very start of the prophetic tradition, with Moses. When others in the camp of the Hebrews begin to prophesy, Moses's assistant Joshua is scandalized. "A young man ran and told Moses and said, 'Eldad and Medad are prophesying in the camp.' Then Joshua the son of Nun, the attendant of Moses from his youth, said, 'Moses, my lord, restrain them.' But Moses said to him, 'Are you jealous for my sake? Would that all the LORD's people were prophets, that the LORD would put His Spirit upon them!' " (Num. 11:27–29 NASB). Clearly, the story does not hold up exclusivity as the ideal. Instead, it tells us that Moses's hope is for the universal spread of the Spirit. If Nietzsche is right and the biblical text simply serves to underwrite the authority of the priestly class, then the authors of Scripture clearly made a major blunder by placing these words on the lips of Moses, the greatest of all Hebrew prophets, at the very inception of the prophetic tradition.

Later prophets echo Moses's hope through their very prophetic utterances. As they imagine the day of the Lord, they do not speak of the mysteries of God being guarded jealously but rather of a day when "the earth will be full of the knowledge of the LORD as the waters cover the sea" (Isa. 11:9; Hab. 2:14). The eschatological vision of the prophets is not of continued passivity and dependence but of steady growth in understanding, culminating in universal accessibility to the Spirit.

> "But this is the covenant which I will make with the house of Israel after those days," declares the LORD, "I will put My law within them and on their heart I will write it; and I will be their God, and they shall be My people.
>
> "They will not teach again, each man his neighbor and each man his brother, saying, 'Know the LORD,' for they will all know Me, from the least of them to the greatest of them," declares the LORD, "for I will forgive their iniquity, and their sin I will remember no more."
>
> Jeremiah 31:33–34 NASB (Cf. Ezekiel 36; Joel 2)

This language runs counter to the practice of "priestcraft"—in which the clerical class jealously preserves the authority of religious privilege. Here the prophet promises, in effect, the end of the prophet as a distinct class of person. "In those days" the Spirit will be poured out on all flesh, and no one will need priest or prophet to teach him. In fact, Peter believes that this ancient hope has been fulfilled with the events of Pentecost (Acts 2:16–18). The Spirit, Paul insists, is not the unique property of a given race or class: "In the one Spirit we were all baptized into one body—Jews or Greeks, slaves or free—and we were all made to drink of one Spirit" (1 Cor. 12:13). The Spirit who gives sight and freedom unseats powers and authorities by empowering "Jews *and* Greeks, slaves *and* free."

Perhaps all of this is just more cynical maneuvering to conceal the agendas of the biblical writers. If so, they have concealed their agenda remarkably well.

The rhetoric of Old and New Testament emphasizes the work of the Spirit in speaking against powers and authorities, including religious authorities. The Spirit gives us eyes to see and sets us free by exposing the violence and self-interest of society. Scripture likewise draws attention to the sovereign freedom of the Spirit. The Spirit can stand with or stand against prince, priest, or people. No class or ideology can claim the Spirit as its own possession. The Spirit can promise us freedom from the web of social constructs and vested interests, because the Spirit stands outside of and apart from these constructs. Likewise, the hope of the prophets is that the Spirit would be poured out on all flesh—not that they would remain in darkness, but that by the Spirit they would be given eyes to see and ears to hear. The very aspiration of the prophet is for a people who need no prophet to teach them: "It is written in the prophets, 'And they shall all be taught by God' " (John 6:45; cf. Isa. 54:13).

The biblical prophets fully recognize human blindness and injustice. Confronted with this imprisoning ignorance they speak the liberating, sight-giving word of the Spirit.

Back to Eddie Van Halen

We still need to make our way back to the point at which we began our discussion of inspiration, however, back at the beginning of chapter 5. That discussion began, not with a series of theological assertions, but with the artist's experience. In speaking of "inspiration" the artist borrows a theological category to articulate something about how the creative act *feels*. Ang Lee, Mark Doty, Eddie Van Halen, and others all insisted that, the song, poem, or creative idea seems to come *to* them—or even *through* them—rather than *from* them. In some instances, our artists report, the work of art feels as if it has been *discovered* rather than planned and crafted. And at times, they tell us, they produce work that seems to exceed their own understanding. The artist can't really account for how it came to be. *Ion* and the postmodern can each explain this experience. The artist is not the one speaking, playing, writing, or acting. The artist is largely passive and is simply acted on and through by another. The other in the case of *Ion* is the Muse. In the case of the postmodern the other is The Other—whether that be construed as Jameson's prison house, the "Big Other" of Belsey, the "ready-formed dictionary" of Barthes, or McClary's unrecognized repositories of cultural beliefs and ideals.

But while these accounts may offer an explanation of the artist's experience, I have argued that they are sharply at odds with a Christian pneumatology. The work of the Spirit is to restore and complete our humanity. And one dimension of restoring humanity is restoring a human voice with which to speak. Where the Holy Spirit is given, men and women find rather than forfeit their voices. "Christ . . . is in me and is my life, but he remains himself and

I continue to be myself."[23] Where the Spirit of freedom dwells, tongues are loosed. The Holy Spirit's work is to remake us after the likeness of the One who is the *Word of God*. It is not surprising, then, that where the Spirit is, human beings are enabled to speak.

But for all of these theological objections, one of the virtues of *Ion* and the postmodern is that they account for the artist's experience of inspiration—that sense that the creative work is coming from outside oneself. How might a Christian pneumatology—drawing particularly on what we have said about the Spirit in the last two chapters—make sense of the kind of comments we have from Ang Lee and Eddie Van Halen?

Before undertaking an answer, we should point out that a theological account that "makes sense of" creativity is different from a complete description or explanation of artistic creativity. Other kinds of descriptions—psychological, physiological, sociological, and so on—could be offered and would generate a much more complete picture (a "thick description"). What the theologian can say is: here is how the artist's experience fits together with what Christians say about God. He may even say that the things Christians say about God can help us understand the artist's experience more completely; in fact, if what Christians say about God is true, we would expect artists to have just the sort of experience they do.

A Christian Theological Framework for Artistic Inspiration

In the act of creating, the artist *does* encounter a voice outside of herself—many voices in fact. In particular, the artist hears both the voice of creation and the voice of culture. As the artist hears and responds to these voices, she may be said to be (in a qualified but important sense) "inspired"—that is, breathed into by God's Spirit. Nevertheless, even in these moments of inspiration the artist's individuality is not lost; her own voice is not drowned out. And though there are other forces at work in her art, their activity does not make her passive. The artwork equally arises from her own voice (and her own labor). All of this reflects a creation brought into being and governed by the God of gift and the Spirit of freedom. This is the broad framework for understanding artistic creativity that is made available by Christian theology. We can develop this vision in more detail through a reading of Psalm 104.

Psalm 104

Bless the Lord, O my soul!
  O Lord my God, You are very great;
  You are clothed with splendor and majesty,

23. Yves Congar, *I Believe in the Holy Spirit*, vol. 1, *The Holy Spirit in the "Economy": Revelation and the Experience of the Holy Spirit*, trans. Geoffrey Chapman (New York: Crossroads, 2003), 33.

Covering Yourself with light as with a cloak,
  Stretching out heaven like a tent curtain.
He lays the beams of His upper chambers in the waters;
  He makes the clouds His chariot;
  He walks upon the wings of the wind;
He makes the winds His messengers,
  Flaming fire His ministers.
He established the earth upon its foundations,
  So that it will not totter forever and ever.
You covered it with the deep as with a garment;
  The waters were standing above the mountains.
At Your rebuke they fled,
  At the sound of Your thunder they hurried away.
The mountains rose; the valleys sank down
  To the place which You established for them.
You set a boundary that they may not pass over,
  So that they will not return to cover the earth.
He sends forth springs in the valleys;
  They flow between the mountains;
They give drink to every beast of the field;
  The wild donkeys quench their thirst.
Beside them the birds of the heavens dwell;
  They lift up their voices among the branches.
He waters the mountains from His upper chambers;
  The earth is satisfied with the fruit of His works.
He causes the grass to grow for the cattle,
  And vegetation for the labor of man,
  So that he may bring forth food from the earth,
And wine which makes man's heart glad,
  So that he may make his face glisten with oil,
  And food which sustains man's heart.
The trees of the LORD drink their fill,
  The cedars of Lebanon which He planted,
Where the birds build their nests,
  And the stork, whose home is the fir trees.
The high mountains are for the wild goats;
  The cliffs are a refuge for the shephanim.
He made the moon for the seasons;
  The sun knows the place of its setting.
You appoint darkness and it becomes night,
  In which all the beasts of the forest prowl about.
The young lions roar after their prey
  And seek their food from God.
When the sun rises they withdraw
  And lie down in their dens.
Man goes forth to his work
  And to his labor until evening.

O LORD, how many are Your works!
  In wisdom You have made them all;
  The earth is full of Your possessions.
There is the sea, great and broad,
  In which are swarms without number,
  Animals both small and great.
There the ships move along,
  And Leviathan, which You have formed to sport in it.
They all wait for You
  To give them their food in due season.
You give to them, they gather it up;
  You open Your hand, they are satisfied with good.
You hide Your face, they are dismayed;
  You take away their spirit, they expire
  And return to their dust.
You send forth Your Spirit, they are created;
  And You renew the face of the ground.

Psalm 104:1–30 NASB

Psalm 104 describes an entire cosmos that has been "inspired." Indeed, *He makes the winds his messengers*. All of creation speaks as the Spirit of God moves through it. It is also a cosmos that has been "gifted." We observed earlier that God both gives and draws us into the movement of giving. "We were created to be and to act like God," writes Miroslav Volf, "and so the flow of God's gifts shouldn't stop as soon as it reaches us. The outbound movement must continue. Indeed, in addition to making us flourish, giving to others is the very purpose for which God gave us the gifts."[24] This is how God relates to humanity, but in Psalm 104 we can see this cascade of giving flooding every part of the created world—human and nonhuman. God's Spirit renews the face of the earth in an outpouring of gift that literally streams down through all creation.

The most fundamental gift God bestows upon the world is the gift of being: *You send forth Your Spirit, they are created*. Plants and fish and birds and soil—all come into being and are held in being by the breath of God. In addition to the gift of being, he also gives his beings gifts. The psalmist pictures water flowing down from God's "upper chambers" (v. 13), a good gift that blesses all it touches along its course—springs, ravines, donkeys, birds, trees, grass, and cattle. It brings delight at each point along the way: the donkeys *quench their thirst* (v. 11), the birds *sing* (v. 12), the trees drink their *fill* (v. 16), and the earth *is satisfied* (v. 13). These creatures and elements of the creation are not simply "resources" for human consumption. They are good in their own

24. Miroslav Volf, *Free of Charge: Giving and Forgiving in a Culture Stripped of Grace* (Grand Rapids: Zondervan, 2005), 49.

right, and God blesses them with gifts for their own benefit. But if the various parts of creation are good *in themselves*, they are not good *for themselves*. The stream of blessing that began in the heavenly chambers extends all the way to humanity, culminating in good products of human culture: cultivated food (v. 14), wine (v. 15), and oil (v. 15). The created world too is gifted in order to give.

This movement of blessing reflects the noncompetitive theology described in the last chapter. The gifts that arise from the created world (bread, wine, oil) are truly gifts *of God*. The whole psalm is a meditation on how the benevolent provision of God extends through all the earth. And yet, these good things may also be said to be truly the *gifts of the creation*. It is truly the Lord who has planted the cedars of Lebanon (v. 16), and it is truly the cedars of Lebanon that offer a home to the birds (v. 16). Creation is not a mere conduit (*Ion*-like) of blessing; creation enriches and, as it were, adds itself to the gift. Through rain, the tributaries water the fields. Through the watered soil, the plant. Through the plant, the grape, and through the grape, "wine that gladdens the heart of man"—but the wine gladdens one's heart in large part through the subtle notes and flavorings carried up from stream and field and soil.

The world is both offered by God, and it offers itself.[25] A current of gratuity is initiated and sustained by a Giver who desires all of his creation to be drawn into the movement of giving. God's giving—his "inspiration" of the created world—*underwrites* rather than negates the reality of the created world giving itself.

In the same way, God's activity of gift-giving does not preclude human activity and labor. "He causes the grass to grow for the cattle, and vegetation for the labor of man" (v. 14). Bread, wine, and oil are both truly given by God and truly produced by human effort. The young lions "roar after their prey," and yet receive their food from God (v. 21). Looking out over the seas, the psalmist sees not only fish and great sea creatures ("the Leviathan") but

25. John Milbank speaks of the "transcendental 'giving' in all things": "All locutions include an implicit 'there is', so they also include a 'something is given', something has arrived, something has been transferred, if only to me, the speaker: so if I were to say, 'I am looking at the clouds', this assumes that in some fashion the clouds have arrived at me, are there for me, are able to give themselves to me. If things could not give themselves to us, if the manifestation of light were not announced through vision, we should not be able to say that they *were* at all. It follows that it is redundant to assume that things are apart from their capacity to give themselves, or to be involved in some sort of spatial or temporal transference whereby they express themselves in and for something else, the 'recipient'. Not necessarily a conscious recipient, although to be conscious is not only the reflexivity of being—being aware, in *this* being, that there is being—but also the reflexivity of what gives—being aware, as *this* recipient, of the general rule of give and take" ("Can a Gift Be Given? Prolegomena to a Future Trinitarian Metaphysic," *Modern Theology* 11, no. 1 [1995]: 121.) Heidegger suggests that all Being is a giving. Being means "presencing," an "unconcealing," in which Being grants its truth. See Martin Heidegger, "Time and Being," in *On Time and Being*, trans. Joan Stambaugh (New York: Harper & Row, 1972), 5–6.

merchants and fishermen—the ships that move along (vv. 25–26). Here are swarms of fish, great predators of the deep, and fishermen skillfully plying their trade, and yet (in noncompetitive fashion) it is also fair to say that "they all wait for You to give them their food in due season" (v. 27). In the fields and on the seas, the psalmist acknowledges human skill and labor and at the same time traces these good works back to the hand of God. "It must be observed," writes Staniloae, "that no one returns to God things he has received from him without his own work having been added to them. The grapes, the bread, the wine, the oil offered to God are more than just God's gift; human work has also left its stamp upon them." Moreover, he adds, "it is God's wish that the human person spends himself in the effort to place his own valuable stamp upon the gifts received and thereby makes of them human gifts as well."[26]

The cultural activities of harvesting and making food and wine also are good in themselves but, as before, they are not good *for* themselves. They "make glad" and "sustain." So the stream of giving as described in Psalm 104 culminates with humanity, but it does not end upon reaching humanity. Cultural activity is also included in the stream of gift-giving initiated and sustained by the Great Giver. The work of the farmer, miller, and vintner bring gladness and sustenance to many others. Culture and human labor are both gifts received and gifts offered. The picture we are left with is that of a cosmos caught up in the movement of gift, in which all things are blessed and set in motion to bless others. The world the psalmist describes is—at the level of both the cultural environment and the material environment—a world in which all creatures receive from others and then extend themselves out toward others.

How Does All of This Apply to the Creative Experience of the Artist?

The world is "gifted," receiving its being out of the gratuitous kindness of God. And the world is likewise "given": "Then God said, 'Behold, I have given you every plant yielding seed that is on the surface of all the earth, and every tree which has fruit yielding seed; it shall be food for you'" (Gen. 1:29 NASB). The inspired creation becomes the inspiring creation; filled with the breath of God, it offers to others something of the life it has received. We can think of the artist, then, as one who first of all *receives* the gifts of a gifted world—gifts of sound, color, light, shape, and scent. The world offers itself to the artist; more than that, the world *speaks*. The winds, Psalm 104 tells us, are God's *messengers* (v. 4); fire and flame minister on God's behalf (v. 4). We saw that where God's Spirit is given to men and women, speech bursts

26. Dumitru Staniloae, *The Experience of God: Orthodox Dogmatic Theology*, vol. 2, *Creation and Deification*, trans. Ioan Ionita and Robert Barringer (Brookline, MA: Holy Cross Orthodox Press, 2005), 25.

forth—in their own voices. The same is true of the nonhuman creation. "By the word of the LORD the heavens were made, and all their host by the breath [*ruach*] of his mouth" (Ps. 33:6), and so, the heavens and all their host tell out the glory of God and pour forth speech (Ps. 19). A common postmodern trope is that all of reality is constructed by *human* language. But this is to deny the creation its own integrity and *its own* voice. Certainly—as Paul reminds us (Rom. 1:19–23)—it is possible to twist, misinterpret, or ignore the testimony of the created world. But the frailty of our hearing does not negate the reality of nature's voice.

Musicians, writers, and visual artists can all testify to the ways in which the material world *speaks*—the sense that *this* note *wants* to go in *that* direction, that *this* color calls out for *that* color as its neighbor. This is an experience shared by both accomplished and beginning artists. Composer Shulamit Ran describes her creative process as "a search, trying to tune into what needs to happen next, where the music wants to go—as though trying to probe its deep secrets."[27] Because the world has been given by a Giver, because the world offers itself, the artist is right to associate creativity with *receptivity*, with encountering something outside of herself. Artistry involves receiving the gifts that are offered by stone and color, by resonating string and wood, and indeed by our own physical bodies. It is right to say both that the lion receives its food from the hand of God and that it roars after its prey. The lion's meal can be said to be both the gift of God and the outcome of its labors. In the same way it is right to say that the artwork is given by God *and* given by the world *and* given by the artist's own labor and creativity. God's Spirit stands at the head of the cascade of giving that flows through the material world and nourishes the creativity of the artist. And because God gives to make us givers, each participant in the cascade of giving contributes its own voice, its own gifts, to the onward movement.

In addition to the voice of the material world, the artist encounters another distinctive voice outside of herself: the voice of culture. Human artworks, as we have seen, do not emerge fully formed from the earth, untouched by human hands or the marks of culture. This way of thinking about artistry would be markedly out of step with the pneumatology we have been developing. God gives gifts, intending that the recipients will become givers as well—and not just conduits or errand runners but true givers. Those who receive gifts shape and add to them (just as the soil and water contribute their distinctive flavoring to the wine). If this is how God has made humanity—not only to receive, but to give—then we should *expect* the emergence of culture, and the emergence of culture that does not merely reproduce nature but creatively extends and develops it. "He makes grass grow for the cattle, and plants for

27. Quoted in *Women and Music: A History*, 2nd ed., ed. Karin Pendle (Bloomington, IN: Indiana University Press, 2001), 285.

man to *cultivate*." Humanity not only receives gifts but cultivates and "re-presents" these gifts to others. Culture itself and its products are made into a gift that is offered—offered to humanity generally, but also offered to the artist.

For this reason as well, the artist is not mistaken when he experiences creativity as receptivity. Culture, society, its products and practices are among the gifts he receives; they are among the voices he hears as he sets out to create. In the case of culture, of course, not all gifts are benign. Some of what is offered up from the community may be oppressive ideology. If the framework of creation is gift, however, this fact does not in itself rob the artist of his voice. A gift is offered rather than imposed. And to claim that the artist is merely a passive receptacle of culture is to stop the chain of gift. It is to deny that the artist can be a giver as well as a receiver. The "wine that gladdens the hearts of men" is shaped by the labor of the winemaker, the fruit of the vine, the character of the soil, and the waters that flow from the chambers of the heavens. Each adds its note to the bouquet. This is a picture of human activity that acknowledges God, acknowledges the created world, acknowledges culture, and acknowledges the reality of individual creativity.

If the artist *receives* gifts—from others, from God, from the created world—it makes sense that part of her artistic experience would be that of *receptivity*. ("The poem is more something we find than something we make."[28]) At the same time, if God's intention is that we not only receive but become givers ourselves, then it makes sense that *not all* of the artist's experience would be that of receptivity. This fits not only with the theology we have outlined, it also fits well with the creative experience—far better in fact than the account offered by either *Ion* or the postmodern. The idea that George Eliot is not really the author of *Adam Bede* and is not responsible for its content; the suggestion that Ion is nothing but a spirit-possessed madman, acting in a divine trance; the belief that Balzac did not say what Balzac said—all of these fly in the face of our deeply held intuitions about creativity. They are not immediately plausible claims. Our sense is that however profoundly the artist may be shaped by a mysterious inspiration, or by other voices, his own voice remains. Eddie Van Halen may not know where the ideas for his guitar solos come from; he may play them in an ecstasy of blind creativity. But it is still undeniably Eddie Van Halen playing. It is not as if at Tuesday's show he (without knowing how) finds himself playing like the great gypsy guitarist Django Reinhardt; at Wednesday's show he (without knowing how) finds himself playing like jazz guitar great Wes Montgomery; and at Thursday's show he (without knowing how) finds himself playing like classical guitar virtuouso Andres Segovia. Even through the mysterious process of creation, even as he is receptive to melodies and ideas he somehow encounters "outside of himself," we continue to hear Van Halen's own distinctive musical voice. Van Halen is not simply "receiving"

28. Mark Doty, in Laufer and Lewis, *Inspired*, 105.

but giving—contributing something of himself in a way that makes his music distinctively *his*.

Likewise, Ang Lee may sense that all he creates is sent to him "from somewhere." Indeed, in a movie like *Crouching Tiger, Hidden Dragon*—a Chinese-language martial arts movie set in nineteenth-century China—Lee draws deeply from a particular artistic tradition, culture, and aesthetic. Nevertheless, the movie has been critically acclaimed because Lee creatively *transforms* these influences and conventions—drawing these Asian influences into conversation with elements from historical romance, cowboy Westerns, and science-fiction films. Lee "drew many of his influences from Asian cinema," his *Variety* biography tells us, but he also "transcended his Taiwanese heritage to make films in such diverse settings as 19th century England and early-1970s Connecticut."[29] Lee is both shaped by and shapes what he has received from culture. He is both a receiver and a giver. This is what we would expect if we live in a world in which openness to another's voice does not silence one's own. It is what we would expect if we live in a world in which we are gifted in order to become givers.

What seems to be the case is that artistic creation includes both cultural influences and personal expression, that it is both mysterious and a process that includes technique and self-discipline, that sometimes the artist creates in a flash of blinding inspiration and sometimes through countless hours of careful study, practice, and revision. Artistic creation involves both receptivity (to the material world and to cultural practices, for instance) and also personal effort. While receiving the gifts of the material world and the gifts of culture, the artist is no passive recipient. Artistic creation involves hard work. For every song and poem that seems to appear in a blinding flash of inspiration, there are dozens more that are cultivated, nurtured, and constructed over weeks, months, and years. And more often, these two processes go hand in hand. A single work of art may emerge from a process that includes bursts of insight, stretches of long slow slogging, careful thought and planning, and connections made from a deep and seemingly preconceptual intuition. But again, this is what we would expect if the world is neither indifferent toward us, nor imposes itself on us, but offers itself. This is what we would expect if humanity's place in the cosmos is neither that of marionette nor that of sovereign master. Our intuition, in other words, is that the artist inhabits a world of many voices and influences, which shape her profoundly, but to which she may also contribute her own voice. Some of the other voices she encounters are benign; some are malevolent. The presence of other voices does not annihilate her individuality, but instead, through learning and listening to these other voices she discovers her own. Our intuitions about the artistic experience reflect the world described by Christian theology.

29. "Ang Lee: Biography," *Variety.com*. Available at http://movies.yahoo.com/movies/contributor/1800025608/bio.

Creative Inspiration as Indwelling

Over the last three chapters we have worked through a single proposed connection between art and spirituality—that of inspiration. Art is spiritual, *Ion* and his descendents have proposed, because the artist is the spirit's mouthpiece. The artist is the vessel through which the divine speaks into the world. Although I have argued against the way that *Ion* develops this idea, we've reached the place where we can affirm the broad outlines of *Ion*'s connection—at least in a limited and qualified sense. The artist is indeed "inspired"—not in the way that *Ion* conceives inspiration, nor even in the way that Christians speak of Scripture being inspired, but nevertheless, truly inspired in a very important sense. The artist lives in a *world* that is inspired—animated by the breath of God. It is a world in which—*because* they have been given being by the breath of God—materials and cultures *speak*, extending themselves toward others. It is a world in which every good gift comes down from above (James 1:17)—gifts of the material world and of culture. Each truly gives itself, and each is truly given by God, the first giver.

Artistic inspiration is also *Spirit*-ual inasmuch as it echoes the Holy Spirit's work of making us fully human. In an earlier chapter, we saw that to be fully and truly human is to be in relationship with other men and women. In Genesis 1, when human beings are described as God's image bearers, it is in the context of mutual relationship: "So God created humankind in his image, in the image of God he created them; male and female he created them" (Gen. 1:27). This same passage, however, speaks about our relationship to the rest of the created world: "Then God said, 'Let us make humankind in our image, according to our likeness; and let them have dominion over the fish of the sea, and over the birds of the air, and over the cattle, and over all the wild animals of the earth, and over every creeping thing that creeps upon the earth'" (Gen. 1:26). Bearing God's image means to be a part of God's creation and to exercise a role within that creation. In the world God creates, humanity is to be a receiver of gifts: "Out of the ground the LORD God made to grow every tree that is pleasant to the sight and good for food" (Gen. 2:9). Likewise, in God's creation, humanity is to be a giver: "The LORD God took the man and put him in the garden of Eden to till it and keep it" (Gen. 2:15). And when sin enters the creation, it is not only our relationship with one another that is broken but our relationship with the physical environment: "Cursed is the ground because of you; in toil you shall eat of it all the days of your life; thorns and thistles it shall bring forth for you" (Gen. 3:17–18).

Drawing all of this together, we can say that God creates us as human beings to live in right relationship with the rest of the created world. This is part of what it means to be made in the image of God. The Spirit's work of restoring our humanity, then, includes restoring us to right relationship with the physical world. We were made to inhabit God's creation and to be both receivers and givers with respect to the world he has created. So, we fulfill an important dimension of our vocation as human beings when we receive the gifts of creation and culture. We also fulfill an important dimension of our human vocation as we give of ourselves, shaping and adding to the material world and the world of culture. As the artist attends carefully to the gifts of the natural world and the social world, and as he actively responds, returning his own gifts to others, he becomes a participant in the grace-filled cosmos described in Psalm 104; he joins in the great chain of giving set in motion by God.

The trinitarian life of the Spirit also gives us a picture of what it means to "live in right relationship" with others. In chapter 4 we saw that Father, Son, and Spirit live together in an eternal relationship of self-giving love. The three persons of the Trinity remain distinct but mutually indwell one another in a relationship of *perichoresis*. It must be emphasized that this eternal relationship between Father, Son, and Spirit is utterly unique. At the same time, however, the created world testifies to a creator in whom participation and indwelling does not mean a loss of freedom. "We live," says theologian Colin Gunton, "in a perichoretic universe. . . . Everything may be what it is and not another thing, but it is also what it uniquely is by virtue of its relation to everything else."[30]

In a "perichoretic universe" my humanity is completed rather than compromised by other voices. We can acknowledge the "Big Other"—society, culture, beliefs, and practices—without insisting upon the death of the author. In a perichoretic universe, I am "indwelled" and "inhabited" by other voices without forfeiting my own. In a perichoretic universe we can recognize that artistic creativity is *receptive*—an experience of "being indwelt"—without abandoning the idea that it is *creative* as well. Psalm 104 describes just such a world in which all of creation flows out *into* others while receiving others *into itself* in a great movement of gift.

This pattern of both receiving and creating is seen supremely in Jesus, the one in whose image we are remade by the Spirit. Jesus "in the Spirit, fashioned and joined a body to himself, wishing to unite creation to the Father and to offer it to the Father through himself and to reconcile all things in his body."[31] The eternal Word of God unites creation to himself, without ceasing to be the eternal Son of God. He *receives* the created world into himself in the incarnation but is not absorbed by it. Having received humanity into himself, Jesus becomes a *giver*, doing the creative and re-creative work of restoring our humanity.

30. Colin Gunton, *The One, the Three and the Many: God, Creation and the Culture of Modernity* (Cambridge: Cambridge University Press, 1993), 173. In this concluding section I am following the broad lines of Gunton's argument on pp. 163–79.

31. Athanasius, *Letters to Serapion on the Holy Spirit*, 1:31, in Khaled Anatolios, *Athanasius* (New York: Routledge, 2004), 232.

PART 3

A World Remade

8

Seeing the Spirit in All Things, Seeing All Things in the Spirit

Discernment and the Restoration of Vocation

The work of God's Spirit is to restore sight: to allow human beings to see truly, no longer blinded by ideology and priestcraft. The work of the Spirit is to restore speech: to allow human beings to speak truly and creatively, no longer passive conduits for the Muse or the Big Other. The work of the Spirit is to restore freedom: to empower human beings to not only receive creation but also to become givers who add to the world. In this way, in enabling us to see and speak, the Spirit also restores another dimension of our humanity—our vocation. In this chapter I will describe this human vocation as one of *discernment.* I will also describe this work of discernment as including both a *responsive* dimension and a *creative* dimension, corresponding to the capacity for sight, on the one hand, and the capacity for speech, on the other. As human beings we have the high calling of, first of all, *seeing the world truly* and, secondly, *speaking of and for the world—faithfully, creatively, and redemptively.*

We will begin considering this first dimension of discernment—responsive discernment or seeing truly—through a reading of Anne Tyler's lovely novel, *Saint Maybe.*

Things Just Work Out

Tyler's novel introduces us to Ian Bedloe. At seventeen, Ian hasn't had to make many major life decisions, and there don't seem to be any on the horizon either.

Life is laid out pretty neatly for him. His family is "Waverly Street's version of the ideal, apple-pie household: two amiable parents, three good-looking children, a dog, a cat, a scattering of goldfish."[1] Ian himself is "large-boned and handsome and easy-going, quick to make friends, fond of a good time."[2] He is on the baseball team, and his girlfriend is the prettiest girl in the eleventh grade. He's not the most devoted student, but Ian is bright and not worried about getting into a good university. "Things would turn out fine, he felt. Hadn't they always?"[3]

Of course things will turn out fine. Life runs along its own reasonable course, flowing steadily down channels already carved out. Ian is the kind of kid—he knows, his teachers know, we all know—who will go on to college, marry a pretty girl, and get a good-paying job; he's the kind of young man who will settle down in an attractive house in a nice neighborhood and, eventually, raise a family as good-looking, successful, and likable as himself.

Over the next several months, however, a series of tragic episodes (for which Ian feels personally responsible) dissipate the halo of good fortune that had encircled his life. Ian finds himself overwhelmed with guilt and suddenly uncertain of the terrain ahead. How will "things turn out fine" *now*? How does one find the way forward when the next step doesn't just materialize—but must be *chosen*? Walking in the early evening, Ian passes a small storefront church.

> He walked on by. Behind him a hymn began. "Something something something lead us . . ." He missed most of the words, but the voices were strong and joyful.
>
> He paused at the intersection, the arches of his sneakers teetering on the curb. He peered at the DON'T WALK sign for a moment. Then he turned and headed back to the church.[4]

Ian, like a sort of suburban mystic, hears voices and sees a sign—one he obeys: "DON'T WALK."

Led by the voices, Ian turns around and steps through the door of "The Church of the Second Chance"—a small, earnest group meeting in a makeshift sanctuary. It is a decision that turns Ian around in a much more far-reaching sense. He embraces Christianity and joins the Church of the Second Chance. He quits college, takes a job as a carpenter, and (as a kind of penance for his guilt) assumes the care of three orphaned children.

What has happened? *Did* Ian see a message from God on that street corner? *Did* he hear the Spirit's voice in the congregation's singing?

Ian's parents are puzzled and concerned by his newfound faith. They are Christians as well but in an altogether reasonable and occasional sort of way. The family makes sporadic forays into God's territory ("Dober Street

1. Anne Tyler, *Saint Maybe* (London: Vintage, 1992), 4.
2. Ibid.
3. Ibid., 5.
4. Ibid., 115.

Presbyterian")—for holidays, weddings, and funerals. But when it comes to their own territory—that is, the ordinary business of daily life and relationships and career—God is, well . . . not so much "unwelcome" as "unexpected." *Things just work out*, after all; or (as Ian discovered) *things just don't work out*. But in either case, events follow their own reasonable and orderly courses. Do your work; get good grades; get into a good university. "Of course we have nothing against religion," Ian's mother insists, "we raised all of you children to be Christians. But *our* church never asked us to abandon our entire way of life."[5] The Bedloes have achieved a sedentary satisfaction with the austere, transcendent deity of their local church. Ian, however, has suddenly embraced a God who is disconcertingly near and active enough to be disruptive. Ian's church believes in a God who *speaks*, not just to saints once a millennium but to school teachers and bus drivers in the course of their everyday routines, not just from mountaintops but through songs and street signs.

On an evening some months later, Ian and his parents are joined for dinner by a woman from the Church of the Second Chance. Sister Harriet is a former school teacher and—like many of those in Ian's new congregation—good-hearted, devout, and slightly odd. "One night I dreamed this dream," Sister Harriet tells Ian and the rest of the family.

> I dreamed I was standing in front of my class explaining conjunctions, but gibberish kept coming out of my mouth. . . . In the dream I couldn't think what had happened, but when I woke up I knew right away. You see, the Lord was trying to tell me something. "Harriet," He was saying, "you don't speak these children's language. You ought to get out of teaching." And so I did.[6]

There is an awkward silence around the dinner table. Ian's parents are stunned, but Ian smiles at Sister Harriet. "I think that was really brave of you," he replies, "to admit the whole course of your life was wrong and decide to change it completely." And he goes on:

> "I wonder," Ian said, "how many times we dream that kind of dream—something strange and illogical—and fail to realize God is trying to tell us something. . . . It's easier to claim it's something else," Ian said. "Our subconscious, or random brain waves. It's easier to pretend we don't know what God's showing us."
>
> "That is so true, so true," Sister Harriet told him.[7]

"*Something, something, something lead us*. . . ." Ian couldn't quite make out the words of the hymn coming from the church that night.[8] Certainly,

5. Ibid., 127.

6. Ibid., 239.

7. Ibid., 239–40.

8. When he walks through the doors of the church a moment later, the congregation is singing "Blessed Jesus! Blessed Jesus!" (ibid., 116), which suggests that the indistinct words Ian

we live in a world full of messages, a globe vibrating with voices. No doubt "something" leads us—our feelings, a good argument, "our subconscious, or random brain waves." But God? By God's Spirit? Should God be included in the class of things that "lead us"? And if we answer in the affirmative, how do we know which "something" is leading us at any particular moment? For Ian's parents, the answer to all these questions is pretty straightforward. The ordinary stuff of the world should be understood to be just that: the ordinary stuff of the world. A feeling is a feeling and not the call of God. A dream is a dream and not a divine prompt to change careers. And a (street) sign is just a sign and not "A *Sign.*"If God actually were to lead us, it would be something big, something obvious, something manifestly "miraculous" (a problematic term). For Ian and Sister Harriet, however, the answer is much more complex. For the members of the Church of the Second Chance a sign may very well be "A Sign."

Responsive Discernment: Discerning the Spirit in All Things

It is easy, in fact, to move through life with little sense that there is anything to be discerned. Like Ian at the beginning of Tyler's novel, many of us simply assume that things will unfold according to their own internal logic—if you're from this family and born with that set of abilities, if you do this and follow through on that, then you'll end up here and do thus and such. Really, there doesn't seem to be that much to be discerned. In the modern West at least, our "default" is generally set for God's absence and noninvolvement—an attitude embodied by Mr. and Mrs. Bedloe. Painting in very broad strokes, we might characterize the Bedloes' personal theology as "functional Deism." A Deist "affirms a divine creator but denies any divine revelation."[9] Similarly, the Bedloes have no problem with belief in God *per se*. Mrs. Bedloe reminds Ian that she has "raised all of you children to be Christians." But she and her husband are dubious—embarrassed, really—by Ian and Sister Harriet's suggestions that God directs and speaks to them. Humanity may very well speak of God, but God does not speak to humanity—at least not that often or in such informal settings.

If our starting assumption is the principle of Enlightenment secularism—*all events shall be presumed God-forsaken unless otherwise proven blessed*—then "discernment" primarily will mean "remaining wary," "staying on one's guard," or even "skepticism." Discernment in this case is cocking one eyebrow at the audacious claim that God is at work. But if the paradigm instance of God's

---

couldn't quite make out were the opening lines of "Savior, Like a Shepherd Lead Us" (hymn lyrics by Dorothy A. Thrupp, 1836).

9. William L. Rowe, "Deism," in *Concise Routledge Encyclopedia of Philosophy* (London: Routledge, 2000), 198.

Spirit at work is Jesus Christ, then this way of thinking about discernment is clearly inadequate. At the heart of New Testament faith is the conviction that God is not only intimately involved in human history; in Jesus, he has actually taken the human condition to himself. In Jesus Christ,

> the incorporeal and incorruptible and immaterial Word of God entered our world. In one sense, indeed, He was not far from it before, for no part of creation had ever been without Him Who, while ever abiding in union with the Father, yet fills all things that are. But now he entered the world in a new way, stooping to our level in His love and Self-revealing to us. . . .
>
> He took to Himself a body, a human body even as our own. Nor did he will merely to become embodied or merely to appear. . . . No, He took *our* body.[10]

No part of creation is without God's presence, Athanasius observes. But in Jesus Christ, God is more than "present" to his creation; here he takes the stuff of creation into his own being, making a human life his own.

And this has serious implications for Ian's traffic signals and Sister Harriet's dream. Sometimes people talk about God speaking to them right in the midst of what they're doing or about God being at work in the ordinary details of their lives. Our culture tends to regard this sort of talk as silly at best and pathological at worst. That's understandable; this sort of claim can be and often is abused. Nevertheless, it is the claim at the center of the Christian faith: in Jesus Christ, God has spoken a word in the midst of human history. In Jesus Christ, God has taken up residence in the midst of ordinary human lives. What is more, Jesus Christ is not (at least in this regard) a "special case"—as if in this one instance God has agreed to violate divine policy and get involved in the ordinary business of the world. Jesus is not the exception but the rule of true humanity. In him we see what God has always intended for us. Humanity was made to be the dwelling place of the Creator; we were shaped in such a way as to be filled by the breath of God.

So—in a world that God has by his Spirit taken to himself in the most intimate way possible, discernment will have as much to do with saying yes as with saying no. The discerning person will not only be judicious but receptive; she will avoid gullibility, yes, but nurture availability. In fact, the most explicit New Testament reference associates spiritual discernment with recognizing what *is* of the Spirit, rather than rejecting what is not: "The man without the Spirit does not accept the things that come from the Spirit of God, for they are foolishness to him, and he cannot understand them, because they are spiritually discerned" (1 Cor. 2:14 NIV).

The first task of discernment, then, is not a closing off but an opening up, what we might call *responsive discernment*. If God's Spirit is present and

10. Athanasius, *On the Incarnation*, trans. and ed. by A Religious of C. S. M. V. (Crestwood, NY: St. Vladimir's Seminary Press, 2003), 33–34.

working in the world, we should live expectantly, looking attentively for the Spirit's activity, listening carefully for the Spirit's voice. Jürgen Moltmann observes that because God's Spirit fills creation "it is . . . possible to experience God *in, with and beneath* each everyday experience of the world."[11] If this is the true shape of the world, then discernment is not a matter of divining those rare instances when God shows up. Instead, it means learning to recognize, as Moltmann writes, "that in everything God is waiting for us."[12] "Spirituality" on this account will not mean turning away from the world (as if this world were "God-forsaken") but turning toward it, with Spirit-renewed vision.[13] Where a narrow scientism sees only "an insignificant planet lost in the great cosmic immensity,"[14] the presence and activity of God's Spirit authorizes us to see the same body as "my Father's world"—

> And to my listening ears
> All nature sings and round me rings
> The music of the spheres. . . .
>
> This is my Father's world.
> He shines in all that's fair.
> In the rustling grass, I hear him pass
> He speaks to me everywhere.[15]

Discernment, then, presumes awareness, sensitivity, and openness—a willingness to "see more" and "look deeper," to "see God in all things."[16]

This, by the way, is another point at which some have suggested a correspondence between spirituality and the arts. Someone who is sensitive, intuitive, creatively perceptive, someone who sees things differently—doesn't this describe the artist as much as the spiritually discerning? Perhaps the arts are "spiritual" because the artist and the mystic alike are open to a larger reality. Each recognize

11. Jürgen Moltmann, *The Spirit of Life: A Universal Affirmation*, trans. Margaret Kohl (Minneapolis: Fortress, 1992), 34.

12. Ibid., 36.

13. For this point see ibid., chapter 4, and Jürgen Moltmann, *God in Creation: An Ecological Doctrine of Creation* (London: SCM, 1985), chapter 3.

14. Jacques Monod, quoted in John C. Eccles, *The Human Psyche: The Gifford Lectures, 1978–1979* (London: Routledge, 1980), 251.

15. "This Is My Father's World," hymn lyric by Maltbie D. Babcock, 1901.

16. John V. Taylor asserts that "the first essential activity of the Spirit is *annunciation*" (*The Go-Between God: The Holy Spirit and the Christian Mission* [London: SCM, 1972], 18, emphasis added). The Spirit opens our eyes and calls us to attend to the world and to one another. So for Taylor as for Moltmann, "discernment" begins with a greater openness to God's presence in the midst of the ordinary: "The Spirit of God is that power of communion which enables every other reality, and the God who is within and behind all realities, to be present to us. . . . All faith in God is basically a way of 'seeing the ordinary' in light of certain moments of disclosure which have been the gift of the Holy Spirit" (ibid., 19, 20).

that there is more to be seen, that all the truth of the world may not be recognized at first glance. Perhaps both the artist and the spiritual person are allied in testifying to a world filled with signs, filled with *sign*-ificance.

The Artist and "God-in-All-Things"

One person who suggested this correspondence is the British art critic Clive Bell (1881–1964). Bell was an early advocate of postimpressionist artists such as Cézanne, Gauguin, and Matisse and wrote several influential works on aesthetics. His treatise, *Art* (1914), would become one of the foundational texts of the position known as "formalism."[17] In Bell we discover another figure from the world of the arts, who—like Coltrane, Kandinsky, and Ang Lee—appeals to the language of spirituality in order to make sense of his artistic experience.

The art world of the late nineteenth and early twentieth centuries was a time of enormous change and transition. Radically new styles and approaches to visual art emerged, each gaining both admirers and antagonists. As a critic operating in this environment, Bell set out to clarify how one determines what is and what is not a work of art. In *Art* he ventures to "put forward a hypothesis by reference to which the respectability, though not the validity, of all aesthetic judgments can be tested."[18] And the starting point for this theory of art, he argues, "must be the personal experience of a peculiar emotion. The objects that provoke this emotion we call works of art. All sensitive people agree that there is a peculiar emotion provoked by works of art."[19]

So true works of art arouse a distinctive response (at least within "sensitive people"), a response that Bell characterizes as the "aesthetic emotion."[20] But *how* do works of art achieve this? Consider the wildly diverse range of works that move us—paintings of different periods and styles, works from different media, sculptures, works of architecture, and so forth. What could be common to all of these different works that allows us to characterize all of them as "art"? "What quality is shared by all objects that provoke our aesthetic emotions? What quality is common to Sta. Sophia and the windows at Chartres, Mexican sculpture, a Persian bowl, Chinese carpets, Giotto's frescoes at Padua, and the masterpieces of Poussin, Piero della Francesca, and Cézanne?"[21]

Bell rules out several possibilities. It is not representational accuracy that makes something a work of art; a painting is not a great painting simply

17. See Noël Carroll, "Formalism," in *The Routledge Companion to Aesthetics*, ed. Berys Gaut and Dominic McIver Lopes (New York: Routledge, 2001), 87–96.

18. Clive Bell, *Art* (n.p.: BiblioBazaar, 2007), 7.

19. Ibid., 16.

20. Ibid., 17.

21. Ibid.

because it "looks like" what it depicts. Nor do we call something a great work of art simply because its subject matter moves us. A painting may record a very touching scene of a mother embracing her child. The tenderness of the scene may bring a lump to one's throat, but this, Bell says, is something different than the "aesthetic emotion." The lump in the viewer's throat is irrelevant to the painting's status as a work of art. No, what arouses aesthetic emotion, and what all great works of art share in common, is "significant form." Precisely what Bell means by "significant form" is never entirely clear (and this remains one of the most important criticisms of his theory). He approaches an explanation of the concept, however, when he ventures beyond the language of art criticism and into the realm of theology (or "metaphysics," as he describes it).

> Now the emotion that artists express comes to some of them, so they tell us, from the apprehension of the formal significance of material things; and the formal significance of any material thing is the significance of that thing considered as an end in itself. But if an object considered as an end in itself moves us more profoundly (*i.e.* has greater significance) than the same object considered as a means to practical ends or as a thing related to human interests—and this undoubtedly is the case—we can only suppose that when we consider anything as an end in itself we become aware of that in it which is of greater moment than any qualities it may have acquired from keeping company with human beings. Instead of recognising its accidental and conditioned importance, we become aware of *its essential reality*, of *the God in everything*, of the *universal in the particular*, of the all-pervading rhythm. Call it by what name you will, the thing that I am talking about is that which lies behind the appearance of all things—that which gives to all things their individual significance, the thing in itself, *the ultimate reality*.[22]

Ordinary people like you and me look at the things in the world around us and see objects that we may use or information we may gather. The artist, on the other hand—at least in moments of inspiration—is able to see her surroundings as "pure form," not as means to an end but as ends in themselves. I look at a tree and think "tree." But the artist, Bell says, looks at it and really *sees it*, sees "its essential reality."[23] He writes, "The habit of recognising the label and overlooking the thing"—in other words, the habit of, like me, glancing at this extraordinary array of browns and greens in front of me and simply thinking "tree"—this, Bell claims, "accounts for the amazing blindness, or rather visual shallowness, of most civilised adults. . . . The habit of using the eyes exclusively to pick up facts is the barrier that stands between most

22. Ibid., 47, emphasis added.

23. "Who has not, once at least in his life, had a sudden vision of landscape as pure form? For once, instead of seeing it as fields and cottages, he has felt it as lines and colours. In that moment has he not won from material beauty a thrill indistinguishable from that which art gives?" (ibid., 39).

people and an understanding of visual art."[24] The great capacity of the artist is the ability to recognize the *significance* of "ordinary things," to perceive the universal in the particular, the God-in-all-things. The artist is able to perceive ultimate reality shining through the veil of material form and gives this perception expression in his art.

It is not too much, then, to say that for Bell, the great gift of the artist is the gift of discernment. And since the reality being discerned is ultimate reality (or God), the true artist is the virtuoso of *spiritual* discernment. Bell believes that more or less the same thing is going on in both true art and true spirituality. He writes that "the mystic [like the artist] feels things as 'ends' instead of seeing them as 'means.' He seeks within all things that ultimate reality which provokes emotional exaltation."[25] Just as the artist gives artistic form to "God in all things," so the truly spiritual person perceives some unnameable reality sustaining all things and attempts to give form to this experience of spiritual ecstasy in some system of religious belief (such as Christianity or Buddhism or Islam). "Art," Bell writes, "is a manifestation of the religious sense."

> If it be an expression of emotion—as I am persuaded that it is—it is an expression of that emotion which is the vital force in every religion, or, at any rate, it expresses an emotion felt for that which is the essence of all. We may say that both art and religion are manifestations of man's religious sense, if by "man's religious sense" we mean his sense of ultimate reality. What we may not say is, that art is the expression of any particular religion; for to do so is to confuse the religious spirit with the channels in which it has been made to flow. It is to confuse the wine with the bottle. Art may have much to do with that universal emotion that has found a corrupt and stuttering expression in a thousand different creeds.[26]

For this reason, Bell judges that "art and religion belong to the same world."[27] In fact, he makes the even stronger claim that "rightly . . . do we regard art and religion as *twin manifestations* of the spirit."[28] The artist, like the truly spiritual person, is able to discern the infinite and transcendent dimension of reality—"the God in all things."[29]

24. Ibid., 55.
25. Ibid., 56.
26. Ibid., 62.
27. Ibid., 56.
28. Ibid., emphasis added.
29. Those who recall our discussion in chapter 1 may recognize a broad resemblance here to the theology of Friedrich Schleiermacher, the great forerunner of nineteenth-century theological liberalism. Schleiermacher, like Bell, will propose a connection between artistry and spirituality. In *On Religion* he makes the striking claim that "poets and seers . . . orators and artists are true priests of the Most High, for they bring deity closer *to those who normally grasp only the finite and the trivial*" (Friedrich Schleiermacher, *On Religion: Speeches to Its Cultured Despisers*, trans. Richard Crouter [Cambridge: Cambridge University Press, 1996], 7, emphasis added). Most of our time is spent on petty and mundane business, but the artist strives "to awaken

When "Intimacy" Becomes "Identity"

Bell's vision certainly is more attractive than the distant and disinterested God of popular deism. His theory of art and his theology insist that God is not far from any one of us. The world is not an alien realm to God but is filled with his presence. The artist and musician, Bell believes, train our eyes and ears to be more attentive. They teach us that the physical world is pregnant with significance and that the ordinary events of sight and sound are portals through which transcendence may at any moment come streaming in. All of this is true and enormously important. Our first word when speaking about discernment is yes, rather than no. "Discerning the Spirit in all things," then, might be a good way of describing an attentive and receptive attitude toward God. There are dangers, however, in making this the only phrase on our lips when we undertake the task of discernment.

Bell so fully affirms God's presence in creation that the two risk being absorbed into one another. On the one hand, the world is robbed of its own voice and distinct integrity. All that is meaningful, significant, and beautiful in the world is immediately promoted to the status of "God." "What lies behind the appearance of all things—that which gives to all things their individual significance . . . [is] ultimate reality."[30]

The actual stuff of the material world, then, is reduced to a thin husk sheltering the presence of God. Ironically, Bell's thesis—which urges us to attend to the world carefully—ends up being a denial of the world. The significance of "the thing in itself" turns out to be *not* the thing itself but the "ultimate reality" lurking within.

On the other hand, God risks being absorbed into the world, becoming simply something like the life force—the electric current on which the universe runs. It is significant that Bell tends toward impersonal terms for God: God is "the ultimate reality," "the all-pervading rhythm," and "that which" (*not* the One Who) "lies behind the appearance of all things."[31] In this kind of religious scheme there might be the possibility of (some variety of) mystical union between humanity and the ultimate reality, but there is little hope of relationship, exchange, and love. And again, this leads us to an irony: in the popular deism of Mr. and Mrs. Bedloe no personal relationship is possible between God and the created order because the distance between the two is so

---

the slumbering seed of a better humanity" (ibid.). As the priest of a true spirituality, the artist "proclaims *the inner meaning* of all spiritual secrets and speaks down from the kingdom of God; this is the source of all visions and prophecies, of all holy works of art and inspired speeches that are scattered abroad" (ibid., 7–8, emphasis added). Schleiermacher, his translator observes, believes that there is "a special affinity between an artistic sensibility and the conditions that make the human soul receptive to religion" (Richard Crouter, "Introduction," in ibid., xxxiv).

30. Bell, *Art*, 47.

31. Ibid.

great. In the religious system of Clive Bell no personal relationship is possible between God and the created order because the distance between the two has been eliminated. Intimacy slides into identity and eliminates the possibility of true intimacy.

God's Spirit is at work in all of creation, in our midst—indeed, as Christians testify, at work in us. The first thing to be discerned is that there is something, someone to be discerned. On the other hand, God's immediacy should not be confused with identity. God may be in all of creation, but "all of creation" is not God. Like a wise and loving parent with her children, God loves his creation enough to allow it to be genuinely *other* than himself. God has created a world in which his creatures speak and speak with their own voices. And while some of what God's creatures say in their own voices is true, some of what is said is not.

Narrative Discernment: Not Losing the Plot

Can we say anything more, then, about seeing truly? Can we offer any advice to Ian Bedloe as the singing voices summon him, his tennis shoes rocking back and forth on the curb? Reverend Emmett, who leads the Church of the Second Chance, confides to Ian at one point in the novel about the many times he has *mis*-read the signs, *mis*-heard God's voice.[32] How can we train our eyes to more readily see whether—in a very specific situation—the Spirit is at work *here* or *there*, leading *this way* or *that*?

One part of the answer is to recapitulate all that we have said in this book so far. The Spirit is above all at work in Jesus—the anointed one, the bearer of the Spirit, the giver of the Spirit. Moreover, the Spirit's work is to make us truly and fully human, refashioning us after the pattern of the perfect humanity of Jesus Christ. The direction in which the Spirit is moving is Jesus. Spirits, John advises the church, are to be tested by their identification with the Spirit-anointed life and work of Jesus. "Beloved, do not believe every spirit, but test the spirits to see whether they are from God; for many false prophets have gone out into the world. By this you know the Spirit of God: every spirit that confesses that Jesus Christ has come in the flesh is from God, and every spirit that does not confess Jesus is not from God. And this is the spirit of the antichrist, of which you have heard that it is coming; and now it is already in the world" (1 John 4:1–3). We know who we are and who we are to be by looking at the incarnate Christ. This has some very practical implications.

Discernment in Light of a Restored Humanity

First, we saw that Jesus, the one upon whom the Spirit rests, is the Word and Wisdom of God. The work of the Spirit, then, is not limited to the realm of

32. Tyler, *Saint Maybe*, 259–60.

"mystery." The Holy Spirit is the Spirit of wisdom and the Spirit of revelation. Conversely, as we saw in chapter 3, the Holy Spirit is the incarnating Spirit and the guarantee of the resurrection of our *bodies*. This suggests that in looking for the leading of the Spirit we are justified in attending to our *whole* humanity. Not only our reason but also our feelings, intuitions, emotions, and physical responses matter. They are not any less a part of our humanity, nor are they any less a concern of the re-creating Spirit. Similarly, the Spirit of wisdom also speaks to the reason. Discerning the leading of the Spirit will not mean ignoring our emotions and physical responses, nor, on the other hand, will it mean ignoring reason and argument in order to wait for an intuited "leading of the Spirit."

In addition to this, we saw that our humanity is not only individual but corporate. We are who we are in the company of others. The body of Christ—in whose image we are remade—is the church, and the presence of the Holy Spirit is made powerfully manifest in the gathering together of God's people. This suggests that one way of discerning the leading of the Spirit is by living among, spending time with, and learning from the community of God's people. Moreover we saw that the eternal plan and purpose of God was to bring about a differentiated community—a community of Jew and Greek, male and female, slave and free. It is this sort of community that Paul commands to sing to one another "in psalms, hymns, and spiritual songs"; it is this sort of community that is the renewed image of God in the world. If our churches have often done a poor job at discernment, perhaps it is in part because they resemble only the unity, and not the diversity, of our triune God.

In chapters 5, 6, and 7, we saw that God speaks in creation, and so, we should *listen*. We should live our lives like people who serve a speaking God. When seeking discernment we should be quiet and expectant in God's presence. And we should attend to the word already spoken by the Spirit. This will mean preeminently looking to Jesus Christ—the living Word of God—and the Scriptures—the written Word of God. At the same time we determined that the Spirit restores rather than robs us of our own voices. God invites us not only to listen but to say something. This means that—after we have prayed and listened, after we have looked to the community, to Jesus, and to the Scriptures—we can act, and act confidently. God's good pleasure is to give us agency in the world. He invites us not only to listen, but to speak and to act.

The Spirit on the Move

Spirit-ual discernment will mean looking to what we see in Jesus, the bearer of the Spirit. But in addition to reiterating these points, we might return to Tyler's novel and think about discernment in the context of our experience as readers. *Saint Maybe* follows Ian Bedloe from the time he is seventeen until he is in his forties. How do we recognize this one character as the same person through the whole story? We couldn't appeal to some simple visual identification ("he looks like *this*"), because over the course of more than two decades, his appearance changes. We couldn't apply some specific situational criteria either ("he's a college student") because again, Ian's situation changes. In fact, his story *is* the story of these and other changes—changes in his appearance, his outlook, his relationships, and so on. It is an understanding of these very developments, adjustments, and transformations that gives us a deep sense of *who* Ian is. Knowing Ian is not a matter of being able to give an exhaustive description of him at some particular point in time. (In fact, this might be misleading. Imagine, for instance, if after Ian's dramatic conversion we were to try to relate to him based on a thorough understanding of his values and perspective prior to his conversion.) We know who Ian is by following his story. Ian Bedloe is the person who has followed this path, who has lived this narrative, who has inhabited this history and experienced these events. And as we follow that narrative, we come to know what we can or cannot expect of him. We are able to recognize what sorts of things are literally "in character" or "out of character" for him. As we become familiar with the path a person has traveled, we see patterns emerge, and we come to know the way that person thinks, speaks, and acts.

In addition to this, a novel allows us to make sense of a character not only with reference to his past but also with reference to his future. We only know whether the story is a happy one or a sad one when we've seen how it ends. The final chapter determines, to a large extent, whether the main character is seen as tragic or heroic, noble or wicked. Of course, when we're reading, we don't get to the end until the end. Nevertheless, once we reach the end, the ending casts its shadow back across all the pages that went before. It is, to a large extent, the ending that determines the meaning, the import, the significance of the earlier events. If the ending of the novel is uplifting and hopeful, then there may be a sense that some of the tragic events from earlier in the story have been redeemed. The wicked events that came earlier are, then, literally, not the last word. Depending upon the story, they may even come to be seen as necessary for the accomplishment of some greater good. Or, conversely, the story may end with a sudden cynical or tragic twist. And in this instance, again, the ending defines the meaning of what has gone before. Suddenly, all the pleasant events, sacrificial acts, and noble intentions of the early chapters seem hollow, meaningless, or even ironic.

In certain spy novels or suspense thrillers the end of the story may reveal that the main character is not the person we thought she was all along. This final revelation sends shock waves reverberating back through all the earlier events. We mentally revisit the events and the words of the previous chapters and see them now in a new and different light.[33]

33. One novel that uses this device to powerful effect is William Golding's *Pincher Martin* (London: Faber and Faber, 1956).

We get to know the characters of a novel, in other words, not by a static examination of their attributes but by "following" their story. We see where they are, where they have come from, and where they are going. And while we see this point with particular clarity in novels, it is also borne out in our own self-understanding. How do we know our own identity or that of others around us? Paul Ricoeur speaks of "narrative identity."[34] "A character," he writes, "is the one who performs the action in the narrative."[35] So, I understand who I am by recounting a particular story to myself—a history that gathers together and plots all the disparate events of my experience. To be me means to have grown up in *that* house, to have been raised by *these* parents, and have had *those* friends; it is to have gone to the schools and had the experiences and successes and disappointments that I have had.

In this light we might also consider the way that God identifies himself throughout the Old Testament. Over and over again, God identifies *who He is* by appealing to *what He has done*. So, for instance, the Ten Commandments begin: "I am the Lord your God, who brought you out of Egypt, out of the land of slavery. You shall have no other gods before me" (Exod. 20:2–3 NIV). This phrase "I am the Lord your God, who brought you out of Egypt" (or something very much like it) occurs nearly sixty times in the Old Testament, in eighteen different books. God announces his identity to Israel by recounting a particular narrative—the history of his saving activity.

This idea of narrative, of knowing a character through the trajectory of her story, is particularly helpful when we begin to think about discerning the Spirit. It is significant that the language used in ordinary conversation about discernment is often the language of movement, travel, and journey. We wonder *which way* the Spirit is *leading*; we ask for *guidance* and look for *direction* so that we know which *path to take* and don't get *off course*. This language is entirely appropriate when speaking about the Spirit whose name means "breath" and "wind." If "the wind blows where it chooses" (John 3:8), then there will be a dynamism to discerning the Spirit; we are looking not for a location or (simply) a static list of identifying characteristics but for a trajectory, a direction of movement.

Jürgen Moltmann describes the "experience of the Spirit" as an event that occurs "between remembered past and expected future."[36] We meet the Spirit, he writes, "when Christ is present and when the new creation of all things is anticipated."[37]

So, there is "remembered past." In discerning the Spirit, we look at the shape of creation in the beginning. We consider God's original intentions

34. See, in particular, Paul Ricoeur, *Oneself as Another*, trans. Kathleen Blamey (Chicago: University of Chicago Press, 1992), 140–63.

35. Ibid., 143.

36. Moltmann, *Spirit of Life*, 17.

37. Ibid.

for humanity. We look also at how God has acted to love, correct, and save his people throughout the Old and New Testament. Then, in addition to "remembered past," Moltmann says, we locate the Spirit with reference to "expected future." The Holy Spirit (we have been saying throughout these chapters) is at work bringing things to completion, working the renewal and re-creation of our humanity and of all God's broken creation. This means that the present work of the Spirit is on the way to the new creation God has promised.

In between these two points, and wholly determining the arc of the trajectory connecting them, is Jesus Christ, the bearer and bestower of the Spirit. We find the Spirit not just between remembered past and expected future but "when Christ is present."

So, then, there is an essentially dynamic character to spiritual discernment. We do not discern the Spirit by running down an inspector's checklist of principles and criteria. Rather, we locate ourselves and our situation within a trajectory that originates in Eden and culminates in the new Jerusalem, and which is oriented decisively by passing through the cross. Since I do not live in Eden nor in the new Jerusalem (and since, needless to say, I am not Jesus Christ), discerning the Spirit's leading means something other than listing out what the garden was like, what the new creation will be like, or the things that Jesus did. Instead, the path of the Spirit is the trajectory between these. We come to know the Spirit's leading by immersing ourselves in his narrative, becoming familiar with his ways and words among his people. We then begin to discern a pattern, to know what sorts of things are "in character" or "out of character." And as we become familiar with this pattern and this path we learn, as Paul says, to "keep in step with the Spirit" (Gal. 5:25 NIV).

Creative Discernment: Discerning All Things in the Spirit

Discernment, we have said, includes responsiveness—seeing where God's spirit is at work and so seeing the world truly. We also began by saying that discernment is a *creative* act. We do not just passively hear and obey. In addition to "discerning the Spirit in all things," humanity has been entrusted with the creative task of *discerning all things in the Spirit*. The Spirit empowers and commissions us to resee and rename, to perceive the same reality differently, and so, to discern things not "after the flesh" but with eyes given by the Spirit.

Discernment and Naming

One of the clearest examples of this kind of creative discernment is found in the creation story of Genesis 2. There we read that "no plant of the field was yet in the earth and no herb of the field had yet sprung up—for . . . there was no one to till the ground" (v. 5); so "the Lord God took the man and put him in the garden of Eden to till it and keep it" (v. 15). Significantly, God charges Adam with the task of adding something to the world—bringing about something that wasn't there before. The human contribution to the created world is made even more strikingly apparent a few verses later: "So out of the ground the Lord God formed every animal of the field and every bird of the air, and brought them to the man to see what he would call them; and whatever the man called every living creature, that was its name. The man gave names to all cattle, and to the birds of the air, and to every animal of the field" (vv. 19–20). God doesn't drop humanity into Eden like toddlers into a playpen ("Whatever you do, don't *touch* anything! I've got it all exactly how I want it"). God's desire is for human beings to *say something*—something new—about the world he has created. God leans forward "to see what [Adam] would call them" (v. 19). This naming is truly creative, then, but not arbitrary. "The significant fact about the life in the Garden is that man is to *name* things," writes Alexander Schmemann. "In the Bible a name . . . reveals the very essence of a thing . . . as God's gift."[38] Naming means recognizing what a thing is most truly and then creatively orchestrating that identity in sound and syllable. Naming is a double act of discernment. It involves (first) recognizing what a creature is most truly, and (second) identifying those sounds and utterances that will most clearly exposit that creature in all its individuality.

The importance of naming in Genesis's account of humanity's creation underlines the point that enabling discernment is one further way in which the Holy Spirit *re-creates* our humanity. The Holy Spirit enables human beings to faithfully carry out their Genesis 2 vocation of *recognizing* and *saying something* about the created world. The full exercise of our vocation means speaking in a way that harmonizes with God's own creative word. The Holy Spirit enables us to discern the shape of God's creative and redemptive work, to discern the character of created reality, and, therefore, to speak and act within creation in a discerning way—a way that is both faithful and creative. Discerning all things in the Spirit will mean speaking and acting redemptively, perceiving things within the trajectory of God's redemptive work.

Commending A Way of Seeing

Again, there is an analogy at this point to the work of the artist. In an earlier chapter we mentioned *mimesis* or representation, a theory that can appeal to its pedigree as the oldest philosophy of art. Mimesis suggests that ultimately the work of the artist is to imitate—to copy or reproduce the world. In yet another chapter we mentioned *expressionism*—the theory of art that one is most likely to encounter when talking with the proverbial "person on the

38. Alexander Schmemann, *For the Life of the World*, quoted in Eugene F. Rogers Jr., *After the Spirit: A Constructive Pneumatology from Resources outside the Modern West* (Grand Rapids: Eerdmans, 2005), 178.

street." The simplified, person-on-the-street version of expressionism holds that, rather than receiving the *impress* of the *external* world, the artist seeks to *express* her *internal* world. The artist seeks out artistic forms that will allow her to pour forth her deepest feelings and emotions.

Each of these theories (as we might expect) says something true about artistic creation, though each on its own says too little. The artist doesn't simply vent raw emotion (as in a crude form of expressionism) but deals in the stuff of the external world—color, sound, event, movement.[39] Neither, on the other hand, does the artist simply offer copies of reality (as in a simplified version of mimesis), but rather, he commends a particular way of seeing, hearing, and experiencing the world. *Consider this color when placed next to that; observe this scene from this vantage point; listen to these sounds in this sequence and arrangement; consider these events within the framework of this story.* In each instance, the artist says not simply "see this color," but "look and see if you can see this color *as*. . . ." The artist issues an invitation to join him in naming part of the creation.[40] And whether the artist speaks truly of creation, whether the artist's vision is consonant with God's redemptive vision for creation, in endorsing a way of experiencing the world, the artist exercises the human vocation of naming. "The first thing to be said about works of art," Anthony O'Hear writes, "is that even where their medium is realistic, as in certain novels or certain genres of painting . . . the aim of the activity is not simply to reproduce the world literally or photographically."[41] Instead, "in a work of art there is a sustained attempt to endow aspects of the world with human value and significance and to present us with ways in which those aspects of the world might be experienced."[42] The artist engages in and commends a way of seeing.

The poet Rainer Maria Rilke suggests that this act of creative naming is, indeed, why we are here:

> Are we perhaps here to say: House,
> Bridge, Well Gate, Jug, Fruit Tree, Window—

39. Of course, there are more sophisticated and interesting versions of both mimesis and expressionism than the discussion here might suggest. There are resemblances, in fact, between the account I develop below and a version of expressionism sometimes referred to as "cognitivism."

40. This may be more obviously true of representative art—art that sets out to portray some bit of the real world. But it is equally the case for abstract or nonrepresentational art. One may commend not only a particular way of regarding a sunset (say), but also a particular way of experiencing "red" or "linearity" or "space" or a particular set of sounds. Indeed, some of the most purely abstract works of visual art, such as color field painting, for instance, seem to me to do just this. Such works place a frame around some element of our ordinary visual experience and invite us to consider *red*—to regard it as not simply the color on the cheek of a portrait subject or one of the hues in a still life, but as something worthy of our attention in itself.

41. Anthony O'Hear, *The Element of Fire: Science, Art and the Human World* (New York: Routledge, 1988), 107.

42. Ibid., 109.

—at most, Pillar, Tower . . . but to say—oh!
to say in this way, as the things themselves
never so intently meant to be.[43]

What Rilke states poetically, Jürgen Moltmann articulates in the idiom of Christian theology, in a powerful passage worth quoting at length.

> There are very many and very various definitions of the essential character of the human being. In the present context we may define him by saying that he is destined to be the eucharistic being. To express the experience of creation in thanksgiving and praise is his designation from the very beginning, and it is also the content of his life in its consummated form. The human being does not merely live in the world like other living things. He does not merely dominate the world and use it. He is also able to discern the world in full awareness as God's creation, to understand it as a sacrament of God's hidden presence, and to apprehend it as a communication of God's fellowship. That is why the human being is able consciously to accept creation in thanksgiving, and consciously to bring creation before God again in praise. . . .
>
> As God's gifts, all his creatures are fundamentally Eucharistic beings also; but the human being is able—and designated—to express the praise of all created things before God. In his own praise he acts as representative for the whole of creation. His thanksgiving, as it were looses the dumb tongue of nature. It is here that the priestly dimension of his designation is to be found. So when in the 'creation' psalms thanks are offered for the sun and the light, for the heavens and the fertility of the earth, the human being is thanking God, not merely on his own behalf, but also in the name of heaven and earth and all created beings in them. Through human beings the sun and moon also glorify the Creator. Through human beings plants and animals adore the Creator too. That is why in the praise of creation the human being sings the cosmic liturgy, and through him the cosmos sings before its Creator the eternal song of creation.[44]

Christian discernment is not merely reproducing a divine blueprint. By the Spirit, the Christian engages in and commends a way of seeing. In particular, we no longer see "according to the flesh" (Greek, *kata sarka*) but according to the Spirit. We see everything anew. "From now on, therefore, we regard no one from a human point of view [*kata sarka*]; even though we once knew Christ from a human point of view, we know him no longer in that way. So if anyone is in Christ, there is a new creation: everything old has passed away; see, everything has become new!" (2 Cor. 5:16–17). This new way of seeing is both an act of receptivity and an act of creativity. It involves both recognizing the pattern of God's activity in the world, and creatively, imaginatively participating in God's work of re-creation.

43. R. M. Rilke, "Ninth Duino Elegy," as quoted in Anthony O'Hear, "The real or the Real? Chardin or Rothko," in *Philosophy, Religion and the Spiritual Life: Royal Institute of Philosophy Supplements*, ed. Michael McGhee (Cambridge: Cambridge University Press, 1992), 52.

44. Moltmann, *God in Creation*, 70–71.

Naming and Renaming

It might be helpful to consider some examples of this kind of redemptive renaming: two from Scripture and three more from the world of the arts.

Renaming David's Cunning Plan

One remarkable instance of this kind of renaming can be found in the way the prophet Nathan confronts King David following David's adultery with Bathsheba.

> The LORD sent Nathan to David. He came to him, and said to him, "There were two men in a certain city, the one rich and the other poor. The rich man had very many flocks and herds; but the poor man had nothing but one little ewe lamb, which he had bought. He brought it up, and it grew up with him and with his children; it used to eat of his meager fare, and drink from his cup, and lie in his bosom, and it was like a daughter to him. Now there came a traveler to the rich man, and he was loath to take one of his own flock or herd to prepare for the wayfarer who had come to him, but he took the poor man's lamb, and prepared that for the guest who had come to him." Then David's anger was greatly kindled against the man. He said to Nathan, "As the LORD lives, the man who has done this deserves to die; he shall restore the lamb fourfold, because he did this thing, and because he had no pity." Nathan said to David, "You are the man! . . . You have struck down Uriah the Hittite with the sword, and have taken his wife to be your wife, and have killed him with the sword of the Ammonites.
>
> 2 Samuel 12:1–7, 9

King David's vision has been fatally distorted by his own sense of power and status. In confronting David, Nathan the prophet first commends a different way of perceiving the situation—a redemptive renaming that allows David to correctly discern the character of his actions. David is renamed. "Powerful king who may demand whatever he wishes" becomes "greedy and grasping man without pity." Uriah is renamed, not "obstacle to the king's desire," but as "poor, loving servant." And Bathsheba is renamed, no longer "one who may satisfy the king's passing lust," but as "the long cared-for beloved of another." Above all, David's actions throughout are renamed. In attempting to cover up his taking of Bathsheba, David, the old guerilla fighter, had devised another crafty plan, but Nathan renames "David's ingenious plan of escape" as "Cruel deceit. Crass manipulation. Heartless calculation. An abomination to the Lord."

Nathan offers David a "reseeing" of his situation that is both creative and faithful; it is both a work of reimagination and a declaration of the situation as seen from the perspective of a holy, merciful, and covenant-keeping God. David looks out on the same facts and the same individuals, but now he perceives the same reality differently. In an act of double discernment he comes to see both God's heart and the individual integrity of the people he has wronged.

Renaming the Samaritan

Another biblical instance of renaming is even better known—Jesus's answer to the question, "Who is my neighbor?"

> Jesus replied, "A man was going down from Jerusalem to Jericho, and fell into the hands of robbers, who stripped him, beat him, and went away, leaving him half dead. Now by chance a priest was going down that road; and when he saw him, he passed by on the other side. So likewise a Levite, when he came to the place and saw him, passed by on the other side. But a Samaritan while traveling came near him; and when he saw him, he was moved with pity. He went to him and bandaged his wounds, having poured oil and wine on them. Then he put him on his own animal, brought him to an inn, and took care of him. The next day he took out two denarii, gave them to the innkeeper, and said, 'Take care of him; and when I come back, I will repay you whatever more you spend.' Which of these three, do you think, was a neighbor to the man who fell into the hands of the robbers?" He said, "The one who showed him mercy." Jesus said to him, "Go and do likewise."
>
> Luke 10:30–37

Who do we name "neighbor"? And how do we name the Samaritan? Who do we perceive as the righteous among us, as those obedient to God? Jesus challenges each of these definitions in this act of renaming. The name of *neighbor* is not "one from among my group" but "one who acts with compassion and fellow-humanity." The Samaritan in the story understands this. He discerns that the name of the traveler by the side of the road is not "inconvenience" or "unclean one" or "enemy." In portraying these actions, Jesus also gives the name "neighbor" to the Samaritan—the one known as "half-breed," "heretic," and "cursed." The story is told in response to the question "what is the greatest commandment?" and so Jesus's answer is also a renaming of "obedience" and "covenant faithfulness." The name of the commandment-keeper is not "priest," "one learned in the law," or "one who is ritually pure." The neighbor, the obedient one, is a Samaritan, and the Samaritan is neighbor and obedient one. Through this renaming, Jesus's hearers come to discern both the character of God's kingdom and the character of their fellow human beings.

Finally, it is worth noting that in both of these instances, the act of discernment or reseeing is facilitated by a story. The imaginative form allows an act of reimagination.

And, of course, artists of all sorts continue to engage in acts of reimagination. Some of these artistic acts bear all the marks of redemptive reimagining—real acts of discernment. Here (too briefly) are three examples I have encountered—local artists discerning the movement of the Spirit in the midst of their community and surroundings.

Discernment and Dance

Patricia Cross has been a dancer all her life, but for the last several years she also has been the director of "Rejoice Ministries" in East Nashville.[45] "Rejoice" provides after-school dance instruction to children from poor families and difficult home situations.

Patricia becomes animated in talking about the first time her students dress in their leotards. The leotards are provided in an assortment of vivid colors—reds, yellows, oranges, blues. "They look like a whole garden of flowers all lined up together," Patricia says. As they prepare for their first recitals, the students stand delighted in front of the studio mirrors and resee themselves. They are colorful; they are beautiful. They are individuals ("I'm orange!"); they are part of a group ("I'm one of 'the blues'!"). As they perform for the local community, both they and their neighbors learn that their presence, their movements, their bodies can bring joy. "Unwanted child" is renamed "dancer." The one named "trouble" is renamed "graceful." The one who on the corner was "loiterer" and "nuisance" in this building is renamed "garden" and "flower." Patricia's ministry says something true about humanity through the dance—a medium that has the power to rename human movement and effect "the transformation of 'ordinary' movements."[46] "For example, the graceful sweeping movement of a road-sweeper might be incorporated into a dance. . . . But the sequence of movement is no longer mere sweeping (however much it resembles it): it has become dance. Following Danto, this could be called 'the transfiguration of the "ordinary" activity' into dance."[47]

In dance we are encouraged to resee the human body and the ordinary stuff of human movement, not simply as functional, nor as something to be possessed sexually, but as something full of worth in itself.

Discerning the Grain

Chris Barber is a Nashville-based cabinet maker and woodworker. Much of his work holds books or stereo speakers, or provides seating space in Nashville area homes; on other occasions it is on display in regional museums. More recently, his work was placed in a gallery space in the church he and I both attend. Members of the congregation gathered before and after services, standing

45. See www.rejoiceschoolofballet.org.

46. Graham McFee, "Dance," in *Routledge Companion to Aesthetics*, Gaut and Lopes, eds., 549.

47. Ibid.

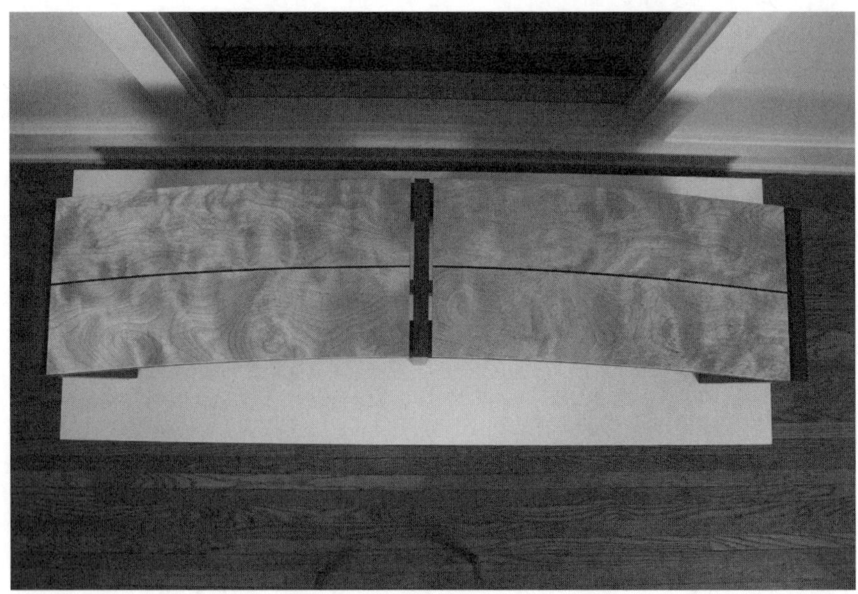

Fig. 8.1. Chris Barber, bench, top view. (Photo by Chris Barber)

Fig. 8.2. Chris Barber, bench, side view. (Photo by Chris Barber)

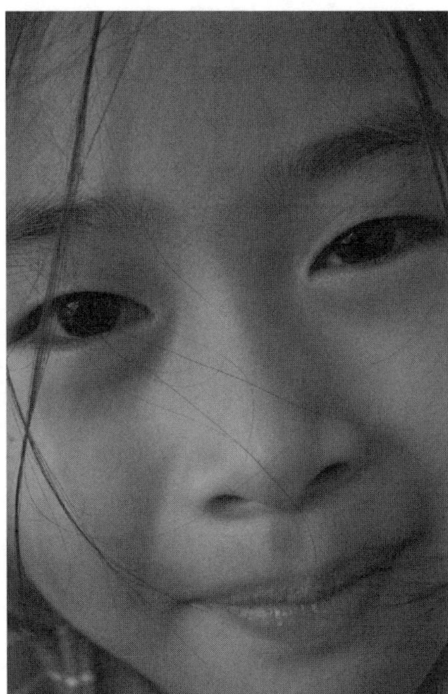

Fig. 8.3. *Red Light: Isan Girl* 2007 by Sarah Bennett. (Copyright 2007, Sarah Bennett, http://flickr.com/gp/sarahbennett/a7W274)

silently in front of Chris's graceful pieces (figs. 8.1 and 8.2).[48] They are remarkable works of both creativity and fidelity—imaginatively exposing and utilizing the grain, color, and texture of each piece of wood.

Chris's pieces are acts of both responsive and creative discernment. On the one hand, they call us to recognize what is there—what is in the wood and what can be seen in the material of the created world. On the other hand, they invite us to resee what is there—to see the material world as not only resource and raw material but as a source of wonder. In bowl, cup, and table, we see that the world both *is* and *is not* what we make it. Here is something *new*—shaped and fashioned by a highly skilled artist. And yet each item makes it unmistakably plain that the world has its own character and integrity—quite literally its own "grain." Human labor is not merely the imposition of our will on a passive creation but a work of dialogue. Moreover, as we stand in front of this work of a laborer's hands, we may resee human labor itself. In each joint and bevel one can discern the dignity and value of human work.

Discerning the Image

While she was still an undergraduate student at Belmont University, Sarah Bennett began traveling to Thailand to work among girls of the Isan people who had been sold into prostitution. A photographer as well as a religion major, Sarah's work was very literally to resee and reimage these women—women made in the image of God but reimagined by society as "commodity" (see fig. 8.3).[49]

In Sarah's photographs, the one named "whore" is renamed "sister," "daughter," and "child of God." Like Adam in the garden, Sarah's camera looks out over the girls of Bangkok and says, "Your name is 'human'; your

48. For further examples of Chris's work, see www.barberwoodworking.com.

49. Sarah Bennett, "An Artistic Response to the Trafficking of Isan Women to Bangkok as Prostitutes" (BA Honors Thesis, Belmont University, Nashville, TN, 2008).

name is 'beloved'; your name is 'image of God.'" In her photographs Sarah both engages in and commends a different way of seeing. And this reseeing arises from having discerned the trajectory of God's redemptive work.

Discernment means seeing truly. And for just that reason, it also means seeing *imaginatively*. The state of the world around us is not the deepest truth about the world. The interpretive frames offered us by our culture and by which we are to make sense of what we see and experience—these likewise are not the deepest truth about the world. The truth of the world includes both its origin in the love of God and its destination in the new creation. And supremely, the truth of the world—certainly the truth of humanity—is Jesus Christ. In him, humanity and all of creation find their fulfillment.

Discernment is to recognize all of this and to speak and act accordingly in our present situation. In so doing, we not only act wisely and make good decisions, but we fulfill an important part of our human vocation: to recognize the truth of the world and speak toward the re-creation of all things.

9

Beautiful, Beautiful Zion

The Spirit and Completion

In all the preceding chapters we have described the Spirit as restoring, completing, and perfecting our humanity. Moreover, the remaking and restoring we have talked about has moved out in ever-widening circles. The Spirit remakes us in our innermost being, in our bodies, in our relationships, in society, and in the rest of the created world. Indeed, we saw at the end of the last chapter that part of our vocation as human beings is to participate in the Spirit's work of remaking all things. The completion of our humanity is one part of the Spirit's cosmic work of completing and perfecting.

All of this draws us to a final way in which art may be considered "spiritual." All of the words listed above—*completing*, *perfecting*, *making things what they are intended to be*—have an *eschatological* character. They speak of movement toward a final goal or *telos*. They also are all words that might be used to describe the work of an artist. If this is so, then, some have suggested, perhaps the artist and the Spirit are about the same work—or at least the same sort of work. Each on this account perfects and brings to completion, each works at refining and purifying, each seeks to bring about a fitting conclusion or a satisfying whole. Each strives toward beauty.

"All Heaven before Mine Eyes"

Certainly, in ordinary Christian piety there seems to be an intuitive connection made between beauty and the new creation. Christians voice their hope in the dialect of beauty. They have read of a city "prepared as a bride adorned for her husband" (Rev. 21:2), a city of "pure gold, clear as glass" (Rev. 21:18).

And so they sing the kind of cheerful revival hymns I sang in church as a boy. We sang of a "bright and cloudless morning when the dead in Christ shall rise"[1] and encouraged one another that we would "meet where flow'rs are blooming; ever fadeless, ever fair."[2] We closed our eyes and stretched out our hands toward "a land that is fairer than day . . . by faith we can see it afar."[3] In the midst of boredom and disappointments and failures we began our hymns, confident that at the end of all things we would continue to "sing on that beautiful shore the melodious songs of the blessed."[4] School teachers, secretaries, and salesmen—from time to time we could picture our pilgrim selves, white-robed and glorious, striding into a brightly remade world.

We're marching to Zion,
Beautiful, beautiful Zion;
We're marching upward to Zion,
The beautiful city of God.[5]

When Christians speak and sing of a new creation, they turn as a matter of course to the language of beauty. "The glory of heaven," Santayana writes, "could not be otherwise symbolized than by light and music."[6] The reverse is true as well. When speaking of beauty or great art, critics and artists reach for the language of transcendent completion. The critic Achille Bonito Oliva, for instance, approvingly describes Joseph Beuys as an artist with "a scheme for transforming the world," who "sets out, through art, spiritually to reconstitute man's unity."[7] Artists and critics of an earlier age might gesture toward paradise. Milton, for instance, writes,

Let the pealing Organ blow,
To the full voic'd Quire below,
In Service high, and Anthems cleer,
As may with sweetnes, through mine ear,
Dissolve me into extasies,
And bring all Heav'n before mine eyes.

Il Penseroso, 161–66

1. James M. Black, "When the Roll Is Called up Yonder," in *Hymns of His Grace*, No. 1 (Chicago: Bilhorn Bros. Music Publishers, 1907), 94.

2. Anonymous, "Shall We Meet beyond the River?" 1911.

3. Sanford F. Bennett, "In the Sweet By and By," 1868.

4. Ibid.

5. Isaac Watts, "We're Marching to Zion," *Hymns and Spiritual Songs* (London: Manning & Loring, 1806.

6. George Santayana, *The Sense of Beauty: Being the Outline of Aesthetic Theory* (New York: Dover, 1955), 29.

7. Irving Sandler, *Art of the Postmodern Era: From the Late 1960s to the Early 1990s* (Boulder, CO: Westview, 1996), 283.

After hearing the opening of Mozart's A major Piano Concerto, the music critic Sir Neville Cardiff exclaimed, "If any of us were to die and then wake hearing it, we should know at once that (after all) we had got to the right place."[8]

Among theologians, figures as diverse as the great Russian iconographer Leonid Ouspensky and the Dutch Reformed theologian Abraham Kuyper have suggested that earthly beauty points toward a glorified world. Kuyper writes that "art has the mystical task of reminding us in its productions of the beautiful that was lost and of anticipating its perfect coming luster. . . . Art points out to the Calvinist both the still visible lines of the original plan, and what is even more, the splendid restoration by which the Supreme Artist and master-Builder will one day renew and enhance the beauty of His original creation."[9] Bishop Richard Harries says much the same thing, claiming the "beauty of that final state of affairs, that new heaven and new earth, is reflected even now in the beauty of our world and in works of art."[10]

Many of us will resonate with this sort of language. Sometimes singing with others, sometimes standing in the midst of an extraordinary architectural structure, or listening as the last words of a poem are read, we feel we have caught a glimpse of a better world, or perhaps, that we have seen a small piece of this world perfected. *This is how things are meant to be*, we might say. Or perhaps, *in a perfect world, this is how things would look, this is how things would sound.*

So, perhaps we might say that in bringing about perfection, completion, or beauty, the artist is doing something spiritual, because this is what the Spirit is about as well. In this chapter and the next, I would like to explore this association. In particular, I would like to consider whether, when Christians describe the new creation as "beautiful," they are saying something *meaningful*—something more, in other words, than just, "the new creation will be great." Does the word *beauty* align well with what Christians want to say about the completing and perfecting work of the Spirit? Before committing ourselves to words like *beauty*, *perfection*, and *completion*, however, we should consider why they have fallen out of favor in the art world of the twentieth century.

The Problem of an Ending

Beauty and *completion* are controversial terms. In particular, critics and philosophers have had little interest in the category of beauty throughout most of the twentieth century. Many have had real contempt for the term.[11] "Beauty

8. Jeremy Nicholas, "Composer of the Week: Wolfgang Amadeus Mozart," at *Gramophone Archive*. Available at http://www.gramophone.net/ComposerOfTheWeek/View/124.

9. Abraham Kuyper, *Lectures on Calvinism* (Grand Rapids: Eerdmans, 1943), 155.

10. Richard Harries, *Art and the Beauty of God: A Christian Understanding* (London: Mowbray, 1993), 147.

11. This is described, for instance, in Arthur C. Danto, *The Abuse of Beauty: Aesthetics and the Concept of Art* (Chicago: Open Court, 2003), 6–8; Dave Hickey, "Enter the Dragon: On the

has fallen into considerable disfavor in modern philosophical discourse," writes David Bentley Hart, in part due to the reduction of "beauty" to "the pretty, the merely decorative, or the inoffensively pleasant."[12]

This distaste for the category of beauty is evident not only in philosophical aesthetics but in twentieth-century art. One obvious example is the work of Francis Bacon (1909–92), a British painter recently featured in a Metropolitan Museum of Art retrospective exhibition (see fig. 9.1). A reviewer notes that Bacon's paintings are characterized by a "strange taste for horror" and "shrinking back from beauty."[13] "After World War II," the review observes, Bacon "believed that the world needed nothing less than a viciously honest figurative art that mirrored man's brutality."[14] Bacon was an idiosyncratic figure, both in his artistic and personal life. But his fascination with horror and brutality and his aversion to beauty are anything but idiosyncratic. In fact, these are among the qualities that mark him as "one of the most significant and influential artists of the 20th century" and "a standard bearer for current art world tendencies."[15]

The Lie of Appearances

One objection to beauty is well captured by the old cliché, *beauty is only skin deep*. Beauty, the saying suggests, presents us with the surface of things—but the surface only. Look for the word *beauty* in a department store catalog, and you will find yourself browsing *cosmetics*—a word that means something "intended to improve *only* appearances; superficially improving."[16] The pleasing surface may be a deception, an attempt to smooth over deep and serious flaws. (Among the categories of items you will find in the cosmetic section of your department store catalog are "cover up" and "concealers.") The external beauty may even be a ruse to conceal a hidden identity or secret agenda.

In this connection, beauty has been characterized by some academics as a kind of *kitsch*.[17] Kitsch, in Milan Kundera's famous definition, is the refusal to

---

Vernacular of Beauty," in *Uncontrollable Beauty: Toward a New Aesthetics*, ed. Bill Beckley with David Shapiro (New York: Allworth, 1998), 15–24; Nicholas Wolterstorff, *Art in Action: Toward a Christian Aesthetic* (Grand Rapids: Eerdmans, 1980), 161–63.

12. David Bentley Hart, *The Beauty of the Infinite: The Aesthetics of Christian Truth* (Grand Rapids: Eerdmans, 2003), 15.

13. Lance Esplund, "A Histrionic Horror Show," review of the exhibition "Francis Bacon: A Retrospective" at the New York Metropolitan Museum of Art, *The Wall Street Journal*, July 9, 2009, Arts and Entertainment section. Here Esplund is quoting comments made about Bacon by the artist Balthus.

14. Ibid.

15. Ibid.

16. "Cosmetic," in *The Concise Oxford Dictionary of Current English*, 9th ed., ed. Della Thompson (Oxford: Clarendon, 1995), 302, emphasis added.

17. Hermann Broch in describing the art world of his day declares, "Only the dilettante and the producer of kitsch . . . focus their work on beauty" (*Geist and Zeitgeist: The Spirit in an Unspiritual Age*, trans. John Hargraves [New York: Counterpoint, 2002], 16).

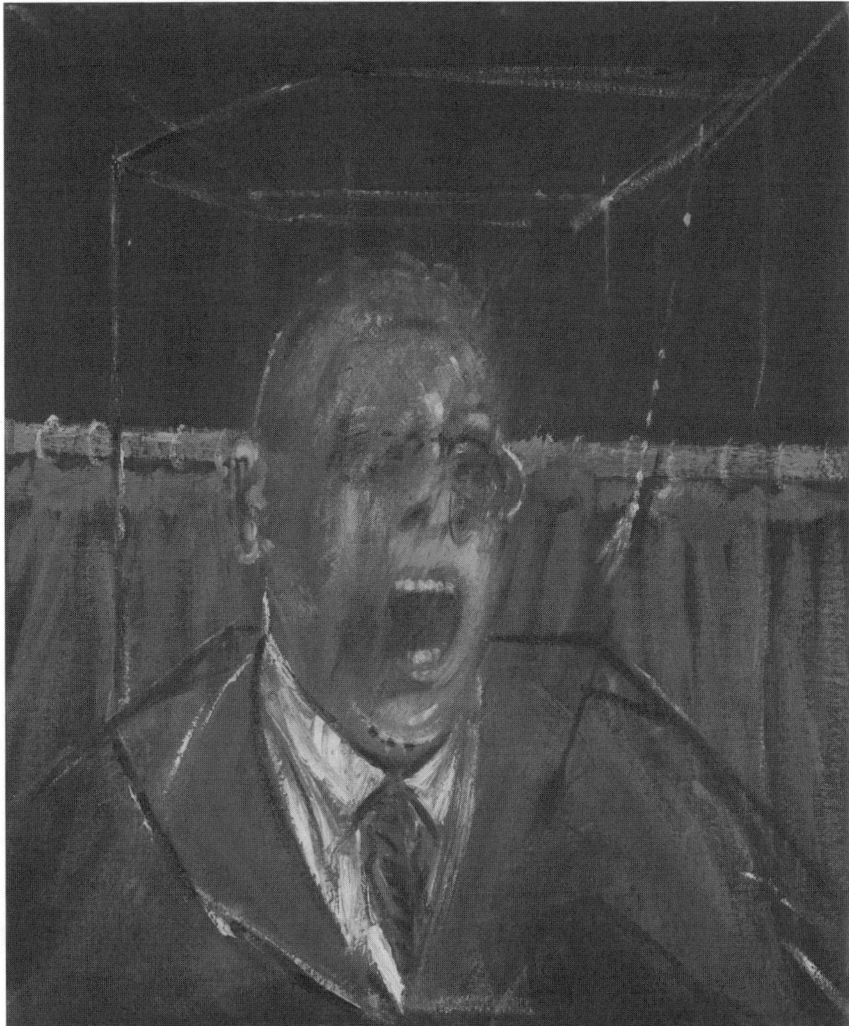

Fig. 9.1. *Study for a Portrait* 1952 by Francis Bacon. (Tate Gallery, London/Art Resource, New York; © 2011 The Estate of Francis Bacon. All rights reserved. ARS, New York/ACS, London)

acknowledge the shit of the world. The coarse language is necessary to make the point. All of the inoffensive euphemisms societies devise for excrement reflect precisely the attempt to conceal the unacceptability of the world as we find it. Kitsch, Kundera concludes, is a *theological* phenomenon, rooted in the Judeo-Christian Scriptures.

> Behind all the European faiths, religious and political, we find the first chapter of Genesis, which tells us that the world was created properly, that human

> existence is good, and that we are therefore entitled to multiply. Let us call this basic faith a *categorical agreement with being.*
>
> The fact that until recently the word "shit" appeared in print as s--- has nothing to do with moral considerations. You can't claim that shit is immoral, after all! The objection to shit is a metaphysical one. The daily defecation session is daily proof of the unacceptability of Creation. Either/or: either shit is acceptable (in which case don't lock yourself in the bathroom!) or we are created in an unacceptable manner.
>
> It follows then that the aesthetic ideal of the categorical agreement with being is a world in which shit is denied and everyone acts as though it did not exist. This aesthetic ideal is called *kitsch*. . . .
>
> Kitsch is the absolute denial of shit, in both the literal and the figurative senses of the word; kitsch excludes everything from its purview which is essentially unacceptable in human existence.[18]

Following much the same reasoning, many artists and critics over the past century—the past century particularly, with its genocides, perversions, corruptions, and cruelties—have recoiled from the category of beauty. A work of art can only be pleasing, attractive, well-formed, by deliberately averting its gaze from all that is offensive, repulsive, and distorted. Beauty is a lie, an act of deception, and a suppression of human reality. What we also should notice, however, is the connection Kundera draws between traditional ideas of beauty—form, order, fullness, perfection—and a particular theological vision. Beauty makes a claim about the shape of reality, and that claim is rejected as a lie. Beauty speaks of order and harmony in a world of shit. It is a cover-up.

The Lie of Universality

A second complaint against beauty is expressed in a second cliché: *beauty is in the eye of the beholder*. This proverb asserts, first of all, that beauty arises not from the world of things outside of us but from our own perceptions. Beauty is not a property of objects but the experience of perceiving subjects (it is not "objective" but "subjective").

A second implication of this cliché is that, since beauty reflects individual tastes, ideas about "beauty" simply amount to an expression of human differences—differences of age, culture, social conventions, personal background, and so on. Different ideas about beauty are a feature of the differences in the "beholders." Someone may point out, for instance, that our contemporary ideal of beauty is very different from that of another age. Often this point is made by comparing the full-figured women painted (say) by Titian to the anorexic models of today's fashion industry (fig. 9.2).

18. Milan Kundera, *The Unbearable Lightness of Being* (New York: Harper & Row, 1984), 168–69.

Fig. 9.2. *Venus and the Lute Player* c. 1565–70 by Titian and workshop. (Copyright The Metropolitan Museum of Art/Art Resource, New York)

These same ideas find expression in academic debates over beauty. "It behooves all of us to recognize," writes art historian Amelia Jones, "that beauty—there's no doubt about it—is in the eye of the beholder."[19] Her essay, which appears in the collection, *Aesthetics in a Multicultural Age*, is a furious rebuke of art critic Dave Hickey, who has recently attempted to rehabilitate the category of "beauty."[20] The problem, Jones argues, is that while aesthetic judgments are "in the eye of the beholder," talk of beauty attempts to "universalize" and "naturalize" these judgments. Those who speak of beauty hope to make others forget the subjective nature of aesthetic experience. They exalt the perspective of one particular group as normative for all people and claim that this socially and historically located perspective is rooted in the very structure of nature. "Of course," the collection's introduction observes,

19. Amelia Jones, "'Every Man Knows Where and How Beauty Gives Him Pleasure': Beauty Discourse and the Logic of Aesthetics," in Emory Elliott, Louis Freitas Caton, Jeffrey Rhyne, eds., *Aesthetics in a Multicultural Age* (Oxford: Oxford University Press, 2002), 233.

20. See Dave Hickey, *The Invisible Dragon: Essays on Beauty*, rev. and exp. ed. (Chicago: University of Chicago Press, 2009).

"what is posited as universal and essential is nothing more than the classical Western canons of art and literature, which were primarily constructed by white male anthologists, literary editors, and genteel intellectuals in the last two centuries."[21] For this reason, Jones hopes "to dislocate and discredit claims for the neutrality of 'beauty' as a label of aesthetic judgment,"[22] to "interrogate what (or whose) interests are served by the rhetoric of beauty."[23] Here again, beauty is accused of being a cover-up, though of a different kind. Beauty (or rather talk about beauty) is denounced as the veil draped over "an ideology of control that is . . . highly successful in sustaining the law of patriarchy."[24]

In this connection, Jones also might want to draw our attention to Titian's "Venus and the Lute Player." Such paintings portray an idealized femininity: soft, white, and vulnerable; naked; enclosed in a domestic space; and available to the male gaze. The lute player enacts the attitude of the viewer, as he—clothed, active, and armed—fixes his eyes upon Venus. She, meanwhile, the idealized feminine, looks away in passive assent. The canonization of these images as beautiful lends authority to their characterizations. Beauty allows those in power to scrawl "the way things are MEANT to be" over images that simply portray the way they *want* things to be.

Again, it is fascinating to note that though Jones is an art historian, her objection to beauty, like that of Kundera, is ultimately theological. At the end of the day, she writes, "it is God—the ultimate patriarch—who secures such claims of beauty. Only God can act as origin and end of beauty, incontrovertible enough to stop the seepage that pollutes the ostensibly closed, otherwise 'pure' system of aesthetic judgment."[25] Both Jones and Kundera, then, claim that the rhetoric of beauty is fatally dishonest, and likewise, both believe that this dishonest claim is theological in nature.

The Lie of Transcendence

There is a third complaint leveled against beauty (and related concepts like perfection and completion), and this has to do with its apparent inadequacy.

At times it seems the category of beauty fits awkwardly or not at all when placed up against actual works of art we admire and value. And so, while it may seem quite appropriate to characterize (for instance) Matisse's *Mme Matisse: Madras Rouge* (*The Red Madras Headress*) as beautiful, it seems a less adequate characterization of Rembrandt's *The Slaughtered Ox*. We might agree after a moment's reflection that, *well*, *yes—in a certain way—it*

21. Emory Elliott, "Introduction: Cultural Diversity and the Problem of Aesthetics," in Elliott et al., *Aesthetics in a Multicultural Age*, 10.

22. Jones, "Every Man Knows," 231.

23. Ibid., 222.

24. Ibid., 220.

25. Ibid., 225.

is *beautiful*. But the hesitation and the "in a certain way" are telling. Though we may admire the painting as a very great work, *beauty* is not the first word that occurs to us in speaking of it. We could make similar observations in the field of music, literature, or dance.

It was just this perceived inadequacy of beauty—particularly in characterizing striking features of the natural world—that led many eighteenth-century philosophers to distinguish between "the beautiful" and "the sublime." One of the most influential expositions of this distinction is Edmund Burke's *Philosophical Enquiry into the Origin of Our Ideas of the Sublime and the Beautiful* (1757).[26] The paradigm of beauty, Burke explains, is feminine. The beautiful is pleasing, comforting, delightful, attractive, and so on. Much of what moves us in the natural world, however, is of a very different character. In encountering the extremes of nature—say, a sheer towering face of granite set imposingly in the midst of a barren landscape—we experience a kind of pleasure that is not at all comforting but mingled with fear and awe. We are overwhelmed; we recognize our smallness before something that surpasses us utterly. Such an encounter, says Burke, is an experience of the sublime. In an essay from 1764, Immanuel Kant provides typical examples of the sublime and the beautiful, respectively.

> The sight of a mountain whose snow-covered peak rises above the clouds, the description of a raging storm, or Milton's portrayal of the infernal kingdom, arouse enjoyment but with horror; on the other hand, the sight of flower-strewn meadows, valleys with winding brooks and covered with grazing flocks, the description of Elysium, or Homer's portrayal of the girdle of Venus, also occasion a pleasant sensation but one that is joyous and smiling.[27]

Whereas the beautiful is soft and enchanting, the sublime is imposing, terrifying, and—notably—more to be esteemed. Burke asserts that the sublime "always dwells on great objects, and terrible; [beauty] on small ones, and pleasing; we submit to what we admire, but we love what submits to us."[28]

And there is another reason the sublime is especially valued. For modern thinkers like Kant and Burke, the experience of aesthetic sublimity is the moment when the subject gazes out beyond what can be grasped by sense and imagination; it is the terror and awe one experiences when standing before the infinite. But the "standing before" is important here. On this account the experience of the sublime is not only darkness but light (albeit a blinding light). In this encounter one "knows" what cannot be known. This is the delight that

26. Edmund Burke, *A Philosophical Enquiry into the Origin of Our Ideas of the Sublime and the Beautiful* (Oxford: Oxford World Classics, 1990).

27. Immanuel Kant, *Observations on the Feeling of the Beautiful and Sublime*, trans. John T. Goldthwait (Berkeley: University of California Press, 2004), 47.

28. Burke, *Philosophical Enquiry*, 103.

one derives from the sublime. "To be able even to think the infinite *as a whole*," Kant writes, "indicates a mental power that surpasses any standard of sense."[29] So the sublime makes us aware of both the "limits and inadequacy"[30] of our own imagination and "the superiority of the rational vocation of our cognitive powers over the greatest power of sensibility."[31] We are able to *conceive* even that which we cannot *perceive*.

This transcendent experience, Kant and others insist, is not tied to beauty but sublimity. Beauty is inadequate to our highest aesthetic experiences. Plato's Ladder of Beauty is overturned. It is not the forms but the *formless* that reflect the infinite and true being. "The sublime (an aesthetic of power) rejects beauty on the grounds that it is diminutive, dismissible, not powerful enough,"[32] writes Elaine Scarry. By replacing form (which is merely pleasant) with the formless, "the sublime cut beauty off from the metaphysical."[33]

For the *modern* philosopher, the category of beauty is simply inadequate to infinite reality. *Postmodern* thinkers have also appealed to "the sublime," and their objections to beauty are even deeper. On their reading, beauty is (once again) a lie. Beauty is an attempt—either foolish or deceitful—to contain and represent a formless and unrepresentable reality. Kundera complains that beauty airbrushes shit. Jones complains that beauty disguises oppressive ideologies. Postmodern philosophers like Jean-Francois Lyotard believe that beauty makes a false promise of harmony in a cacophonous world. Beauty is seen as an attempt to set limits and boundaries, to comprehend an incomprehensible world. It is a futile quest for rational proportions amid the eternal flux of experience.

The modern philosopher values the experience of the sublime because this is the moment in which one *apprehends* that which exceeds comprehension. The postmodern philosopher, however, values the sublime as the moment when we are confronted with incomprehensibility itself. In meeting the sublime we do not stand (like Kant) in the *presence* of what is beyond us; rather, we experience the sublime as the *absence* that is beyond us. The postmodern sublime represents unrepresentability and speaks unspeakability. "The postmodern," writes Lyotard, "would be that which . . . denies itself the solace of good forms . . . which searches for new presentations . . . in order to impart a stronger sense of the unpresentable."[34]

29. Immanuel Kant, *Critique of Judgment*, trans. Werner S. Pluhar (Indianapolis: Hackett, 1987), 111, emphasis in translation.

30. Ibid., 114.

31. Ibid.

32. Elaine Scarry, *On Beauty and Being Just* (Princeton: Princeton University Press, 1999), 84, 85.

33. Ibid., 85.

34. Jean-Francois Lyotard, *Postmodernism: A Reader* (New York: Harvester Wheatsheaf, 1993), 46.

Lyotard offers the novels of James Joyce as an example of this aesthetic. Joyce, he writes, "makes us discern the unpresentable in the writing itself, in the signifier. A whole range of accepted narrative and even stylistic operators is brought into play with no concern for the unity of the whole."[35] If there *is* no metanarrative, if there is no unity of the whole, then the great deception of beauty is to present us with forms, with unities. What is rejected is the idea that there is any final form or goal, any completion toward which all things are moving.

Once again, as with Kundera, as with Jones, we should notice that Lyotard's rejection of beauty is not aesthetic *per se* but theological. Even as they censure the idea of beauty, the critiques we have surveyed intensify the pairing of beauty with eschatology. Each dismissal of beauty is likewise and in the same manner a rejection of teleology and of eschatology. (In fact, it might be more accurate to say that in the instances we have considered, beauty is condemned *because* it implies a teleological eschatology.) The objection to beauty is an objection to the claim that there is a single overarching story (with a single ending) to be told. What is denied is the idea that the world can be narrated or represented, that a single ending can be written. Unities and endings are rejected alike because they exclude and bring "closure"—not in the positive, therapeutic sense in which the term is popularly used, of course, but in the sense of closing off and shutting out stories that do not fit the grand narrative.

Like the airbrush-artist who smoothes over blemishes, eschatology is indicted as the theologically authorized spin-doctoring of history, a supposedly happily-ever-after ending told in advance, in which all wrongs are righted and everything is redeemed in beauty—to the praise of a wise and benevolent creator. The claim that all things can be summed up in a single beatific vision is rejected in the same manner as the claim that the infinite chaos can be given form, captured in words, or placed on canvas. For the critics of beauty as well as its champions, then, the questions of beauty and eschatology are intertwined.

The Defeat of Chaos

What should we make of these complaints? First of all, however forceful the objections to final unity, it is difficult to imagine any sort of Christian eschatology in which chaos and formlessness is awarded ultimacy. In fact, looking back to the last chapter, we could say that in its *remembered past*, in its *expected future*, and in *the presence of Jesus Christ*, Christianity tells the story of the defeat of chaos.

35. Jean-Francois Lytoard, "An Answer to the Question, What Is the Postmodern?" in *Postmodernism Explained: Correspondence, 1982–1985* (Minneapolis: University of Minnesota Press, 1992), 14.

Remembered Past

The beginning of the biblical narrative describes a primeval confrontation between God, who acts by his word and his Spirit (cf. Ps. 33:6), and chaos—the *tohu wabohu* of formlessness and emptiness.

> The earth was a formless void [*tohu wabohu*] and darkness covered the face of the deep, while a wind [*ruach*] from God swept over the face of the waters. Then God said, "Let there be light"; and there was light.
>
> Genesis 1:2–3

The remainder of the chapter details the steady, methodical overturning of the *tohu wabohu* and the watery depths of chaos. In the creation story of Genesis 1 God gives form to formlessness and brings fullness to the void. On the first three days God gives form to what was "formless" [*bohu*]—separating, limiting, setting boundaries, and establishing relations. On day one, God separates light from darkness and day from night; on the second day, God separates the "waters above"—the expanse of the sky—from the "waters below." The waters below the sky are separated from dry land on the third day. On the following three days of creation, God *fills* each of the domains he has *formed*. The account of days five and six in particular draw attention to the abundance and the manyness of God's activity of filling. On day four, the day and night are filled with the sun, moon, and stars. On day five, the sea is filled with "swarms of living creatures" (v. 20) and the sky with "every winged bird of every kind" (v. 21). Finally, on day six, God fills the earth with "everything that creeps upon the ground of every kind" (v. 25). Humanity is listed last of all among the works of day six: the crown of creation. This world God creates is marked by *peace* (rather than chaos) and *abundance* (rather than nothingness).

Day*	Forming	Filling	Day
1	Day, night	Sun, moon, and stars	4
2	Waters above, waters below	Fish, birds	5
3	Water, land	Animals, humanity	6

*Adapted from Rikki E. Watts, "Making Sense of Genesis 1." Accessed online at http://www.asa3.org/ASA/topics/Bible-Science/6–02Watts.html. See also a similar chart in Gordon J. Wenham, *Exploring the Old Testament: A Guide to the Pentateuch* (Downers Grove, IL: InterVarsity, 2003), 19.

By their making, Word and Spirit push back the unmaking chaos of formlessness. The *form* of creation, however, is not the restrictive, sterilizing imposition of limits. Rather, the forms of day and night, sky and firmament, sea and land are nothing less than open space in which all the teeming, blooming diversity of creaturely being can flourish. The destructive, malignant chaos of *tohu wabohu* is supplanted by peace (*shalom*), the ordered fullness of right relationship.

Expected Future

The final chapters of the Bible likewise describe an apocalyptic confrontation with the *tohu wabohu* and waters of the formless void. The thirteenth and fourteenth chapters of Revelation describe the beasts and the dragons—the "monsters of chaos"[36] who rise "out of the sea" (Rev. 13:1). When these have been defeated, there is "a new heaven and a new earth; for the first heaven and the first earth had passed away, and the sea was no more" (Rev. 21:1). The sea, Richard Bauckham observes, represents the "waters of the primeval abyss . . . the source of destructive evil, the possibility of the reversion of creation to chaos."[37] With the creation of the new heavens and the new earth, the voracious nothingness of *tohu wabohu* and the uncreating, unmaking chaos are overcome forever.

The Presence of Jesus Christ

If these are the opening and consummating scenes of the Christian story, then its decisive climax is the life, death, and resurrection of Jesus Christ. Here too chaos is overcome. Jesus strides out over the waters of the abyss (John 6:18–20). And like God in his creative act, Jesus speaks to the winds and waters, so that they return to their ordered places (Mark 4:37–39). Additionally, as we have seen, in Christ's body and by his Spirit a fractured and fragmenting humanity is re-*formed* into a community of peace. He creates "in himself one new humanity in place of the two, thus making peace . . . [reconciling] both groups to God in one body through the cross, thus putting to death that hostility through it" (Eph. 2:15–16). Likewise, through Christ an empty and barren humanity is *filled* with the Spirit of God and drawn into the abundance of God's life.

> For in him the whole fullness of deity dwells bodily, and you have come to fullness in him.
>
> Colossian 2:9–10

> And he has put all things under his feet and has made him the head over all things for the church, which is his body, the fullness of him who fills all in all.
>
> Ephesians 1:22–23

> He who descended is the same one who ascended far above all the heavens, so that he might fill all things.
>
> Ephesians 4:10

The modern sublime suggests that form cannot contain what is ultimate. The postmodern sublime says that form is a lie in a world of chaos. The New

36. Richard Bauckham, *The Theology of the Book of Revelation* (Cambridge: Cambridge University Press, 1993), 89.

37. Ibid., 53.

Testament, however, asserts that in Jesus Christ the infinite and eternal has indeed taken form: "We declare to you what was from the beginning, what we have heard, what we have seen with our eyes, what we have looked at and touched with our hands, concerning the word of life—this life was revealed, and we have seen it and testify to it, and declare to you the eternal life that was with the Father and was revealed to us" (1 John 1:1–2). This form is not an oppressive limitation, or the closing down of possibility, but a declaration of peace (Eph. 2:14, 17) and fullness (John 10:10).

The Spirit and Resurrection

The Spirit, we have said, is at work re-forming creation and bringing all things to completion. We have also said that in Jesus Christ, the infinite has *taken form*. In Jesus our humanity has been completed. It is right, then, to say that Jesus is the *eschatos*. If we want to know the shape of the new creation, we should look at Jesus. This, in fact, is an idea we find throughout Paul's letters. The resurrection of Jesus Christ, more than any other event or teaching, shaped the church's understanding of the new creation.[38]

Many (though not all) Jews of the first century hoped for the resurrection of the dead.[39] Those who did would have recognized it as the great final act of God's redemptive work. Those who looked for the resurrection of the dead were hoping for far more than individual immortality; they were awaiting the consummation of history. The raising of the dead would be accompanied by the vindication of the righteous, the judgment of the wicked, the undoing of death and corruption, and the uniting of all things under the reign of God. It would be the moment when all of creation would shake off its shroud and stand in the light of God's kingdom.[40] This, Peter declares, has in fact happened in the person of Jesus of Nazareth:

> God raised him up, having freed him from death, because it was impossible for him to be held in its power. . . . This Jesus God raised up, and of that all of us are witnesses. Being therefore exalted at the right hand of God, and having received from the Father the promise of the Holy Spirit, he has poured out this that you both see and hear.
>
> Acts 2:24, 32–33

38. Gordon D. Fee, *God's Empowering Presence: The Holy Spirit in the Letters of Paul* (Peabody: MA: Hendrickson, 1994), 803–5.

39. For a discussion of the range of eschatological views current in the first century, see N. T. Wright, *The Resurrection of the Son of God* (Minneapolis: Fortress, 2009), esp. 32–200.

40. See, for instance, ibid., 127–28, 204–6; George Eldon Ladd, *A Theology of the New Testament*, rev. ed. (Grand Rapids: Eerdmans, 1993), 407–10; Gordon D. Fee, *Paul, the Spirit, and the People of God* (Peabody, MA: Hendrickson, 1996), 49–51; Hans Schwartz, *Eschatology* (Grand Rapids: Eerdmans, 2000), 286–87.

For the early church, the resurrection of Jesus is not simply a symbol or a foreshadowing of the new creation but its manifestation. The resurrection has taken place. The power of death has been broken. God's anointed one has been publicly vindicated, enthroned, and has received the promised Holy Spirit. This promised Holy Spirit has been poured out upon God's people. Each of these statements insists: the last days have arrived.[41] In the risen Jesus, humanity, and indeed creation, has been perfected and has reached its promised end: perfect communion with God.[42] As Jesus bursts from the shattered tomb humanity and the stuff of the material world are, in his person, carried beyond death and into the life of God's new creation. At the same time, Paul can write that we "groan inwardly while we wait for adoption, the redemption of our bodies" (Rom. 8:23). The resurrection, says Paul, has *already* happened. And—we wait for the resurrection that has *not yet* arrived, with patience. This "already–not yet" tension is one of the most characteristic features of New Testament eschatology. The kingdom has arrived, and we pray "thy kingdom come"; death has been defeated, and we await the defeat of death; Jesus is Lord and King, and we look eagerly toward the day when "every knee shall bow and every tongue confess that Jesus is Lord." The new creation is "already," even now, in our midst. At the same time, this world yet awaits transformation.

We cannot eliminate the tension between the "already" and the "not yet" of New Testament eschatology by dividing its parts between Christ and the church. In other words, it is not that the new creation is simply *already* a reality for Jesus but *not yet* a reality for his followers. The first Christians "behaved as if they were in some important senses already living in God's new creation."[43] They believed that even as they inhabited "the present evil age" (Gal. 1:4) they were those "on whom the ends of the ages have come" (1 Cor. 10:11). Paul could say both that "we *will be* changed" (1 Cor. 15:52) and that "you *have been* raised with Christ" (Col. 3:1; cf. Eph. 2:6).

The Holy Spirit is the key to understanding these two, apparently contradictory affirmations. Paul refers to the Spirit as "first fruits" (Rom. 8:23), "pledge" (2 Cor. 1:22; Eph. 1:14), and "seal" (2 Cor. 1:22; Eph. 1:13), and each image testifies that the new creation is both a present reality and a future hope.[44] "The Savior is created in the flesh and becomes a beginning of those who are recreated,"[45] Athanasius writes. And the same Spirit of the resurrected One

41. "A new moment has opened in the divine plan for Israel and the world, because the long-promised, long-awaited event has occurred: 'the resurrection of the dead' has in a sense already happened with the resurrection of Jesus. . . . In and through [Jesus] a new era in Israel's history, in world history, had dawned" (Wright, *Resurrection of the Son*, 452).

42. Schwartz, *Eschatology*, 284.

43. Wright, *Resurrection of the Son*, 578.

44. Fee, *God's Empowering Presence*, 806.

45. Athanasius, *Orations against the Arians*, in Khaled Anatolios, *Athanasius* (New York: Routledge, 2004), 159.

is alive within his church. As "first fruits," the Spirit is the power of God at work in his people by which they experience even now the dawning future. As "pledge," the Spirit is the abiding promise that the cosmic work of re-creation initiated in Jesus Christ will be brought to completion. Calvin draws attention to this role of the Spirit, writing:

> God raised his Son from the dead, not to make known a single example of his power, but to show toward us believers the same working of the Spirit, whom he calls "life" while he dwells in us because he was given, to the end that he may quicken what is mortal in us. . . .
>
> Christ rose again that he might have us as companions in the life to come. He was raised by the Father, inasmuch as he was the Head of the church, from which the Father in no way allows him to be severed. He was raised by the power of the Holy Spirit, the Quickener of us in common with him. Finally he was raised that he might be "the resurrection and the life." . . . In this mirror the living image of the resurrection is visible to us.[46]

Jesus, Calvin suggests, *is* the *eschatos*: the "goal toward which all creation moves"[47] and a living image of the transfigured creation. Moreover, the Spirit is the realized presence of this new creation in "us believers." The same Spirit who is "Quickener" of the risen Christ lives in us as the *vinculum caritatis*—the "bond of love"—joining us not only to our Lord but to the new creation as well. "When we are sealed in this way, we properly become sharers in the divine nature," Athanasius exclaims, "and so the whole creation participates of the Word, in the Spirit."[48]

A Crucified Beauty

What light is shed on our discussion of beauty by acknowledging Jesus as the new creation (and the Spirit as first fruits and pledge of the new creation in us)?

Cross and Resurrection

First of all, the "already–not yet" tension that we have encountered alerts us not only to the presence of God's Spirit in our midst (the "already") but to the fact that the kingdom of this world has not yet become the kingdom of God in its fullness. Because we await the new creation the present work of the Spirit is not only to abide and empower but to purify. This suggests that there is indeed reason to be cautious in too quickly promoting earthly

46. John Calvin, *Institutes of the Christian Religion*, 3.25.3, trans. Ford Lewis Battles (Philadelphia: Westminster, 1960), 991.

47. Schwartz, *Eschatology*, 284.

48. Athanasius, *Letters to Serapion on the Holy Spirit*, in Anatolios, *Athanasius*, 223.

beauty to eschatological beauty. The critics of beauty have good reason to be skeptical. Human judgments concerning beauty are no less fallible than human judgments of truth, goodness, and justice. We absolutize and universalize personal preferences and idiosyncratic opinions. Those who hold power and influence often wield concepts like "beauty" as a weapon. The suppression of dissenting voices is disguised as the simple upholding of aesthetic standards. But, of course, to acknowledge all of this is simply to acknowledge the fallen condition of humanity. The Christian least of all should resist the suggestion that works of art—even very great ones—are marked by the blindness, vice, and prejudice of their creators.

Indeed, the resurrection tells us not only that the stuff of the world will be transformed, not only that the transformation has begun, but also that transformation is *necessary*. "The end to the creation's 'bondage to decay' can come about only by a radical remaking,"[49] writes Colin Gunton. The cross testifies to just how radical this remaking is. The image of "first fruits" might remind us of Jesus's image of the kernel of wheat. "Very truly, I tell you, unless a grain of wheat falls into the earth and dies, it remains just a single grain; but if it dies, it bears much fruit. Those who love their life lose it, and those who hate their life in this world will keep it for eternal life" (John 12:24–25). The shape of the new life we see in Jesus Christ—the shape of the Spirit-life—is death and resurrection. There is no gospel without *both* cross and empty tomb. We have no reason to expect that our ideas of "beauty" are exempt from this radical remaking. The "not yet" of New Testament eschatology reminds us that there will be discontinuity between the values of this creation and the values of the next.

Crucified Beauty: Against Cover-Up

Having said this, if the cross testifies to *discontinuity*, the resurrection also witnesses to *continuity* between this creation and the new creation. One way of imagining eschatological beauty, then, would be as a realm in which every trace of past sorrow and suffering has been removed, in which the entire sorry history of human misery has been scraped away in order to provide a blank canvas for new creation. This is one of two tendencies that Miroslav Volf observes in Christian eschatology.[50] Some in the Christian tradition have emphasized the emphatic judgment and censure of this present creation, in an *annihilatio mundi*. This vision imagines a radical discontinuity between creation and new creation, with all vestiges of the present world being consumed in a great cosmic conflagration. This eschatology might just be guilty of the charges that

49. Colin Gunton, *The Christian Faith: An Introduction to Christian Doctrine* (Oxford: Blackwell, 2002), 153.

50. See the discussion in Miroslav Volf, *Word in the Spirit: Toward a Theology of Work* (Oxford: Oxford University Press, 1991), 89–102.

Kundera and others raise against beauty. As we saw, Kundera objected that beauty excludes or conceals what is ugly and offensive. Beauty, then, appears to be a kind of deception, only telling part of the story and artfully veiling the rest. Kundera might complain: if the beauty of the new creation is built on the ashes of an *annihilatio mundi*, then this final "harmony," this "completion," is a lie. Nothing has been harmonized, nothing reconciled. The final "peace" is achieved simply through the violent obliteration of all that has come before. This resembles the paradise of the totalitarian state: all is well as long as one controls the media and the history books and destroys any contrary evidence.

There is another stream within the tradition, however, that allows for continuity as well as discontinuity between creation and new creation. This eschatology includes censure but healing as well, not only destruction but re-creation, in a *transformatio mundi*. While each of these traditions can claim some biblical support, Pentecost and Jesus's resurrection point emphatically toward eschatological transformation rather than eschatological annihilation.

This is seen vividly in the extraordinary Pentecost outpouring of tongues. Pentecost has been described as a "reversal of Babel," but this is not quite right. Babel—with its profusion of human languages and the subsequent elaboration of diverse cultures—is not undone at Pentecost, but transfigured:[51] "How is it that we hear, each of us, in our own native language? . . . In our own languages we hear them speaking about God's deeds of power" (Acts 2:8, 11). At Pentecost the multiplicity of human language and the richness of human culture is welcomed by the Spirit even as the division, confusion, and separation associated with that multiplicity is excluded. Human history, with all of its ambiguities and brokenness, is not erased but transformed by the Holy Spirit.

The testimony of Pentecost is articulated with even greater power and poignancy in the risen Christ. "It is I myself!" the risen Jesus declares to his disciples (Luke 24:39). The resurrected Jesus is transfigured—"I was dead, and see, I am alive forever and ever; and I have the keys of Death and of Hades" (Rev. 1:18)—and yet, the transfigured one is Jesus of Nazareth. He calls out to his disciples, "Cast the net to the right side of the boat, and you will find some" (John 21:6). With these words he not only reminds Peter of one of their first meetings (Luke 5:4–10) but also beautifully reassures him that the journey through death has not removed the traces of their shared history. The particular history of Jesus is taken up into the world of God's new creation.

"The contribution made by spiritual human beings," writes Staniloae, "by the great creators of art, the scholars, and by many just views and experiences of peoples and individuals—all these will remain inscribed on this final all-

51. Colin Gunton, *The One, the Three and the Many: God, Creation and the Culture of Modernity* (Cambridge: Cambridge University Press, 1993), 216.

comprehensive image of reality and of human existence, filled in its entirety with the infinite God."[52]

Crucified Beauty: Against Kitsch

Jesus's resurrected body bears the marks of his preresurrection life. Nowhere is this more clearly seen than on his scarred hands and feet. Before breathing on his followers with the Holy Spirit (John 20:22), "he showed them his hands and side" (John 20:20). The marks of human history, indeed of human sinfulness, depravity, and injustice, are indelibly inscribed upon the flesh of the resurrected Lord, carried into the life of the new creation by the Spirit and transfigured. These marks in no way tarnish the glory of the new creation, but rather "those wounds, yet visible above" are "in beauty glorified."[53]

If the risen Christ is an image of the *eschatos*, then we also can say that the beauty brought about by the Spirit is not a bland, facile "prettiness." Neither is the beauty of the new creation achieved through suppressing and concealing awkward facts or embarrassing episodes. Rather, the transfigured wounds of Christ and the redeemed languages of Pentecost are connected to God's *presence* among his people by the Spirit. The Spirit, we have seen, is God's personal presence in creation and among his people. And an active, abiding *dwelling-in-the-midst-of* means more than a timeless, ahistorical "spiritual" encounter; it means journeying through a shared history. As God's Shekinah glory dwells in the tabernacle and in the temple, God himself journeys out with his people into the desert. With the destruction of the temple and the dwelling place of the Shekinah, God shares in his people's exile.[54] Similarly, Jesus as God-among-us, as bearer of the Spirit, is God's presence in the midst of evil and suffering. This presence of God in the midst of his creation manifests in history the character of the new heavens and the new earth. But the "eschatological good" of shared history *necessarily* includes shared scars and shared suffering. The resurrected world bears the marks of history—even tragic history—in part because these wounds are the testimony of God's presence in the midst of his people across time. Because of this, even they share the character of the new creation.

52. Dumitru Staniloae, *The Experience of God: Orthodox Dogmatic Theology*, vol. 2, *Creation and Deification*, trans. Ioan Ionita and Robert Barringer (Brookline, MA: Holy Cross Orthodox Press, 2005), 53.

53. Matthew Bridges, "Crown Him with Many Crowns," 1857.

54. For this point, see the discussion in Jürgen Moltmann, *The Spirit of Life: A Universal Affirmation*, trans. Margaret Kohl (Minneapolis: Fortress, 1992), 48–62.

10

Perfection, Proportion, and Pleasure

The Spirit and Beauty

Beauty and eschatology belong together—both the language of Christian devotion and the critics of beauty agree on this point. We have also addressed some important concerns about beauty by considering the character of the eschatological work of the Spirit. The critics of beauty recognize—correctly, it seems to me—that the Christian eschatological vision demands an affirmation of beauty. A Christian eschatology asserts that history, humanity, and the cosmos look forward, not only to an ending, but to a *telos*—to completion, fulfillment, and a kind of perfection. The objections to beauty confirm, in a backhanded sort of way, the imagery of Scripture and the intuition of Christian devotion. To hope for the kingdom of God in its fullness is to hope for beauty.

Naming Beauty

What we haven't yet done is say what beauty *is*. Some would say that this isn't possible. Certainly, an attempt even to survey the various accounts of beauty would require a book much longer than this one. Still, having said something of what beauty is *not* (it is not essentially denial, propaganda, or limitation, for instance), it seems important to give some positive description of beauty—however brief and partial. Perhaps the work of the Spirit is to beautify creation, but for this to be a meaningful statement, we need to be able to give some sort of content to the term "beauty." We began the last chapter with hymns about "beautiful, beautiful Zion." Christian piety has an intuitive sense that God's new creation will be beautiful. I would like to think about some of the ways Christians might be *right* to speak about the new creation in this way—some of the ways it might be true and meaningful to describe the new creation and the Spirit's work as *beautiful*. I will argue that when we look at some of the features that are most characteristic of beauty, we can see that in some important ways Christian intuition is correct. When Christians call Zion beautiful, they are saying something more meaningful, more insightful, and more precise than simply "heaven will be great." And when Christians describe the eschatological work of the Spirit as beautifying, this is more than a rhetorical flourish.

We will take as our guide a well-known description of beauty from St. Thomas Aquinas:[1]

> Species or beauty has a likeness to the property of the Son. For beauty includes three conditions, "integrity" or "perfection," since those things which are impaired are by the very fact ugly; due "proportion" or "harmony"; and lastly, "brightness" or "clarity," whence things are called beautiful which have a bright color.
>
> *Summa Theologica* I, q. 39, art. 8[2]

One virtue of this definition is that it explicitly associates beauty with Jesus Christ. The beauty of the new creation is the beauty of Jesus Christ because Jesus *is* the *eschatos*. He is the new creation, the pioneer of the resurrection from the dead that God intends for all creation. And the eschatological work of the Spirit can be characterized as "beautifying" because his work is to remake us in the likeness of the altogether beautiful humanity of Jesus Christ.

A second attractive feature of this definition is that it gestures toward two of the most significant traditions in philosophical aesthetics. Jennifer McMahon suggests that, historically, theories of beauty can be divided into these broad traditions: the Pythagorean and the pleasure-principle.[3] The Pythagorean emphasizes proportion, harmony, and *ratio*-nality. The tradition of the pleasure-principle, on the other hand, focuses on delight, attraction, and the sensual appeal of the beautiful.

We will consider three facets of beauty suggested by Aquinas's definition. These three characteristics do not provide a complete account of beauty or

1. I am not, however, intending to provide a thorough exposition of Aquinas's description or an account of his ideas on aesthetics.

2. *The Summa Theologica of St. Thomas Aquinas*, 2nd and rev. ed., 1920. Literally translated by Fathers of the English Dominican Province Online Edition, copyright © 2008 by Kevin Knight.

3. Jennifer Anne McMahon, "Beauty," in *The Routledge Companion to Aesthetics*, ed. Berys Gaut and Dominic McIver Lopes (New York: Routledge, 2001), 227. In similar fashion Umberto Eco describes the two fundamental impulses of medieval aesthetics as the aesthetics of *quantity*—proportion, order, form, and number—and the aesthetics of *quality*—color, brightness, and beauty's sensual appeal and delight (*Art and Beauty in the Middle Ages*, trans. Hugh Bredin [New Haven: Yale University Press, 1986], 42, 43, 47–49).

"necessary and sufficient conditions" for beauty. They do, however, give us an outline of some of its most distinctive features.

Perfection

Aquinas's first condition of beauty is perfection (*perfectio*) or integrity (*integritas*). If the beauty of Christ and the beauty of the new creation is to be characterized as "perfection," however, this must be—as we've already seen—a perfection that can accommodate scars. The perfection of the kingdom of God is not the airbrushed sheen of the fashion magazine. In the same way, Pentecost prevents us from thinking of eschatological "perfection" as a sterile uniformity—like soldiers on parade. These shallow conceptions of perfection are inadequate to a theological account of beauty, and they are also inadequate to an artistic account of beauty.

The artwork that masks difficulty (as Kundera points out), that covers over scars and struggles, is not beautiful, but kitsch. We are deeply dissatisfied, for example, with a film or novel that brushes away all the tensions and crises of the plot and concludes with an abrupt "and they all lived happily ever after." Such an ending does not complete but undermines the beauty of the work. Even if the superficial polish of the ending pleases us at first, we are left with the nagging objection: *but that isn't true*; *that isn't honest*. More than "happily ever after," readers hope for an ending that—whether happy or sad—is coherent, satisfying, well-formed; one that is suited to what has come before and draws things together in a way that is complete and whole. We seek what critic Frank Kermode calls "*pleroma*, fullness, the fullness that results from completion."[4] It is just this kind of completion that a clumsy happy ending fails to provide. The story hasn't been faithful to its own materials and trajectory. It hasn't carried its characters and history through to completion but has tossed their development aside in favor of wrapping things up neatly. The ending doesn't arise organically out of what has come before, and so there is no sense of wholeness. This "perfection" of polish and uniformity is a lie.

Against such a superficial perfection, Aquinas elaborates *perfection* as *integrity*—a word that is a synonym of *honesty*. The perfection of integrity is *wholeness* and *completeness* (goals that kitsch abandons in favor of a kind of false and superficial perfection). Integrity means "the presence in an organic whole of all the parts which concur in defining it as that which it is."[5] (This is the way we use the term in a moral sense as well. The speech and actions of a person of integrity have an "organic wholeness." Such a person does not suddenly abandon a part of herself in order to impress, to get out of a difficult

4. Quoted in Paul S. Fiddes, *The Promised End: Eschatology in Theology and Literature* (Oxford: Blackwell, 2000), 4–5.

5. Eco, *Art and Beauty*, 78.

situation, or to achieve a particular end. She doesn't act one way in public and a radically different way in private, but what she is, she is "all the way through.")

Perfection-as-integrity does in fact seem to be something we value in many works of art. Great works of art often are characterized by wholeness or completion, and in one of two ways. First, many great works of art give the impression of "wholeness." They are whole in that they lack nothing, nor do they have any extra or gratuitous elements. Every part is fully integrated (hence it has "integrity"). The great Renaissance architect Alberti defined beauty as "a sort of chordal combination, a harmony between the different units which does not allow anything to be added or taken away without having an injurious effect upon the whole."[6] Aristotle makes this a condition of a beautifully formed plot: "the structural union of the parts being such that, if any one of them is displaced or removed, the whole will be disjointed and disturbed. For a thing whose presence or absence makes no visible difference, is not an organic part of the whole."[7]

In addition to this, in many works of art one feels that the artist has brought the material elements of her art to completion, that in her art she has been able to unfold the qualities and character of her material to greatest effect. Whether she is a worker in sound, color, shape, or word, her art makes manifest what these elements are most truly. A striking example of this is the work of Brian Gladwell, an artist who works with corrugated cardboard. Gladwell turns disposable materials—the kind of stuff they ship refrigerators in—into fine furniture and, in the process, reveals the extraordinary qualities of a seemingly ordinary material.[8]

It is right to speak of the new creation and the eschatological work of the Spirit as "beautifying" if by this beauty we mean the perfection of *integritas*. The work of the Holy Spirit is to perfect the creation by bringing it to completion, making humanity and each created thing what it most truly and fully is.[9] Basil the Great writes,

> Only when a man has been cleansed from the shame of his evil, and has returned to his natural beauty, and the original form of the Royal Image has been restored in him, is it possible for him to approach the Paraclete. Then, like the sun, He [the Holy Spirit] will show you in Himself the image of the invisible, and with purified eyes you will see in this blessed image the unspeakable beauty of its prototype. Through Him hearts are lifted up, the infirm are held by the hand and those who progress are brought to perfection.[10]

6. Quoted in Knud Jeppesen, *Counterpoint: The Polyphonic Vocal Style of the Sixteenth Century*, trans. Glen Haydon (New York: Dover, 1992), 83.

7. Aristotle, *The Poetics of Aristotle: With Critical Notes and a Translation*, 1.8. 4th ed., trans. S. H. Butcher (London: MacMillan and Co., 1917), 35.

8. Images of Gladwell's work are available at www.briangladwell.com.

9. Colin Gunton, *The Christian Faith: An Introduction to Christian Doctrine* (Oxford: Blackwell, 2002), 156.

10. St. Basil the Great, *On the Holy Spirit*, trans. David Anderson (Crestwood, NY: St. Vladimir's Seminary Press, 1980), 44.

In the Spirit, and in the new creation, the human being is "returned to his natural beauty . . . the unspeakable beauty of its prototype." Where chaos and division has disrupted our humanity, the Spirit brings wholeness and *integritas*.

Proportion

Aquinas's second condition of beauty is "due proportion or harmony" (*debita proportio sive consonantia*). For much of Western history, this has been the aesthetic ideal *par excellence* and has been particularly associated with music. The ideal of proportion or harmony is usually traced back to the ancient Greek thinker Pythagoras and his study of musical intervals. For Pythagoras, a kind of harmonious and proportionate arrangement of elements was the key to understanding not only music but all of reality. The same universal ratio that orders musical tones and relates them to one another, according to Pythagoras, extends outward to the heavenly bodies and inward to our own souls. This in fact is why music moves us as deeply as it does. We meet there the kind of organizing, beautifying principle that in-*forms* the very heavens.

> Among all things however disparate
> there reigns an order, and this gives the form
> that makes the universe resemble God. . . .
>
> And in this order all created things,
> According to their bent, maintain their place,
> Disposed in proper distance from their Source; . . .
>
> This is what carries fire toward the moon,
> This is the moving force in mortal hearts,
> This is what binds the earth and makes it one.[11]

"Harmony" figures prominently in Plato's dialogues as well. While it always retains its aesthetic sense, the word is used to describe the balanced relationship between the various elements of one's own person,[12] between the various parts of society,[13] and even to describe the diverse unity of the cosmos and the soul.[14]

What we must not miss is that harmony in this sense is not uniformity or unanimity but the beauty that emerges from different elements in right relationship. There is something of this in Czeslaw Milosz's wonderful short

11. Dante, *The Divine Comedy*, vol. 3, *Paradise*, Canto I, 104–17, trans. Mark Musa (London: Penguin, 1984), 4.

12. See, for instance, Plato, *Republic*, 443d–e.

13. Ibid., 432a.

14. Plato, *Timaeus*, 32a–37d, 47c–d.

poem, "When the Moon." Milosz, in one glance, sees both the rising moon and women strolling by in flowery dresses. He finds himself suddenly seized by "their eyes, eyelashes, and the whole arrangement of the world."[15]

It is, in Dante's words, "an order" from "things disparate." We see a world in which there is not just "a moon" and "women" and "flowery dresses" but a breathtakingly varied concord in which all of these together are somehow part of "the whole arrangement of the world"—each shining on, filtering through, and reflecting off of the others.

St. Augustine inherited and made use of this Pythagorean tradition. One of the first works he composed after his conversion to Christianity was the treatise *De Musica*, a book that describes the proportions and ratios that make music possible and considers the significance of these for theology.[16] Music is theologically meaningful, Augustine will explain, because there we discover "*what proportion is* and *how great is its authority in all things*."[17] The important thing about proportion or harmony is that it describes a particular *relationship*. A single number cannot be a proportion in this sense, for instance. "Five" isn't a proportion. The relationship between five and fifteen is, however—namely, the proportion "one-third." "One-third" describes (in this instance) the relationship that arises when five is five and fifteen is fifteen.

This kind of proportion is also essential to music, Augustine argues. In a piece of music, particular notes and rhythms become what they are according to how they are related to all the other musical events around them. Consider what it means to hear a group of notes as a melody. I can begin the melody of a particular song—let's say, Parliament's "Give up the Funk (Tear the Roof off the Sucker)"—on the note B, or E, or F sharp, in fact, on any pitch at all. This simple act of transposition is possible because the tune "Give up the Funk" does not consist in a certain set of pitches (B followed by B, followed by C sharp, followed by E, and so on) but in a certain set of *relationships* between tones (or degrees of the scale). When we hear a melody *as* a melody, the question our ear asks of each sound is not, "Are you an A or a C sharp?" but "Where do you stand in relation to the other tones in this melody?"[18] This is an interesting feature of music.

15. Czeslaw Milosz, "When the Moon," *New and Collected Poems (1931–2001)* (New York: Ecco, 2001), 222.

16. For further discussion, see Steven R. Guthrie, "Augustine's *De Musica* and the Ratio of Redemption," in a forthcoming volume edited by Ned Bustard (Square Halo Publishing), and Steven R. Guthrie, "Carmen Universitatis: A Theological Study of Music and Measure" (PhD diss., University of St. Andrews, 2000).

17. St. Augustine, *De Musica*, 1.12.23, in *The Fathers of the Church: A New Translation*, vol. 4, trans. Robert Catesby Taliaferro (New York: Fathers of the Church, Inc., 1947), 200, emphasis added.

18. "What makes a melody is not, properly speaking, the tones but the relations between tones. . . . To hear a melody is thus first of all to hear a sequence of tones which stand in specific

If I were to paint my house red, I would use different stuff than if I were to paint my house blue—namely, red paint instead of blue paint. But different melodies and rhythms don't arise from different stuff (as if some used notes and beats and others didn't) but from different relationships between notes and beats. A particular melody or a particular rhythm *just is* that particular set of relationships between musical events.

For Augustine this musical harmony and proportion is a powerful image of a universal truth. Living a holy life, like playing a pleasing melody, means being differently *ordered*, rightly related, and proportioned. There now is a harmonious and proportionate relationship between me and God, me and my neighbor, me and the community, me and the physical world, and so on. Augustine describes such a person as an "ordered soul." "That soul keeps order," he writes, "that, with its whole self, loves Him above itself, that is, God, and fellow souls as itself. In virtue of this love it orders lower things and suffers no disorder from them."[19]

This, Augustine believes, is some of what we can learn from music. First, music teaches us that things take on their distinctive character through relationship. The difference between a "right note" and a "wrong note" is the difference in that note's relationship to the other notes around it. The function of proportion in other arts makes this clear as well. As we look at a building we might say that a particular column is "too tall" or "too wide." We don't mean that there is something wrong with the column itself, however. If the building itself were taller, or wider, or whatever, its dimensions might be perfect. Its "too-tall-ness" is a function of its relationships to the other architectural elements of the building. Similarly, Augustine believes, we as human beings are "in tune" or "out of tune" by virtue of our proportions with other things—how we are related to God and the whole harmony of relationships in God's world.

Second, we learn that we live in a cosmos in which relationship is *possible*. Music teaches us that we live in the sort of world in which acoustic vibrations, cultural practices (like singing songs), our physical senses, and our mental processes can all be enlisted and drawn together in a single experience. Not only is such a thing possible, in fact, but it is *beautiful*. Each created thing can look to God and all the rest of creation and repeat the old lovers' cliché: *we were meant for each other!* In the same way, Augustine believes we are moved by the unified but multivoiced complexity of the musical experience because it speaks to us of a world of relation.

Third, and closely related to this, music teaches us that the differences and diversity of the world are not a problem to be overcome but an essential

---

relation to one another in respect to pitch and tones" (Victor Zuckerkandl, *Man the Musician* [Princeton: Princeton University Press, 1973], 91).

19. St. Augustine, *De Musica*, 6.14.46, in *Fathers of the Church*, 368.

component of beauty. Harmony is only possible if the elements of that harmony *both* come together *and* remain distinct. ("And in this order all created things, *according to their bent*, *maintain their place*," writes Dante.) When all things *are what they are* in all their glittering variety, and when all of these are joined together in a cosmos—in a *uni*verse—it is beautiful.

It is not surprising, then, that when in *The City of God* Augustine describes the new creation ("the celestial city"), he describes it as a place of harmony, proportion, and right relation.

> The peace of the body . . . consists in the duly proportioned arrangement of its parts. The peace of the irrational soul is the harmonious repose of the appetites, and that of the rational soul the harmony of knowledge and action. The peace of body and soul is the well-ordered and harmonious life and health of the living creature. Peace between man and God is the well-ordered obedience of faith to eternal law. Peace between man and man is well-ordered concord. Domestic peace is the well-ordered concord between those of the family who rule and those who obey. Civil peace is a similar concord among the citizens. The peace of the celestial city is the perfectly ordered and harmonious enjoyment of God, and of one another in God. The peace of all things is the tranquillity [sic] of order. Order is the distribution which allots things equal and unequal, each to its own place.[20]

Augustine believes that the new creation will be characterized by a universal restoration of right relationship—and for this reason, he can also characterize the new creation as beautiful.

In this sense too, the eschatological work of the Holy Spirit can meaningfully be described as "beautifying." The bringing about of right relation that we've described, the creation of "harmony," is an apt description of the Spirit's work. Within the body of the church the Spirit is the giver of many diverse gifts (1 Cor. 12:4–11) and, in this sense, the author of the many-ness of the body. This diversifying and particularizing work of the Spirit is an essential counterpart to Christ's role as *eschatos*, second Adam, and the form of the infinite. Athanasius describes Jesus's remaking of our humanity, likening him to a great artist:

> You know what happens when a portrait that has been painted on a panel becomes obliterated through external stains. The artist does not throw away the panel, but the subject of the portrait has to come and sit for it again, and then the likeness is re-drawn on the same material. Even so was it with the All-holy Son of God.[21]

20. Augustine, *City of God Against the Pagans*, 19.13, in *The Select Library of The Nicene and Post-Nicene Fathers of the Christian Church*, vol. 2, ed. Philip Schaff, trans. Marcus Dods (Grand Rapids: Eerdmans, 1983/1871), 409.

21. Athanasius, *On the Incarnation*, trans. and ed. by A Religious of C. S. M. V. (Crestwood, NY: St. Vladimir's Seminary Press, 2003), 41–42.

Thomas Smail applies a similar analogy to the work of the Spirit, adding a crucial point.

> [One may] think of the Spirit much more personally and creatively as an artist whose one subject is the Son, and who is concerned to paint countless portraits of that subject on countless human canvasses using the paints and brushes provided by countless human cultures and historical situations. . . . It is Jesus, the incarnate Son of the Father, and no other that the Spirit seeks to portray. Each portrait is successful and creative, not because it makes of him what he is not, by forming him in our likeness and conforming him to our preferences and predilections, but because it uses ever new cultural approaches and historical situations to bring out more of the infinite variety of saving truth that is in him.[22]

Athanasius's illustration emphasizes Christ as the form of the new humanity. Smail, on the other hand, provides an essential complement, by drawing attention to the particularizing work of the Spirit. The artistic analogy is apt. The Spirit is not an automated die-press, punching out stacks of Jesus-copies, one after another. The Spirit's perfecting work is creative and sensitive to the character of the material before him. Those filled by the Spirit are one body of Christ, renewed in his image; yet "varieties of services" (1 Cor. 12:5) and diverse gifts (1 Cor. 12:6–10) are given "by one and the same Spirit, *who allots to each one individually* just as the Spirit chooses" (1 Cor. 12:11). The work of the Spirit is both particularizing (or "diversifying") and unifying. The distinctiveness of each member does not destroy the unity of the body; the unity of the body does not annul the distinctiveness of each member: that, in essence, is *proportio* and *consonantia*. The new creation will be beautiful because there will be harmony and right relationship between God and humanity, among humanity, and among all that God has made. Each thing will be most truly what it is, and—what is more, and amazing—the utterly distinct character of each being will contribute to the beauty of the whole.

Pleasure

Aquinas's third condition of beauty is "brightness or clarity, whence things are called beautiful which have a bright color." Here Aquinas draws our attention to the immediate impression that beautiful things make upon our senses. The medieval love of color and light, Umberto Eco writes, is connected to "a most lively feeling for the purely sensuous pleasure of things."[23] For this reason we can paraphrase this third condition as "pleasure"—an important term in

22. Tom Smail, *The Giving Gift: The Holy Spirit in Person* (London: Darton, Longman & Todd, 1988), 77.

23. Eco, *Art and Beauty*, 44.

another of Aquinas's definitions of beauty:[24] "beautiful things are those which please when seen. Hence beauty consists in due proportion; for the senses delight in things duly proportioned."[25] In this definition Aquinas once again highlights the importance of proportion but also draws attention to the fact that "beauty" doesn't only refer to a quality in *things*; it also identifies a type of response in *us*. Beauty "pleases when seen." Beauty delights.

Many philosophers—particularly those writing since Kant—have described the distinctive sort of delight associated with beauty as "disinterested pleasure."[26] A sculpture sitting on my desk might please me because it reminds me of an old friend who gave it to me as a gift. It might delight me because I am aware that it is worth a small fortune. Perhaps if I were an art historian, it might give me pleasure because it provides all sorts of interesting insights into a particular sculptor, his techniques, and so on. It might even please me simply because it holds down my papers, or looks impressive, or makes visitors to my office think that I'm kind of "artsy." In each of these instances, however, my delight is in something other than the sculpture. You could ask me, "Why do you care so much about that sculpture?" and I could point to some good thing I value that lies *outside of* the work itself (happy memories, its financial worth, or its historical interest, for instance). But what if what pleases me is just the work of art *for its own sake*? What I value in that case is not some other good thing outside the sculpture but just the work itself and the experience of looking at it. The work of art is not drawn in to satisfy some other concern I am pursuing or enlisted to serve my practical interests.

There is a silly exaggeration of this idea, expressed in Oscar Wilde's dictum: "All art is quite useless."[27] Also, various distortions have arisen by making "disinterestedness" the sole criterion of art.[28] But these caricatures and misappropriations shouldn't undermine the valid point being made: sometimes we take pleasure in something for its own sake, and this is one of the interesting

24. "Classical authors, Aquinas, Hume and Kant, are in general agreement with respect to the main point, namely that what is beautiful is the cause of notable pleasure and that this is enough to differentiate beauty from at least some other forms of goodness" (Mary Mothersill, *Beauty Restored* [Oxford: Clarendon, 1974], 373). Kant's influential discussion of the issue can be found in *Critique of Judgment*, Part I, Book I "The Analytic of the Beautiful."

25. Aquinas, *Summa Theologica* I, q. 5, art. 4, ad. 1.

26. "Few ideas in the history of aesthetics have been more pervasive than that of the disinterestedness of the aesthetic attitude. It has figured prominently, in various guises, in the writings of eighteenth-century English empiricists and of nineteenth-century German idealists, and in much twentieth-century writing. The idea can be traced back to Lord Shaftesbury (1671–1713) but Kant was the first to incorporate it into a theory about the logical character of aesthetic judgement" (David Whewell, "Kant, Immanuel," in *A Companion to Aesthetics*, ed. David E. Cooper [Oxford: Blackwell, 1992], 251).

27. Oscar Wilde, *The Picture of Dorian Gray* (London: Penguin, 1985), 4.

28. Nicholas Wolterstorff's *Art in Action* is an extended argument against elevating "disinterested pleasure" to a necessary and sufficient condition for granting an artifact the status of "work of art" (*Art in Action: Toward a Christian Aesthetic* [Grand Rapids: Eerdmans, 1980]).

features of aesthetic pleasure. Rather than drawing the beautiful object into the orbit of my concerns, *I* am the one drawn in; the work *captures* rather than *serves* my interest. "To be interested in beauty," writes Roger Scruton, "is to set all interests aside, so as to attend to the thing itself." In these instances, "we take an interest that is not governed by interest but which is, so to speak, entirely *devoted* to the object."[29] This experience of pleasure has literally an ecstatic quality to it. When I delight in beauty I stand outside (*ek-stasis*) myself for a moment, and am taken up with another. Elaine Scarry describes this ecstatic character of beauty as a "radical decentering."[30] In our delight with the beautiful object "we cease to stand . . . at the center of our own world. We willingly cede our ground to the thing that stands before us."[31] A disinterested pleasure is characterized by *delight in another*.

A disinterested pleasure is also one that is characterized by *freedom*. Genesis declares that after the three days of forming and the three days of filling, creation culminates in Sabbath, the "feast of Creation."[32] "The whole work of creation was performed *for the sake of the Sabbath*,"[33] writes Moltmann. This day alone receives its own blessing from the Lord and is hallowed by him (Gen. 2:3). The orientation of all creation, then, is toward this day of delight.[34] In his profound study of the Sabbath, Jewish scholar Abraham Heschel repeats the words of the Sabbath morning liturgy:

> To God who rested from all action on the seventh day
> and ascended upon His throne of glory.
> He vested the day of rest with beauty;
> He called the Sabbath a delight.[35]

The delight of the Sabbath is the delight of freedom. It is a day of freedom for all creation: "You shall not do any work—you, or your son or your daughter, or your male or female slave, or your ox or your donkey, or any of your livestock, or the resident alien in your towns, so that your male and female slave may rest as well as you" (Deut. 5:14; cf. Exod. 20:10). The very ground of the earth is to be hallowed with Sabbath rest (Lev. 25:1–5) so that on this day God's people regard one another, animals, and the land as something other than "producer" or "consumer." On this day I am reminded that the world exists

29. Roger Scruton, *Beauty* (Oxford: Oxford University Press, 2009), 26, 27.

30. Elaine Scarry, *On Beauty and Being Just* (Princeton: Princeton University Press, 1999), 111. Scarry draws the phrase and this insight from Simone Weil.

31. Ibid., 112.

32. Jürgen Moltmann, *God in Creation: An Ecological Doctrine of Creation* (London: SCM, 1985), 277.

33. Ibid., emphasis original.

34. Abraham Joshua Heschel, *The Sabbath: Its Meaning for Modern Man* (New York: Farrar, Straus and Giroux, 1951), 14. See also the discussion in Wolterstorff, *Art in Action*, 79–83.

35. Heschel, *The Sabbath*, 24.

apart from my intentions for it. In this way, my observance of the Sabbath grants freedom to others and the world. Likewise, the one celebrating Sabbath receives and celebrates freedom. "Remember that you were a slave in the land of Egypt, and the Lord your God brought you out from there with a mighty hand and an outstretched arm; therefore the Lord your God commanded you to keep the sabbath day" (Deut. 5:15). On the Sabbath, the creation is not wielded like a tool or "worked" like the soil, but it is *received*. "See! The Lord has given you the sabbath, therefore on the sixth day he gives you food for two days" (Exod. 16:29).

For Jews and Christians, this Sabbath rest is not only a remembrance of the beginning of creation, but an anticipation of its completion. "The essence of the world to come is Sabbath eternal, and the seventh day in time is an example of eternity."[36] New creation, like creation, will culminate in a feast (cf. Isa. 25:6; Rev. 19:9).

The pleasures and beauties of Sabbath, of creation, and of new creation reflect the character of God. But they also are meant to nurture what humanity is to become. "Call the Sabbath a delight," writes Heschel, "a delight to the soul and a delight to the body. . . . 'Sanctify the Sabbath by choice meals, by beautiful garments; delight your soul with pleasure and [the LORD] will reward you for this very pleasure.' "[37] According to Heschel the pleasure of the Sabbath, this act of finding-pleasure-in, has a *sanctifying* quality.

Of course, as a moral and spiritual good, "pleasure" has a pretty ambiguous reputation. Roger Scruton observes a distinction between pleasure *from* and pleasure *in*.[38] It is possible to "*take* pleasure *from*" someone or something in a kind of hedonistic theft. In such an act the object is only accidentally related to the pleasure derived. The moral fault is precisely in the fact that the hedonist is indifferent to the source of his pleasure. "Pleasure from" is oriented away from the object in question and back toward the one taking pleasure. "Pleasure *in*," on the other hand, is wholly oriented toward the beautiful object. But to find pleasure in another (rather than simply in a hedonistic fashion to take pleasure from another) is to be moved outside of myself.

It is meaningful, then, to speak of the eschatological work of the Spirit as "beautifying" because beauty has to do with pleasure. The new creation, the Sabbath feast the Spirit is bringing about is pleasant, delightful, and abundant. More than that, the new creation will be marked by a free pleasure—not "taking pleasure from" but "taking pleasure in." This sort of pleasure is anticipated in our experience of beauty.

The pleasure and delight of the new creation is a beatitude in which each being's pleasure arises in praise of rather than at the expense of another. In

36. Ibid., 74.
37. Ibid., 19.
38. Scruton, *Beauty*, 30.

God's eternal presence his people find "pleasures forevermore" (Ps. 16:11). In dwelling among God's people the redeemed likewise enjoy perfect communion with those "in whom is all [their] delight" (Ps. 16:3). The pleasure of the new creation, in other words, is nothing other than a manifestation of the love of God and love of our neighbor, which are commanded of us. When carried on the winds of the Spirit, pleasure is a means of grace.

The Beautifying Spirit

Christians are indeed justified in speaking of the new creation as beautiful. And it is right to describe the work of the Spirit who is the pledge and firstfruits of that new creation as "beautifying." In saying these things and making these associations, Christians are saying something meaningful and substantive about the Spirit and his work. The Spirit is the perfecter of creation, bringing wholeness and completion. The Spirit is the giver of proportion, nurturing harmony and right relation. And the Spirit can rightly be associated with pleasure—particularly that sort of delight that takes pleasure in others and is marked by freedom.

In the same way, the artist is justified in honoring the experience of beauty as "spiritual." This doesn't mean that art becomes a kind of surrogate Holy Spirit. Our ability to identify "perfection," "proportion," or "pleasure" is no less fallible than our human ability to recognize truth and goodness.

"Music," writes Thomas Carlyle, "is well said to be the speech of angels; in fact, nothing among the utterances allowed to man is felt to be so divine. It brings us near to the Infinite; we look for moments, across the cloudy elements, into the eternal Sea of Light, when song leads and inspires us."[39] This may strike us as a slightly hysterical bit of Romantic hyperbole—and at one level, it is just that. The "not yet" pole of the New Testament's "already–not yet" seems to have been forgotten. Music alone out of all creation has been exempted from passing through the cross and grave on the way to new creation. And yet, there is something right in what Carlyle says. The Spirit is the firstfruits, bringing the new creation into our presence even now and steadily drawing all things toward consummation. When we truly experience beauty, particularly beauty that is marked by perfection, proportion, and clarity, we may sense that we have encountered something "spiritual," perhaps even something of the new creation. We are right to feel this way.

39. "The Opera," in Thomas Carlyle, *Critical and Miscellaneous Essays* (New York: Peter Fenelon Collier, 1897), 508.

Epilogue

The Museum of Spirituality

Imagine that an alien has landed in your backyard. This alien is in fact an extraterrestrial anthropologist, and he has come to investigate human culture. Our visitor has heard reports of human artistic practices and is intensely curious. "Please—" the alien asks, "I would like to hear people playing music. I would like to see dance and works of art. Can you help me?"

I sometimes present this scenario to students in my classes. Where would you direct such an alien, one who has touched down here in Nashville, Tennessee? Where would you send him to find art and music and dance?

"He should go to the Schermerhorn"—Nashville's state-of-the-art symphony center—a student will suggest. "Or maybe the Grand Ole Opry!" someone else might offer. "He should go to the Frist"—Nashville's art museum—another student will say, "they have an exhibit of the Dutch Old Masters right now." A fourth person volunteers, "The university ballet is putting on a performance Friday night."

Here is what our extraterrestrial anthropologist might conclude: human art lives in concert halls, museums, theaters, and arenas—purpose-built structures, specially designated for aesthetic enjoyment. It is produced and performed by a fairly select bunch of highly trained specialists: world-renowned painters, professionally trained musicians and dancers, or celebrity recording artists. And, art occurs within a relatively limited window of time, on specific, scheduled occasions. Art, in other words, is something that happens in a special place (like a concert hall) at a special time (such as 7:30 Friday evening) through the efforts of special people (like professional artists). This is the way of thinking about art that occurs to us most naturally, and, taking the scope of human history and culture into account, it is utterly idiosyncratic.[1]

Art Outside of Life

In the last chapter I spoke about disinterested pleasure—a powerful idea, and a helpful one. But it is also an idea that, as it has worked itself out, has had some unhelpful consequences. Recall for a moment the question, what is beauty? In the West in the modern era, one answer has been dominant. Beauty, it is said, is the experience of disinterested pleasure. The experience of beauty involves reflecting on and contemplating the aesthetic qualities of a work for the intrinsic pleasure they afford. We experience beauty when we consider and delight in a thing in itself, rather than simply regarding it as a means to some other end. Corresponding to this, art came to be associated with one particular function: art exists for the purpose of aesthetic contemplation.

These ideas have helped to shape our artistic culture in all sorts of ways. One aspect of that culture to which they have contributed is the development of the gallery and the concert hall. These are institutions that appeared on the scene relatively recently—the oldest concert hall in Europe, for instance, is the Holywell Music Room, in Oxford, built in 1748. New York's famed Carnegie Hall opened in 1891. Before this time, art adorned the walls of the wealthy, the public square, or the space of worship. Music accompanied dance or worship or social rituals of other kinds. But if art is *only* art, if it is to be contemplated aesthetically, then it is an insult to employ it simply for "decoration" or as "background music" for some other activity. If the aesthetic qualities are to be contemplated for their own intrinsic merit, then it makes sense to create a space specifically for contemplation. Such a place would be free of distractions and specifically designed for the presentation and appreciation of art. It would be a place not used for any other purpose—in fact, specifically *not* a "useful" space—but solely set apart for the activity of reflection. Nicholas Wolterstorff writes, "If the action of perceptual contemplation is to be performed at all satisfactorily, particularly when its satisfactory practice requires mental concentration, rather special physical conditions are required. To listen to a work of music intently one needs a quiet place—exactly what a concert hall undertakes to furnish. To look at a painting intently one needs a well-lighted space—exactly what a gallery undertakes to provide."[2]

Noble as all this may be at one level, it has contributed to the rather unwelcome picture of art we have communicated to our alien friend. Art has come to be increasingly segregated from everyday life. Rather than being

1. Over the next several paragraphs I am summarizing the argument of Nicholas Wolterstorff, *Art in Action: Toward a Christian Aesthetic* (Grand Rapids: Eerdmans, 1980), esp. 3–39.

2. Ibid., 25.

something that happens in the *midst* of life, connected with all its activities, art came to be regarded as something that happens *outside* of ordinary life—in special places (like museums), at special times (like concerts or exhibits), and performed by a special class of people. So, only singers sing, only dancers dance, and only painters paint. Few opportunities remain for people to make music together. Even fewer opportunities exist for people to dance with one another. Our cities and buildings are "purely functional," with aesthetic considerations subcontracted and farmed out to another sort and another set of institutions.

Art and beauty, which have for centuries served to enrich and enable ordinary life, have come to be thought of as something altogether separate from ordinary life. I say that we have come to *think* of them in this way, though, in reality, art and beauty continue to permeate our existence. We read stories to get our children to sleep and listen to music on the way to work. Human beings, whether or not they are "artists," are irrepressibly artistic. We need not only a roof and four walls, but paint, pictures, and décor. We need not only clothing, but adornment. We need not only food, but flavor, spices, and cuisine. Human beings make things sparkle, not only jewelry, but saucepans. In our most ordinary communication we think not only in definitions and logical relations, but in cadence, prosody, and metaphor. Art and beauty have not ceased to be a significant part of our lives, but in many ways the peculiar history of our culture keeps us from *recognizing* its persistent presence. In such an environment the opportunities for art to happen are steadily narrowed down or eliminated.

The Museum of Spirituality

I offer all of this as a kind of analogy—one more point of resemblance between art and spirituality in our culture. Too often we think of spirituality as something strange and esoteric. Spirituality is something radically "other" than ordinary life. It is practiced in monasteries, on the top of Tibetan mountains, or in Egyptian deserts. Its practitioners are hermits, mystics, monks, and priests. The spiritual experience on this account is also rare, a "once in a lifetime" type event—arising perhaps in a moment of profound personal crisis, or even as a result of a near-death experience. "Spirit" and the "spiritual," in other words, have at times been conceived—like "art"—as something that happens at special times, in special places, to very special people. The result—again as has often been the case with our thinking about art—is that we imagine that the spiritual is something altogether other than and set apart from daily existence and ordinary experience.

Of course this is not the case. If we are speaking about *Spirit*-uality, then Christians believe that the Holy Spirit is not only near to us, but alive *in* us. The Spirit is "the Lord, the giver of life." If God were to withdraw his Spirit, all of creation would return to dust. He is not far from anyone of us, then, for in him we live and move and have our being (Acts 17:28). Nevertheless, if we *think* of spirituality and the Holy Spirit as something mysteriously other than life, then we may fail to attend to his presence in our midst. The Holy Spirit, whose work is to empower and enable life, is separated from our daily life.

For this reason there is something very welcome and very right about the popular interest in "spirituality" that we mentioned at the very beginning of this book. Books, television shows, and lectures extol the spirituality of sex, cooking, yoga, running, gardening—and art. There are a couple of very important and (potentially) very Christian insights here. First, an "everyday spirituality" recognizes that the Spirit is not distant from us. The Spirit is "the Lord, the giver of life," and since there is no other alternate source of life apart from God, all that has life is held in being by the Spirit of God. Second, this kind of whole-life spirituality is consonant with the idea that the work of the Spirit is to complete (rather than unmake) our humanity. The work of the Holy Spirit is to make us just the sort of beings who make art and make love, who garden and enjoy food, who enjoy the strength and health of their bodies and participate in the goodness of nature. The transcendent meaningfulness we experience in these activities is a kind of *Spirit*-uality. We sense something of God's good intention for us in the beginning and something of the good end toward which the Spirit is drawing us.

But there is also a danger that accompanies the popular discussions of spirituality. It is a danger that arises *because of* rather than *despite* the Spirit's intimate involvement with our humanity. The involvement of the Spirit in all of life is ultimately an expression of God's desire to dwell in the midst of his people in a *relationship* of intimacy and love. If "museum spirituality" risks losing the Spirit by keeping him so far apart from daily life, an unbaptized "everyday spirituality" risks losing the Spirit by bringing him *so close* to daily life—so close in fact that he ends up being *absorbed* into cooking, yoga, gardening, or music. From the perspective of the biblical texts, the Holy Spirit is not a nameless, impersonal force, adding goose bumps to our various experiences. Rather, the Holy Spirit "is none other than the fulfillment of the promise that God himself would once again be present with his people,"[3] Gordon Fee writes. "The coming of the Holy Spirit in and among us means that the living God, in the person of the Spirit, is indeed with us."[4] It would be tragic, then, if in acknowledging the presence of the spiritual we lost sight of the God who by his Spirit is present with us.

As we have repeated throughout this book, the work of the Spirit is to perfect and complete our humanity, a work the Spirit has in fact already accomplished in the glorified humanity of Jesus Christ. Jesus is the ground and the confirmation that the Holy Spirit is concerned with our humanity,

3. Gordon Fee, *Paul, the Spirit, and the People of God* (Peabody, MA: Hendrickson, 1996), 22.
4. Ibid., 34.

but for just that reason Jesus Christ in all his concrete, historical specificity cannot be set to one side in favor of a generic, abstract spirituality.

To say all of this is not a demotion of art or beauty or the powerful experience we have of these. It is not even to limit them to secondary importance or to characterize them as "mere signs" (things that can and should be safely set aside once they have done their work of pointing us onward and upward). We do not need to diminish the world in order to exalt the Spirit. In a noncompetitive, perichoretic universe, in a world informed by gift, things are *more* rather than *less* fully themselves by being related to one another. God's Spirit does not threaten but establishes and upholds the creation in all of its distinctive reality. When the dust of the earth is filled with the breath of God, it becomes a place of glory.

Subject Index

abstract art, 53–55, 60, 169n40
Adam, 65, 74–75
adoration, 15, 16
Adorno, Theodore, 82, 91
aesthetic contemplation, 212
aesthetic emotion, 159–60
aesthetic experience, 19
aesthetics, of quality and quantity, 198n3
age to come, 66, 191
Alberti, 200
allusivity, 16–17, 20
"already-not yet," 191, 192–93, 209
anger, 27
annihilatio mundi, 193–94
annunciation, 158n16
anointing, and glory, 37–38
Aristotle, 200
Arius, 40, 83
Armstrong, Louis, 28
art, xii–xiii
  as communication of emotion, 26
  and everyday life, 212–13
  as expressive, 25
  and ideology, 104–6
  and ineffability, 16–18
  mirrors work of Spirit, 70
  and spirituality, 161
artist, voice of, 147–48, 150
artistic genius, 27
artistry, "from below" and "from above," 103
ascending, 66
Athanasius, xii, 12–13, 14, 15, 36, 40–41, 42, 65, 67, 83, 125, 157, 191, 192, 205
atonal music, 55, 57n33, 59
Augustine, xiii, 115–16, 119, 123, 202–4

Babel, reversal of, 194
Bach, Johann Sebastian, 27, 104, 105, 106–7, 110
Bacon, Francis, 180
Baillie, Donald, 75n10
Balthasar, Hans Urs von, 84
Balzac, Honoré de, 131, 147
baptism, 15, 90, 91
Barber, Chris, 173–75
Barth, Karl, 6–7, 120
Barthes, Roland, 131, 132, 140
Basil the Great, 13, 15, 83, 200
Bauckham, Richard, 118n6, 124, 134–35, 189
beauty, xii–xiii, 16, 18, 50–53, 58, 60, 105, 177
  critics of, 179–87, 193
  and eschatology, 187, 197
  in eye of beholder, 182–84
  as intellectual, 58
  and new creation, 177–79
Beethoven, Ludwig von, 3, 26, 102
Begbie, Jeremy, xviii
Bell, Clive, 159–63
Belsey, Catherine, 108–9, 132, 133, 140
Bennett, Sarah, 175–76
Berkhof, Hendrikus, 19
Beuys, Joseph, 178
Bezalel, 116–17
"Big Other," 107–9, 111, 113, 115, 124, 140, 150
blindness, 133, 135, 136, 138, 140
body
  as temple, 78
  vs. spirit, 61
Bonaventure, 50
bourgeois ideology, 106–7, 132
breath, 8, 12, 35, 113, 166
breath of God, xvi, 40, 41, 43, 149
Broch, Hermann, 180n17
Brown, J. Carter, 95
Brueggemann, Walter, 135
Burke, Edmund, 185

Calvin, John, 41–42, 192
Cameron, Julia, xiii
captivity, 133
Caputo, John, 7, 11, 12, 14, 15
Cardiff, Neville, 179
Carlyle, Thomas, 209
celebrity, 123
Chambers, Ross, 103n23
chaos, defeat of, 187–90
charisms, 117, 122, 123
charity, 123
Charlemagne, 70
church, 164
  and music, 81–82
  as new creation, 76–77
circumincessio, 84
clerical power, 138
cognitivism, 169n39
Collingwood, R. G., 19
Coltrane, John, 28–34, 129–30
communication, 12
Communion, 89
community, xiv, xvi, 164
  identity in, 72–73
  and music, 81–82, 90–91
  as noncompetitive, 124
  remaking of, 75–77, 80, 91–92
  and song, 85
competition, 111, 122, 124
completion, 179, 199, 208
concert hall, as cultural institution, 211–12
Congar, Yves, 127
consummation, 43

contemplation, 212
control, 111, 123, 184
Cooper, David, 16
Copland, Aaron, 2
creatio ex nihilo, 120
creation, 64–65
  continuity and discontinuity with new creation, 193–94
  as gifted, 143–45
  voice of, 141, 146
creation account, 74–75, 188
creative discernment, 153, 167–70
creativity, 96, 141
  denied by postmodernism, 131, 132
  as gift, 150
  as gift-giving, 147–48, 150
  humility of, 128
  mysteriousness of, 112
  as nonrational, 97–98, 106
  as passive, 101
  and receptivity, 118, 146–48, 150
Cross, Patricia, 173
cultural artifacts, art as, 102, 103
culture, 102, 145
  voice of, 141, 146–47

dance, 173
Dante, 202, 204
darkness, 88
Davis, Jon, 20
Davis, Miles, 28, 31, 129
day of the Lord, 139
deep feeling, 25, 27
dehumanizing view of arts, 112
deification, 40n32, 42n39
Deism, 156, 162
delight
  in beauty, 206–7
  in new creation, 208–9
differentiated unity, 89
Dillard, Annie, 51–52, 60
Diotima, 49–50, 52, 53
discernment, xiv, 153, 156–59, 162, 173–76
disinterested pleasure, 206–7, 212
diversity, and beauty, 204–5
divinization, 42
doctrinal formulations, 5
domination, 111, 123, 126
Doty, Mark, 111, 140
drink, 14
Dunn, James, 39n31
dust, 35, 40, 41, 43, 49

Eco, Umberto, 198n3, 205
Eden, 74, 167–68
Eliot, George, 108, 109n49, 132, 133, 147
Ellsworth, David, 3, 7
Elshtain, Jean Bethke, 44
emotion, xiv, 25–28, 164
enfleshment, 37
Enlightenment, 138, 156
eschatology, xiv, xvi, 193
  and beauty, 187, 197
Esplund, Lance, 180n13
Eucharist, 89
everyday spirituality, 214
evil, 75
Exodus story, 116
experience, 6–7
exploitation, 126
expression, xiv
expressionism, 25–28, 168–69

fall, 74–75
false prophets, 137
Fee, Gordon, xv, 88, 214
feeling, 6
Flanagan, Tommy, 29
flesh, 48
  salvation of, 68
  vs. spirit, 61–64
Ford, David, 78n15, 87
formlessness, 187, 188–89
Foster, Frank, 29
fountain, 14
freedom, xvi, 88, 122, 132, 133, 136, 140, 153, 207–9

Gaines, Jamal, 20
gallery, as cultural institution, 211–12
generosity, 123
gift, Holy Spirit as, 115, 119, 124
gifts, giving, 123, 144–45, 150
Gillespie, Dizzy, 129
Gladwell, Brian, 200
glorification, 40, 41, 43, 127
glory, 37–38
God
  as gift-giver, 121, 144–45, 149
  glory of, 37–38, 39, 42
  as impersonal, 162–63
  incomprehensibility of, 4
  ineffability of, 13
  presence in creation, 157, 163
  presence in ordinary, 158n16, 161
God-in-All-Things, 159–63
godliness, 77
Golding, William, 165n33
Gordon, Dexter, 129
grace, 120
Gregory of Nazianzus, 13, 15
Gunton, Colin, 21, 150, 193
Hahl-Koch, Jelena, 53
Hampson, Daphne, 118, 125, 126
harmony, 80–81, 84, 86, 201–5, 209
Harries, Richard, 179
Hart, David Bentley, 180
Hawkins, Coleman, 129
heart of flesh, 69–70
Heidegger, Martin, 144n25
Heschel, Abraham, 134, 207–8
heteronomy, 118–19
Hickey, Dave, 183
hierarchy, 126
Hodges, Johnny, 129
Hoffmann, E. T. A., 3
holiness, 1, 77
"holy lie," 137, 138
Holy Spirit, xv–xvii
  anointing by, 38–40, 43
  beautifying work of, 200, 208
  as boundary-breaker, 9
  as carrier, 12
  descends and remains, 125
  dynamism of, 10–11
  filling of, 78–79
  as firstfruits, 191–92, 209
  as gift/giver, 115, 119, 124, 125, 130
  and incarnation, 37
  makes us truly human, 42–43, 92, 140, 149, 168, 177, 214
  as person, 20–21
  as plan-disrupter, 9–10
  and resurrection, 190–91
  as surprise-bringer, 10
  as teacher, 11
  work of, 7–8
Homer, 97–100, 102, 107, 108
homoousios, 83
honesty, 199
Honigsheim, Paul, 71
humanity
  glory and frailty of, 35, 41, 53
  re-creation of, 35, 43, 92, 140
  and the spiritual, 34, 64
humiliation, 126–27
humility, 126, 128

ideology, 104–6, 109n49, 112, 124, 132, 133, 134, 147, 153, 186
illumination, of Holy Spirit, 11
image of God, xvii, 36, 38, 42, 73, 82, 121–22, 149
  re-creation of, 75–77
image of Jesus Christ, 14, 42
immediacy, 32, 34
improvisation, 34
inbreaking, 66
incarnation, 12, 36–37, 42, 60–61, 68

incurvatus in se, 122
individuality, 84, 124, 141, 148
indwelling, 65–66
ineffability, xiv, 2, 3, 5, 10, 11, 16–18, 20
infection metaphor, 26
injustice, 140
inner meaning, 54–57
inspiration, 96, 98, 101, 105, 112–13, 140–41, 149
integrity, 199–201
internal meaning, of art, 59
intimacy, 163
inwardness, as prison, 122
Ion (Plato), 96–101, 106–7, 110–12, 115, 117–18, 122–23, 127, 130, 131–32, 140, 147
Irenaeus, 68

Jackendoff, Ray, 58
Jameson, Fredric, 103n23, 132n8, 140
jazz, 31
Jesus
  baptism of, 38–40, 41, 68, 125
  beauty of, 198
  driven by Spirit, 10
  healing by, 68–69
  as image of God, 14
  resurrection of, 191, 194
  as Second Adam, 44
  self-surrender of, 126
  speaking to Nicodemus, 8
  as True Human, 40–41, 42, 43, 122, 125
  two-fold glory of, 41
Jews and Gentiles, 9, 85, 90
Johnson, Sy, 30
Jones, Amelia, 183–84, 186
Joshua, 139
Joyce, James, 187

Kahn, Ashley, 30
Kandinsky, Wassily, 53–57, 58–60, 61, 62, 65, 66
Kant, Immanuel, 185, 186
kenosis, 126, 130
Kermode, Frank, 199
kingdom of God, beauty of, 197
kitsch, 180–82, 195, 199
knowledge, 15, 20, 21, 99, 107, 110
Kramer, Lawrence, 105n31
Kundera, Milan, 180–82, 184, 186, 194, 199
Kuyper, Abraham, 179

ladder of Beauty, 50–51, 186
Led Zeppelin, 30
Lee, Ang, 95, 140, 141, 148
L'Engle, Madeleine, 4, 7, 14, 19
Lerdahl, Fred, 58
Levitin, Daniel, 71
liberation, 133. *See also* freedom
light, 14
listening, 164
location, of art, 103, 104, 109
love, 15, 19
Love Supreme, A (Coltrane), 28–34, 44, 45
Luther, Martin, 122
Lyotard, Jean-Francois, 186–87

Marsalis, Branford, 30
Marsalis, Wynton, 95
material
  moving beyond, 65–66
  vs. spiritual, 61
Matisse, Henri, 184
McClary, Susan, 103, 104, 105, 106–7, 108, 109n49, 110, 133, 140
McGuinn, Roger, 29
McMahon, Jennifer, 198
Mercer, Michelle, 91–92
messiah, 37–38
metanarrative, 187
Michelangelo, 35, 128
Milbank, John, 144n25
Milosz, Czeslaw, 44, 201–2
Milton, John, 178
mimesis, 51, 168
modern art, 55
Moltmann, Jürgen, 73–74n7, 123, 158, 166–67, 170, 207
Monk, Thelonious, 129, 130
mortification, 67–68
Moses, 43, 137, 139
Mothersill, Mary, 18
Mozart, Wolfgang Amadeus, 96, 104, 179
Murray, David, 29
"museum spirituality," 211–15
music, 6, 85–86. *See also* singing
  and painting, 57
  and proportion, 202–3
  and unity, 89
  as voice of church, 81–82
mutual indwelling, 83–84, 150
mystery, xiv, 3–5, 7, 10, 11, 14, 18

naming, 167–71
narrative, 166, 187
narrative discernment, 163–67
Nathan, confronts David, 171
natural theology, xv
neighbor, 172
new creation, 76–77, 166–67, 170, 190–95, 200
  beauty of, 177–79, 198, 204, 209
new heavens and new earth, 189
new humanity, 76, 80, 85
New Musicology, 103, 104–6, 107, 109n49, 112
New Testament, on the flesh, 62–64
Nicene Creed, 134
Nietzsche, Friedrich, 36, 103n23, 137, 138, 139
noncompetitive theology, 144

O'Hear, Anthony, 169
Oliva, Achille Bonito, 178
one voice, 80–81
ordered, 203
organic wholeness, 199
O'Siadhail, Micheal, 17–18
Ouspensky, Leonid, 179

Parker, Charlie, 28, 102
Parthenon, 27
participation, 17–18, 19
passion, 25
passivity, of artist, 98, 101, 110, 140
patriarchy, 126, 184
Paul, 10
  on the flesh, 62–64
  on resurrection, 191
  on the Spirit, xv–xvi, 9, 11, 191
Pentecost, 8, 9, 20, 139, 194
perfection, 197, 199–201, 209
performance, 34
perichoresis, 84, 121, 215
persecution, 127
personhood, 20–21
Peter, at Pentecost, 9, 139
Philip, 9–10
Pinker, Stephen, 52
Plato, xiii, 49–53, 54, 60, 82, 96–101, 106, 109, 186, 201
Platonism, 110–12
pleasure, 198, 205–9
pleroma, 199
pneuma, 8, 12, 136
pneumatology of freedom, 132
pneumatology of gift, 115, 123, 132
pneumatology of possession, 115, 127
Pneumatomachoi, 15
poiema, xvii
Pollock, Donald Ray, 128–29
popular culture, 71
possession, vs. gift, 115, 117
postmodern critical theory, 105, 106, 107, 110–12, 115, 123, 131, 140, 147
  on captivity and blindness, 133
  on construction of reality, 146

critique of beauty, 186–87
denies creative genius, 131–32
poststructuralism, 108, 111
power, 105, 106–7, 193
prayer, 33
present age, 66, 191
priestcraft, 138–39, 153
prophets, 134–40
proportion, 201–5, 209
Pythagorean tradition, 198, 201–2

Ran, Shulamit, 146
rationalism, 12–14
reason, 4, 164
reception, of art, 110
receptivity, and creativity, 97–98, 118, 127, 130, 146–48, 150
re-creation, xvi, xvii, 38
redemption, and re-creation, xvii
Redman, Joshua, 33
reimagination, 134–36, 172
relationship, 203–4
Rembrandt, 184
renaming, 171–72
repentance, 126
representation, 51, 168
representative art, 169n40
responsive discernment, 153, 156–59
resurrection, 40, 44, 67–68, 190–91
revelation, 138
Ricoeur, Paul, 166
Riley, Terry, 30
Rilke, Rainer Maria, 169–70
Rimbaud, Arthur, 16
Ringgold, Faith, 112
ritual, 71–72
river, 14
Romanticism, 3, 27
Routley, Eric, 77
ruach, 8, 10, 12, 35, 38, 136

Sabbath, 207–8
Sacks, Oliver, 72
Saint Maybe (novel), 153–56, 164–65
Salieri, Antonio, 96
Samaritan, 172
sanctification, 41
Santayana, George, xiii, 178
Scarry, Elaine, 18, 186, 207
scars, of suffering, 195
Schiller, Friedrich, xiii
Schleiermacher, Friedrich, xiii, 5–7, 161–62n29
Schmemann, Alexander, 168
Schoenberg, Arnold, xiii, 55, 57–60
scientism, 158
Scruton, Roger, 16–17, 59, 86, 207, 208
secularism, 156
seeing, 168–69
Seerveld, Calvin, 16
self, 131–32
self-denial, 118, 128, 130
self-expression, 128, 130
self-surrender, 126
sensual, as unspiritual, 48
service, 123
sexual relations, 90, 91
Shaffer, Peter, 96
Shepp, Archie, 29
Sheppard, Anne, 18
sight, 134, 153
significant form, 160
signification, 108
signs, 159
silence, 19–20
sin, 74–75, 122
singing, 72, 79–80, 85–88
Skekinah glory, 195
Smail, Thomas, 126, 205
Small, Christopher, 102
Smith, Patti, 29
social character, of artistic creation, 112
social construction, of reality, 109–10
Socrates, 49, 51, 97–101, 107–8
song. *See* singing
soul, Platonism on, 64
sovereign dynamism, 11, 12, 136–38
speech, 12, 19, 20, 153
spirit. *See also* Holy Spirit
and humanity, 34, 64
vs. body, 48–49
vs. flesh, 62–64
spiritual discernment, 158, 161
spirituality, xi, xv–xvii
and arts, 1–2
of daily life, 214
spiritual journey, Platonic vs. biblical metaphors for, 66
spontaneity, 32, 34
Staniloae, Dumitru, 85, 119n11, 145, 194
Stapert, Calvin, 72
sublime, 185–86, 189
submission, 86–89, 128
suffering, 195
surface beauty, 57, 58, 180
surrender, 118–19, 121, 128, 130

tabernacle, 37, 38, 79, 195
table fellowship, 90
Tarsi, Boaz, 57–58
taste, 182
Taylor, John V., 12, 158n16
teleology, 187
temple, 78, 195
theological systems, 5
Theophilus, 84
theosis, 42
theosophy, 53–54
Thomas Aquinas, on beauty, 198–99, 201, 205
Tillich, Paul, xiii
Timothy, 10
Titian, 182, 183, 184
tohu wabohu, 188–89
Tolstoy, Leo, xiii, 25–26, 34, 44, 51
tonality, 57
tongues, 118n6, 141, 194
Torrance, Alan, 14n53
Torrance, T. F., 13n46, 14
tradition, 102
transcendence, 52, 104, 110, 186
transformatio mundi, 194
Trinity, 13, 83–86, 150
twelve-tone system, 57
Tyler, Anne, 153–56, 164–65
Tyner, McCoy, 32

unison singing, 85
unsayable-ness, 2, 3, 7, 11, 16

Van Halen, Eddie, 112, 140, 141, 147
"Veni Creator Spiritus" (hymn), 47–48, 50, 61
violence, 75, 140
vivification, 68
vocation, xvi, 153
voice, of artist, 110, 147–48, 150
Volf, Miroslav, 84, 119n11, 143, 193
vulnerability, 34

Westermann, Claus, 74
wholeness, 199–200
Wilde, Oscar, 206
Williams, Raymond, 103n23
wind, 8, 166
wisdom, 21
Wolterstorff, Nicholas, 72, 99, 128, 206n28, 212
wonder, 60
worship, 15, 16, 25, 89
Wuthnow, Robert, 2–5, 7, 10, 11, 12, 14, 20, 61

Young, Lester, 129

Zion, 198

Scripture Index

Genesis

1 64, 188
1:2 38
1:2–3 188
1:20 188
1:21 188
1:25 188
1:26 149
1:26–27 73
1:27 149
1:29 145
2 35, 64, 74, 167, 168
2:3 207
2:5 167
2:7 35, xi
2:9 74, 149
2:15 149, 168
2:18 74
2:19 168
2:19–20 168
2:21–24 84n39
2:23 74
2:24 90
2:24–25 74
3–6 76
3:7 74
3:10 74
3:12 74
3:17–18 149
3:19 36
4:8 75
4:19–24 75
4:23–24 75
6–8 38
6:3 62
6:11 38, 75
6:12–13 62
6:13 75
8:1 38

Exodus

1–15 116n5
14:21 8n42
16–25 116n5
16:12 62
16:29 208
20:2–3 166
20:10 207
24:16–17 37
26–40 117n5
29:42–43 78n14
29:46 116
34:29 37
35:30–36:2 117
35:31 117
35:32 117
35:34 117
36:1 117
36:2 117
40:34 37

Leviticus

10:11 117
25:1–5 207

Numbers

11:27–29 139

Deuteronomy

5:14 207
5:15 208

Judges

14:6 10

2 Samuel

12:1–7 171
12:9 171
23 37
23:1–2 38

1 Kings

8:10–11 37

Job

34:14–15 35, 120
34:15 62

Psalms

8:5 35, 37, 41
16:3 209
16:11 209
19 146
33:6 146, 188
34:8 19
90:3 35
104 141, 145, 150
104:1–30 143
104:4 145
104:11 143
104:12 143
104:13 143
104:14 144
104:15 144
104:16 143, 144
104:21 144
104:25–26 145
104:27 145
104:27–30 35

Ecclesiastes

3:20 35

Isaiah

6:10 70
11:9 139
25:6 208
40 135
40:6–7 135
40:6–8 63
40:15–17 135
40:22–23 135
42:20 133
42:22 133
43:8 70
54:13 140

56:10 70
61:1 38, 39

Jeremiah

17:5 63
23:16–17 138
31:33–34 139

Ezekiel

12:2 70
36 70, 139
36:26–27 70

Joel

2 139
2:28 119

Amos

6:1 136
6:4–9 136

Habakkuk

2:14 139

Zechariah

8:4–8 136

Matthew

1:20 12, 37
3:16–17 121
7:11 122
12:28 40
13:15 70
18:11 68
26:39 125

Mark

1:9–11 121
1:12 10, 121
3:22 10
4:37–39 189
8:18 70
8:35 127
10:29–31 127
10:30 66
10:45 122, 125
13:11 12

Luke

1:34–35 10
1:35 12, 37, 68, 121
3:21–22 38, 68, 121
4:1 39, 68, 121
4:14 39, 68
4:16–21 39
4:18 133
4:18–19 68
4:39 69
4:40 69
5 69
5:4–10 194
6 69
9:28–32 40
9:34–36 40
10:30–37 172
12:12 12
24:39 194

John

1:14 12, 37, 38, 60
1:18 12
1:32–33 121
1:33 125
1:46 19
2:19–22 78
3:5 39
3:5–8 8
3:8 133, 166, xv
3:30 118
4:34 122
6:18–20 189
6:45 140
10:10 190
12:24–25 193
14:16 116n3
16:13 11
16:14 11, 12
20:20 195
20:21–22 65
20:22 116n3, 125, 195
21:6 194

Acts

2:1–2 8
2:3 10
2:4 8, 12
2:8 194
2:11 12, 194
2:16–18 139
2:17–18 9
2:24 190
2:32–33 190
2:33 65, 116n3, 119, 121, 125
2:38 116
4:8 12
4:13 12
8:26 10
8:39 9
10 90
10:44–48 9
10:47–48 12
15 90
16:7 10
17:28 214
20:22 10
28:27 70

Romans

1:4 121
1:19–23 146
8 61
8:4–9 61
8:11 10, 43, 121
8:23 191
8:26 11
15:5–11 80

1 Corinthians

2:13 11
2:14 157
3:1 61
3:16 41
4:7 120
6:16 90
10:11 191
10:17 80, 89
11:18 89
11:20–22 89
12:3 122
12:4 116
12:4–11 204
12:5 205
12:6–10 205
12:7 122
12:8 11
12:8–9 116
12:11 205
12:13 9, 90, 91, 139
12:27 78
12:31 118
14:1 118
14:2 118
14:14–15 118
14:18–19 118
15:49 43
15:52 191

2 Corinthians

1:21–22 43
1:22 191
3:16–18 43
3:17 115, 133
3:18 xi
5:16–17 170

Galatians

1:4 66, 191
2:11–14 90
2:16 62
2:20 118
5:16–17 61
5:25 167

Ephesians

1:13 191
1:14 191
1:21 66
1:22–23 189
1:23 78
2:3 88
2:6 191
2:10 76, xi, xvii
2:14 91, 190
2:14–16 76
2:15 76, 80, 85n40, 124
2:15–16 80, 189
2:17 190
2:21 78
2:21–22 78
3:5 77
3:6 124
3:9 77
3:10–11 77
3:11 77
3:18–19 78

4:1–6 91
4:3 125, 132
4:3–4 85
4:3–16 124
4:7 85
4:10 189
4:11 85
4:16 124, 125
4:18 70, 88
4:19 70, 88
4:22–24 76
4:24 76
5 81, 87
5:18 78, 79, 87n44
5:18–21 77
5:19–20 87n44
5:19–21 79, 87n45
5:21 87
5:22–6:9 87, 87n44
5:28–32 87n47

Philippians

2 127
2:3 127
2:5 126
2:6–8 125
2:7 119
2:7–8 122
2:9 126
2:9–10 126
2:15 127
3:3–7 64
3:8–9 64
3:10 127
3:11 127

Colossians

1:20–22 75
2:9–10 189
3 76n12, 81
3:1 191
3:10–11 76n12
3:14–16 81

1 Timothy

3:16 62

Titus

2:12 66

Hebrews

1:3 14, 41

James

1:17 123, 149

1 Peter

3:18 67

1 John

1:1–2 61, 190
4:1–3 163

Revelation

1:10 118n6
1:18 194
4:2 118n6
13:1 189
19:9 208
21:1 189
21:2 66, 177
21:18 177